Letting Go

Also by Karen Hayes

Summer Poem

LETTING GO

Karen Hayes

SIMON & SCHUSTER

LONDON · SYDNEY · NEW YORK · TOKYO · SINGAPORE · TORONTO

First published in Great Britain by Simon & Schuster Ltd, 1994
A Paramount Communications Company

Simon & Schuster Ltd
West Garden Place
Kendal Street
London W2 2AQ

Simon & Schuster of Australia Pty Ltd
Sydney

A CIP catalogue record for this book is available from the British Library.

ISBN 0-671-71839-8

Typeset in Plantin
by Florencetype Ltd, Kewstoke, Avon
Printed and bound in Great Britain by
Butler & Tanner Ltd, Frome and London

Acknowledgements

For her constant support, perception, advice, and empathy, I would like to thank my editor Joanna Frank.

I would also like to thank Sue Dean for her many readings of the first draft and urging me to continue; Jacki Boreham for her early readings of my manuscripts; Nigel, Julia, Adrian and Jeremy Boreham for their continuous interest and enthusiasm; and Serafina Clarke for her encouragement.

For Katheryn Susan Povey

Chapter One

Rain demoralizes the city as people run for buses, for taxis, for the comforting shelter of home, a cup of tea or a gin and tonic, dinner.

'Shouldn't you wait until the rain stops?' Belinda asks politely of the man she has been living with for two years.

He considers, looking through the window at the deluge on the pavement outside. 'I think not,' he says, equally politely. 'It's best I go now.'

She nods, then turns to look out of the window also. What had promised to be a fine spring day has disintegrated into blustery chaos, making her incredibly sad.

'Our picnic was a disaster,' she says wondering why she is making small talk when the man she loves is walking out on her.

'Yes. The first time for ages we've had an afternoon off at the same time and look what happens.' They are not, of course, talking about the weather, but they pretend that they are.

They turn again to the window. An inch of water is rushing torrentially down the gutter, umbrellas are turned inside out with the wind, cars steam like boiling vegetables as they simmer down the busy road. It is truly a diabolical day.

Max, ready to go, hesitates. He is not sure whether to kiss Belinda goodbye or not, and wishes he had left an hour ago when he was still angry. He says, indecisively, 'Belinda . . . I guess there is nothing more to say?' He looks at her small forlorn face with the short hennaed hair plastered to her head from the damp and the rain, at her puffy eyes and reddened nose, and wishes he were wrong, wishes she would suddenly come to her senses, say the words that will enable him to unpack his clothes and books and compact discs and not have to go out in this god-awful storm.

And Belinda does speak. 'I can't believe this,' she says and he knows she is getting angry again, knows she still will not say the words he is waiting to hear. 'This morning we were living happily together, seemingly in love, our lives in order – and now you're going.'

'Belinda – '

'And all because I won't have a baby.'

'Belinda, we've been through all this – '

'Ironic, isn't it? It should be the other way around. How many other scenarios like this are being enacted all over the western world, I wonder, only it's the *woman* sobbing: *I want a baby, I want a baby.*'

Max risks a smile. 'Well, you've always preached equality.'

'Oh God, how can you make jokes?'

'I'm just trying – '

'You are walking out on me because I am not enough for you. Not me, myself, Belinda; not just the woman who loves you, wants to be with you, live with you – it's not enough, you want the trappings. Marriage, babies – '

'With *you*, Belinda. Don't forget that.'

'Oh hell, don't give me that! If you want it with me, why are you going? To find someone else to give you babies, obviously!' She is crying again, sloppy, sodden tears, and Max swears under his breath, wishing he had not stopped to sort out two years of living together before he walked out that door. The price, he knows, is going to be another scene.

'I'm leaving because we have decided today that our relationship is going nowhere. I want children, you don't.'

'Why does our relationship have to go somewhere? You're just thirty, I'm not even that yet. Can't we just enjoy being together for a time? Aren't I enough for you?'

'I want more. I'm ready for more. God, aren't you? I still can't believe you don't want kids. I was sure you'd be as excited as I was when I brought it up today. I'm not asking

2

you to quit your job at the hospital – you can still work, be a mother as well. I thought that's what women want these days – everything.'

Belinda shakes her head sadly. 'I want what we had, Max. A nice, easy, loving relationship. I want you, no one else.'

Max, moved, goes to her and takes her hand. 'You can have me, darling. You can have lots of little baby me's as well.'

'Oh God. How can you be so flippant? You know how I feel about kids. I can't bear them coming into hospital, their mothers and fathers beside themselves with grief. When I speak to the parents, nurse the children, I know it's not for me, Max. Not for me.'

'It's not the norm, Belinda,' Max says gently. 'What you see is not the norm. The vast majority of kids grow up healthy, grow up just as you and I did.'

'I know, rationally I know that. Maybe I'm in the wrong profession; maybe it's made me too much of a pessimist. All I know is I don't want the risk. I don't want the emotional risk of having children. I couldn't cope with it. Can't you accept that, can't you accept *me*?'

She looks at him dully, her tired eyes still damp with tears. He shrugs his shoulders in a helpless way, starts to touch her, then collects himself. 'No, I'm afraid I can't,' he says quietly, walking away from her. 'I'm ready to settle down, move out of this god-awful city, maybe somewhere in the country. Get a house, populate it with a dog perhaps, even a cat – '

'And two point four children. Is that what it is these days, the average nuclear family?'

He looks at her coldly. 'Now *you're* being flippant. I think we've said enough, Belinda, I think we've both said it all. I'm going now, all right?'

She doesn't even look at him. She turns her head away from him, towards the window, towards the rain drumming with fat fingers on the thick glass. Staring helplessly at the back of her head, at her rigid shoulders, Max thinks, harshly, that at least it solves the dilemma of whether to kiss her goodbye or not. Wordlessly, he walks out of the room, out of the flat, out of her life.

The last Belinda sees of him is the back of his raincoat, his narrow shoulders hunched against the wind, his thick blond hair already saturated with the rain that drips drips drips relentlessly down his neck as he hurries away from her in first a fast walk, then a trot, and finally breaking into a purposeful run, whether from the rain, or from her, Belinda is not quite sure.

It is raining also in the country, in the Devon countryside miles away from Birmingham. Steve Dunstan, guitar maker, is hastily pulling on his clothes: old, comfortable jeans, a collarless shirt, a colourful hand-knit jumper from one of his many admirers. One of these admirers, a young woman named Kim, is in his bed right now, quite naked.

When he is fully dressed Steve kisses Kim perfunctorily. 'Great to have you back,' he says. Kim is the lead singer with a struggling band and has been in Cornwall doing gigs.

'Oh sure,' Kim says sarcastically, pulling the duvet over her head. 'That's why you can't wait to get out of bed and away.'

Steve groans, albeit inaudibly. He has a rush order on a guitar; he needs to work at least five or six more hours tonight. Kim's sudden arrival took him by surprise, threw him off his schedule. He certainly can't afford to lose any more time this evening, so he decides to ignore Kim's sarcasm and says, innocently, 'It's only eight o'clock, you're not in bed for the night, are you?'

'Lay off, I'm exhausted.'

'I thought you were going back to see your mother tonight?'

Kim pokes her head out of the dark green printed duvet and grins beguilingly, red lips twitching with mischief. Her smooth face with the bleached yellow half-inch haircut becomes nothing but a framework for that sexy smile which she uses to great advantage on the stage.

She says to Steve, 'I thought, since you missed me so much when I was away, that maybe you'd like me around a bit more. Like, what about me moving in? We've been hanging out together off and on for a year now.'

All Steve can think is: Oh hell, I'll never get that guitar finished tonight. Sitting on the edge of the bed he says, as gently as he can, 'It wouldn't work, Kim. I'm no good with anyone twenty-four hours a day, my ex-wife would vouch for that.'

'Jesus Christ. Would you stop giving me that crap? All that wounded-by-my-marriage shit. How do you know we wouldn't get on; how do you know, unless you give it a try?'

'Kim, please, can we talk about this another time? I've got this guitar to finish – '

'Jesus, those bloody guitars! Whenever you don't want to face something, you rush into your workshop. It's your ashram, your abbey, your Tibetan hilltop – nobody can touch you there.'

This has quite an element of truth in it, so Steve keeps quiet. Kim, after a moment, smiles again enticingly and rises fresh and naked and appealingly out of the duvet like the Phoenix from the flames and throws her arms around Steve. 'Please, Stevie?' she wheedles. 'Please can we have a go at living together?'

He knows it wouldn't work, knows it as sure as he knows that in fifteen minutes' time he's going to be back in his workshop, handling the smooth hard wood of the guitar he's working on now. But he says, procrastinatingly, 'Kim, we're going on holiday together, in only a month's time. Let's see how we get on then, okay? If we stick it in a tent together for three weeks, maybe there's a slight chance for us. I think by then you'll be wanting your own space as much as me, but let's wait and see.'

He kisses her affectionately, but firmly, and walks out of the bedroom. He goes down the stairs, through the beamed kitchen with the Rayburn steaming, through the cobbled old farmyard dripping with rain, and into his workshop, once a cowshed which he painstakingly converted himself. Taking down his current guitar he cradles it fondly, like a baby, running his calloused fingers up and down the Indian rosewood at the sides and back as gently as he would caress the smooth silky skin of an infant. He does this for several long moments, before finally switching on his portable stereo from which an old Dire Straits tape wails into life. Then, with great concentration he begins to work.

On the edge of Dorset, in the picturesque coastal town of Lyme Regis, the storm rages with particular venom on the Cob that meanders out into the sea. Half a mile inland, in an elegant Edwardian house with a rhododendron drive, another storm rages. Anna Beer, a widow of thirty-five, is having what her mother, Eleanor, delicately calls 'words' with her father, Stuart Callington.

'It's no good, Dad, I'm doing it my way.'

'Your way is assinine, Anna. Think of your child. Sophie is not a normal eleven-year-old – '

'I hate it when you say that! She *is* normal, I've been fighting for years to get people to treat her as normal – '

'She's not well, dear,' Eleanor Callington interjects appeasingly. 'That's all your father is saying, that she is not the healthy eleven-year-old we would all like her to be.'

Anna takes another sip of her Scotch; it's the only time she drinks spirits, when she is with her parents in their spacious, elegant home. Her father and mother both have a whisky before dinner, and Anna, when she is visiting, usually has one and very often two. She sees it as a lifeline.

Dinner is late because they have been arguing. Sophie, getting over a cold, was fed early and is upstairs in bed, watching television. Anna drinks more of her Scotch and

6

says, to change the subject, 'Listen to the rain, it's torrential. What a depressing start to spring.'

This is the wrong thing to say to her father. Stuart seizes on it like a dog with a bone and says, 'And what if it's like this when you take Sophie camping? You can't rely on the weather; May can be as wet and cold as December.'

'Dad, I'll be in Spain.'

'Northern Spain can be as bad as the Welsh hills.'

'Sophie wants to go there. She's done a project on Spain at school. I've been teaching her Spanish.'

'What's wrong with France?'

'Nothing, nothing at all, and we'll probably stay there a while, driving through on the way home.'

Eleanor, who has disappeared into the kitchen, comes back to call them into the dining-room. She has a pillow-like body and a soft pliable face; her hair is pale grey and soft also, and is waved gently around her benign face. 'Dinner simply won't keep another moment,' she says, lightly scolding.

They eat politely, formally, as if they were at a dinner party with awkward strangers. This is how we always ate when Mike and I were growing up, Anna thinks: nothing unpleasant or controversial was ever allowed to be discussed at meals. And this is what it would be like, she muses, were Sophie and I to go on holiday with them, to stay at a luxurious hotel somewhere in the South of France as Eleanor and Stuart have suggested. They cannot believe that Anna has refused, that she is insisting on her long-planned camping holiday with her daughter. But like the civilized people they are, neither Stuart nor Eleanor broach the subject again during the meal. Instead, they talk about rhododendrons, about some blight that has befallen the trees in the drive, about the weather. They cannot talk politics, because they disagree too vehemently; they cannot talk books, for Stuart reads only medical journals, and Eleanor the glossier women's magazines. The family is taboo also;

7

neither Anna nor her brother have quite lived up to their parents' expectations.

But when they are comfortably seated once again in the drawing room Stuart says, 'Anna, I am still shocked and amazed that you are refusing my offer to come with your mother and me to France for your holiday. We naturally assumed you would be delighted.'

'Look, it's kind of you to offer, and I appreciate it, but we've already made our own plans.'

'You cannot possibly take that child camping.'

'I can and I will.'

'You are being wilful and obstinate. As Sophie's only parent, you have a grave responsibility to her.'

'Exactly, Dad. Remember that. She is *my* child, *my* responsibility.'

'Your mother and I feel you are being unnecessarily rebellious and ungrateful, turning down this chance.'

Anna looks with despair at her father, rigid as a stone lion, his white hair thick like the mane of a great beast and his grey face cracked and pitted with age, like granite. She suddenly feels tired, tired and angry. She has just nursed Sophie through a nasty head cold and throat infection and she always feels weak, debilitated, after a bout of illness. Spreading her hands out in an unconscious gesture of supplication, she cries, 'Dear God, what can I say, how can I get through to you? I assure you of my gratitude. I assure you I am not being merely stubborn or rebellious, as you call it. I am Sophie's mother: I have a right to do what I think is best for her. Just because I am on my own, because Richard is dead, you feel you must run my life; you think I have no plans, no ideas, no sense of my own. Stop it, do you hear? Stop trying to run my life, mine and Sophie's!'

Eleanor half rises from her chair, but it is too late, Anna has got up and is already at the drawing-room door. Before she walks out she says, with as much control as she can manage, 'I'm grateful, I'm grateful, I'm grateful, I really am, for all you do for Sophie. But please, do there always have to be strings attached?' She walks quickly out of the room.

Eleanor and Stuart look helplessly at each other. 'I wonder if she realizes,' Eleanor says slowly. 'I wonder if she knows just how much we love that child.'

It is still raining, but this time only a light drizzle, a month or two later in the Asturias, the hilly coastal region of Northern Spain. Anna is lying awake in her tent, uptight and irritable, listening to the English voices rising like the tide as they swell with anger. Mostly it is the woman's voice, strident with scorn and fury: the man's is more appeasing, more reasoned. Anna pulls her sleeping bag over her head and wonders how her daughter can sleep through it all, but the child seems to be still and peaceful.

At last Anna dozes: then, suddenly, the harsh explosive sound of a motorbike starting up just a few yards away kills any hope of sleep for the rest of the night. Anna struggles out of her sleeping bag, pulls open the zip of the tent, and watches with impotent rage as the bike roars off, far too quickly, out of the campsite.

The man from the tent opposite is watching, also. He looks Spanish, with his olive skin, curly black hair, droopy revolutionary moustache, but Anna knows he is English because she has been listening to him and his young woman shouting at each other off and on for the past hour. He looks at Anna ruefully and walks over to her tent, smiling apologetically.

Anna's nerves snap. Sophie is still asleep but she has the rest of the night to get through. 'You've woken the whole campsite,' she hisses at him. 'Everyone here now knows the sordid details of your life with that woman.'

'No they don't, almost everyone here is Spanish,' he says unperturbed. 'In fact I think you're the only English campers, apart from us. Anyway, I'm sorry. Dreadful scene, that.'

He looks so woebegone that Anna's anger vanishes. 'Well, perhaps your friend will be back soon.' She gives him a sudden grin. 'But I hope not before morning.'

'She's not coming back at all: she's going back to England. And it's my bloody motorbike.'

And then, suddenly, he laughs. At first it is silent, his whole body twitching soundlessly: then he cannot contain his laughter and it comes out in great gulps of delightful, raucous noise which would be contagious if it were not the middle of the night, were not Anna too tense to appreciate it.

'Oh God,' the man cries between belly laughs, 'I did warn her, I warned her we'd get on each other's nerves before the holiday was out. I didn't realize it would be quite this soon.'

There is another hiss of a zip opening, from the tent on the other side of Steve's. A voice calls out, politely but firmly, '*Callense por Dios, queremos dormir.*' Quiet, we are trying to sleep.

The man abruptly stops laughing, looks stricken. He apologizes profusely in excruciating Spanish, getting himself in a terrible tangle, so Anna takes pity on him and helps him out, trying to appease the disgruntled occupants of the next door tent. Finally the zip shuts again and the man turns to Anna and whispers, 'Look, I'll never sleep after that. Do you feel like a walk on the beach? My name's Steve, by the way, Steve Dunstan.'

Anna smiles. 'I know,' she whispers back. 'Your name is Steve and you are thirty-six and you are useless at relationships which you blame on a bad marriage. You use that as an excuse to avoid any real commitment and you cannot handle deep relationships because you are a workaholic, and you love your guitars far more than you will ever love her – are you a musician, by the way?'

Steve groans, mortified. 'No, I make guitars. God, how embarrassing.'

'What, to make guitars?'

'That you heard all that. Look, I'm sorry, I did try to get her to lower her voice, but – '

'It's okay, I'm sorry too, I shouldn't be flippant about it. I couldn't help overhearing though.'

Steve smiles. It's a nice smile, it makes Anna feel wistful. 'I don't know your name,' he says.

'Anna. Anna Beer.' They look at each other appraisingly in the Spanish moonlight. Anna is tall, and Steve is about the same height. She thinks that he probably doesn't weigh much more than she does either, and wishes she could make him a nice thick nourishing soup. Wondering sadly why years of caring for Sophie hasn't eradicated the nurturing instinct in her, Anna turns to go into her tent.

'What about that walk, Anna?' Steve says. 'The rain's stopped. It's a lovely evening.'

'I can't leave my daughter. She's asleep in the tent.'

Steve has seen this woman's daughter, has spoken to her briefly shortly after he and Kim arrived at the campsite only eight or nine hours ago. He knows the child is not that young so he says, tentatively, 'The beach is only a few yards away. We don't have to walk far: we could just sit by the water and talk.'

Once again Anna feels it: a sweet sad nostalgia rummaging through her emotions like hands at a jumble sale. She shakes her head regretfully and says, 'Sorry, Steve, I just can't.' She goes inside, zips the flap behind her. After a while she hears him walking away, presumably down to the sea at the bottom of the campsite.

Sophie is awake when Anna climbs into their makeshift bedroom. 'Mum, you should have gone with him for a walk on the beach,' she says sleepily. 'You like the sea at night.'

Anna leans over and kisses her, rumples her hair which is thick, dark brown, tangled. 'You are a wicked child,' she says lightly. 'Eavesdropping again. Go to sleep now or you'll be tired in the morning.'

Sophie pushes Anna's own tangled hair, the same texture

but lighter, curlier than her daughter's, away from her eyes and tries to peer into them in the dark. 'Mum,' she says seriously, wide awake now, 'is it because of me? Is that why you won't take a walk with that man? He seems so nice. He was chatting to me earlier when you were washing the dinner plates.' She sounds regretful: what is it, Anna thinks desperately, what is it about these Spanish hills, cascading prettily down to the sandy sea, that makes us both long for things we can never have?

Anna kisses her daughter again, automatically feels her forehead for any sign of a temperature. Sophie feels cool, healthy: Anna is grateful for this blessing. 'I didn't feel like a walk tonight,' she lies to Sophie without a qualm. She is not about to land her daughter with guilt over herself; the child has enough problems.

She crawls into her own space but doesn't sleep. Only when the first streaks of morning light daub at the tiny plastic window of the tent does she fitfully begin to doze, her dreams both troubled and relentless as she curls like a foetus in the humid warmth of her old, shabby, comforting sleeping bag.

Down at the beach Steve does not sleep either. The sky has cleared and a new moon hangs precariously over the sea, tipping on its end as if it is about to trip over itself and fall into the water. It's a good night, peaceful and mysterious. The hills behind the campsite are hidden in the darkness but Steve can feel them, pulsing like giant hearts behind him. He closes his eyes to stave off a sudden spasm of loneliness, the old persistent longing for his ex-wife, Tess, which invades him when he lets up for a moment, relaxes, has time to think.

He keeps his eyes shut for a long time but he doesn't sleep, and at last, as the stars fade, he walks slowly back up to his tent. Before he goes in he stops for a moment at Anna's tent, listening for a sign that she might still be awake, but there is nothing, nothing at all. He suddenly envies her

her child, and realizes that above all he would like to be here with Sam, with his own son. A sense of loss permeates him, as real as the smell of the sea, the damp of the dew. He goes into his tent, throws himself down on top of his sleeping bag, and silently pounds his fist again and again against the soft resilient padding.

Chapter Two

THE rain wakens Anna. It is thumping like rabbits on the old green canvas tent and forcing its way in through the sides. Oh God, she thinks despairingly, why couldn't her parents have bought her a new tent instead of offering to pay for a holiday with them in some balmy French resort town? She shakes the thought from her mind; they're not like that, she knows. When they deem something is necessary for Sophie's welfare, they insist on providing it, are extremely generous: but it has to be on their terms, always.

But oh, how Anna wishes for a new tent! She feels with horror the wetness next to her sleeping bag and struggles to her feet, pulling on warm track suit bottoms and a jumper because it is cold as well as wet. Sophie is miraculously still asleep: her side of the tent seems dry and she looks cosy enough on her air mattress, wrapped not only in her sleeping bag but also in a thick wool blanket. Anna rummages through the grey morning light for her waterproof jacket, grabs her washbag, and runs through the rain to the clean but Spartan washroom at the top of the campsite. Finding a coin in the pocket of her track suit she decides to warm up in a shower. It is hot, relaxing, and she concentrates hard on it, feeling her skin heat and redden, feeling her body blend with the water and the steam, losing herself with a fierce intensity in this simple, commonplace activity. Suddenly her coin runs out and the water turns cold, and she is slapped with a shiver back to reality.

Feeling much better she rubs herself dry with a rather damp towel and confronts herself in the mirror as she brushes her teeth. Her hair, thick like Sophie's but crinkly rather than straight like her daughter's, has grown too long, messy. She looks at it critically as it frizzes in all directions away from her serious, still face which has turned a rather dull red from the past four days in the Spanish sun.

'*¿Ya viene la lluvia, no?*' says a woman who is washing her feet in the next basin. The rains have come. '*Sí, por desgracia,*' Anna replies – such a pity – and they chat for a few minutes about the weather, which the woman assures her is forecast to remain dire for at least the rest of the week. 'It's like that in the Asturias,' she says mournfully. 'When it begins to rain, it does not like to stop.' While she talks she meticulously, diligently, soaps and scrubs between each toe. Anna watches, mesmerized, fascinated, until a sudden clap of thunder breaks the spell. As she rushes back out into the rain she wonders if she is going mad, obsessed by the trivialities of life, a woman cleaning her toes, the comfort of a shower. Perhaps it is my way of coping with the other things, the things that are beyond trivia, Anna thinks: the things I have to face every day but yet cannot face, will not face.

The mountains behind the campsite are almost invisible in the cloud and the sea in the distance is white and soapy. As Anna walks to the edge of the campsite to her tent, she sees Sophie, her head poking out of the unzipped flap, laughing and talking to Steve who is pulling a plastic groundsheet over the leaking side of the tent.

'Morning, Anna,' Steve says, tying the sheet firmly into place. 'This should stop the rain for a bit, as long as it doesn't get too windy.'

Anna thanks him and goes into the tent, chasing Sophie into the sleeping quarters to get dressed. 'I've asked him in for breakfast,' she whispers. 'His tent is so tiny he can't cook in it and it's far too wet to light the camp stove outside.'

Sophie disappears to get changed at the same time as Steve appears at the door of the tent. He is wet through: his dark moustache droops pathetically, like a drenched little furry animal. Anna feels wistful again; wistful, and angry too. She doesn't need another creature to worry about now, and it infuriates her that he's landed himself on her. Oh God, she thinks, will I ever have normal feelings, normal emotions? She supposes not: not now, not ever. Like Sophie, she is damaged, but hers cannot be pinned down, named, dissected, as Sophie's is.

Steve, still standing in the rain half in, half out of the tent, is looking at her quizzically. 'Thank you for patching up our leak,' Anna says, not exactly warmly. 'Come in and get dry,' she adds grudgingly.

He is in the tent, squatting by the camp stove, warming his hands on the bright flame. 'Bit of a change in the weather, isn't it?' he asks rhetorically. Anna nods, preoccupied. As she busies herself filling a saucepan with water from a container, putting it on the burner, Steve watches her. He likes her hair, thick and damp and tangling all over her head in an overgrowth of tight frizzy curls: and he likes her eyes, brown and wide and with a perpetual question mark blazing out of them, as if life has no answers, as if she hasn't any answers.

As if reading his thoughts she fumbles in her pocket, finds a pair of glasses, puts them on quickly. They balance loosely and precariously on her long fine nose as she bustles around, finding mugs, opening a carton of long-life milk, getting out a bag of sugar. Then Sophie comes out of the sleeping area, dressed in a blue track suit. She has her mother's eyes, Steve thinks, but her smile is more trusting, she uses it more often. He likes Sophie's smile, it is wide and appealingly open, with her white, slightly protruding teeth and her endearingly childish lips. With a pang Steve thinks again of Sam.

But then he notices Anna, staring at her daughter, her face white, drained: her body tense. Anna is noticing the child's abdomen, swollen more than usual: she is noticing her skin, obviously yellow even in the dull light of the rainy morning. Anna's heart contracts: *not yet*, she thinks. *Please, not yet.*

Steve, following Anna's stare, looks at Sophie curiously. He senses something is wrong but is not sure what. Then, realizing that Sophie has caught him staring at her, he says, embarrassed, 'I'm sorry.'

Sophie smiles at him. 'It's okay,' she says graciously. 'I'm used to it.'

She puts on her waterproofs and goes off towards the washroom. *She's not used to it*, Anna wants to shout at Steve. People always stare, and you never get used to it, never. Even when they stare with compassion rather than stupidity, pity rather than curiosity, you never get used to it.

The water is bubbling furiously in the saucepan. Anna makes tea in a chipped blue enamel teapot and gives Steve a cup. He seems to be waiting for her to speak so she makes a banal comment on the weather. She senses he wants to ask questions but is too polite, too English.

Sophie returns and Anna scrambles eggs in the iron skillet while Steve disappears for a moment, then comes back with a fresh loaf of white crusty bread which he cuts in large, hunky slices. Anna dishes out the eggs and Steve eats his quickly, gratefully. Anna thinks drily that he's obviously not missing either his woman or his motorbike enough to go off his food.

The rain pounds on the canvas of the tent mercilessly as they have more tea, and fresh bread and jam. Sophie looks both cold and feverish at the same time, though she says she feels fine. Anna looks stressed, and Steve concerned, like someone wanting to help but unable to until someone explains just what the problem is. Anna, knowing there is no help, suddenly wants Steve to go, wants to be alone with her daughter. 'Thanks for lending us the groundsheet,' she says, abruptly and dismissively. 'I'll give it back soon: we'll be packing and going shortly.'

Sophie is dismayed. 'But it's so beautiful here.'

18

'I know, love, and we've had four lovely sunny days, which apparently is lucky for these hills: they are notorious for heavy rainfall. I think we should move on a few days sooner, out of the hills, to a warmer, sunnier coast.'

'Kim and I were going to do that,' Steve says. 'Before the, uh, the disagreement. If the weather turned nasty we were just going to follow the sun.'

Anna wonders what he will do, now, on his own, without a motorbike, without transport. Well, there are buses, she thinks, and trains, and anyway that's not my problem. She is about to say goodbye to him when Sophie says, excitedly, 'Why don't you come with us, Steve? We have lots of room in the car.'

Anna stares at her with exasperation. Does she so need a father, this child, that she must pick up every man who looks at her kindly? Anna shakes her head slightly, and says, as gently as she can, 'That's not such a good idea, Sophie. I'm sure Steve has his own plans, and we have ours.'

Both Sophie and Steve look so crestfallen that Anna takes umbrage again. She is dismayed by her daughter, who at the age of eleven still hasn't learned that fathers in her life never stay around long: she is cross with Steve because he seems a decent man and he doesn't understand that she is saving him pain by dismissing him now. Most of all, she is angry at herself for not being able to control her irascible nature. Whatever Sophie needs, she doesn't need this.

Anna takes a deep breath and tries to smile as she thanks Steve again, wishes him luck. He looks at her, puzzled: he has never met a woman giving off such complicated signals as this one. 'Keep the groundsheet, I have a spare,' he says as Anna once again says she will return it when they take down the tent. 'Bye then, Sophie,' he says, giving her an affectionate pat on the shoulder.

Then he is gone, and Sophie and Anna look at each other, almost desperately. Before Anna can speak, Sophie goes to her and hugs her impulsively. 'It's okay, Mum,' she says. 'Don't worry. The rain will have to stop eventually.'

But now, hours later, it has not. Anna and Sophie are still listening to the rain strumming on canvas, only this time it's the canvas of the 2CV roof as they drive along the winding roads out of the hills, Sophie cosy and dozing in the bed Anna has made for her in the back of the car. Anna removed the back seats while still in England, fitting in a small mattress so that Sophie could rest or sleep in warmth and comfort whenever she felt ill or just tired.

They have at last left the dangerous mountain roads and are on the plains heading towards the Pyrenean border when Sophie, sitting up behind Anna in her makeshift bed, shouts, 'Mum, stop, a hitchhiker!'

Anna nearly runs him down. Her daughter's sudden cry makes her jump, brake suddenly, and skid on the wet, slippery road. Luckily, the hitchhiker jumps back: luckily, there are no other cars on the road and they end up shaken but unharmed in a shallow ditch on the verge.

'Bloody hell, I don't believe it,' Steve says.

'Hiya, Steve!' Sophie cries happily, serenely, as if she had instigated this whole encounter herself.

Steve grins. His dark hair is plastered to his head with the rain, his moustache looks drowned and forlorn. But he smiles, and Anna, still shaking, tremulously smiles back. 'Well, Sophie,' Steve says, peering in the open car door over Anna's shoulder. 'Do you think that if I help your mum out of this ditch, she'll give me a lift?'

It takes over an hour to get the 2CV out of the ditch: though it's a small car, it's wedged awkwardly. By the time it's on the road again Steve and Anna are soaking wet and filthy; only Sophie is dry and happy, snug in her back seat bed.

'I wondered where you had gone,' Sophie says as Anna, with Steve beside her, starts the car and slowly resumes their journey. 'You packed your tent and left so fast I didn't have a chance to ask you where you were going.'

'Didn't see any point hanging around. I thought if I'm going to hitchhike back to England I'd better get an early start.'

'Haven't got very far, have you? We left ages after you.'

Steve laughs. 'I have to confess I spent some considerable time in a café trying to dry off a bit. It's one hell of a day for hitchhiking.'

Anna looks sideways at him, feeling guilty. He's watching her, amused at her discomfiture: then they both, suddenly, laugh. They drive along for a bit, silently, comfortably. Anna is amazed how easy, how restful, she feels, driving along the empty roads of the Spanish countryside with this stranger at her side. She decides she likes this man, he's laid-back, soothing. She herself is exhausted from the lack of sleep, the worry over Sophie, the long drive through the treacherous hills in the interminable rain. But something about the presence of the man beside her relaxes her, calms her.

They drive and drive. Sophie dozes in the back. Steve and Anna talk a bit, but mostly they are companionably silent. The rain at last stops, and sunny Spain rolls around them like a bright yellow ball: great wide fields of wheat reflecting the late afternoon sun. When Sophie wakes, ravenous, they stop the car at the edge of the empty road and collapse, hot and sticky with the sudden heat, and devour their sandwiches under some straggly pines on what appears to be an endless, dusty plateau. After quenching their thirst with lukewarm mineral water and the dregs of tea from Anna's flask, they begin to explore, to stretch their limbs after the confines of the tiny car. They walk for about ten minutes until they find a welcome shady copse, and behind this, surprisingly, they spot some ancient granite steps leading up to a crumpled and deserted monastery. Intrigued, they climb the steps, turn a corner, and there tucked away behind the ruins is a tiny thriving village, all stone and slate cobbles, with old men playing chess in the shade of a walnut tree and two goats tethered to the shop selling cheese and bread and vegetables. Steve buys them juice and ice-cream, and they sit on the steps of the monastery filling themselves up like sponges with the streams of sun cascading through the leaves on the trees and drenching them with welcome, warming heat.

'Oh, this is so much better than the rain,' Sophie says contentedly.

'Hmm.'

'I hope your friend didn't get too wet,' she continues politely.

Steve says, 'You mean Kim, the woman I was with? She should be fine: she's used to motorbikes, has been all over Europe on one.'

'That's all right then . . . Oh, look, look at that huge, fluffy white cat over there! It looks like Samantha.' Sophie rushes off across the square to investigate.

'Samantha is our cat back home,' Anna explains. Then, hesitantly: 'She rather left you in the lurch, didn't she? The woman you were travelling with?'

'She's rather gone off me, I think,' Steve says drily. He leans back, lifts his face and lets the sun wash over him.

Anna peers at him quizzically. 'You're nonchalant about it all, aren't you?'

Steve shrugs, thinking of Kim, of the precarious, ephemeral attraction that had initially brought them together, and says finally, 'The relationship was doomed anyway. She talked me into this holiday, to see if we could live together. We realized when we were still on the ferry it would never work.' He smiles a sudden, mischievous smile. 'It's the motorbike I'm missing most.'

'Callous sod.' But Anna smiles as well.

Steve, his eyes closed to the sun, says, 'I've lived alone for too long. You get to like it.'

Anna stands up: Sophie is calling her from across the square, wanting her to see the cat. 'I know what you mean,' she says to Steve. 'I only have Sophie, but that's enough.

We've been on our own for a long time – I can't imagine it any different.' She walks across the square, her hair frizzed and standing out like a dry bush after being soaked and then dried haphazardly by the sun and the heater in the car. Steve stretches, then stands up to follow her, but suddenly stops. Mother and daughter are squatting on the cobbles, framed by the sunlight behind them, stroking the fat white cat with such concentration, such collaboration, that it would be an intrusion to join them.

Thoughtfully, he sits back on the steps, takes out his tobacco and rolls a cigarette, watching the tableau on the other side of the square. It seems a long time before Anna straightens, helps Sophie up, and then, almost as an after-thought, beckons to Steve to join them. By the time he crosses the square they are already ahead of him, on their way to the car, their arms linked casually, their steps in unison. Steve, behind them, feels oddly obliterated by their solidarity, and wonders whether he should collect his ruck-sack from the 2CV and say goodbye, make his own way back to France, and then to England.

But then Sophie turns. 'Coming, Steve?' she calls, her smile directed like a torch, full-beam, upon him.

'Coming, Sophie,' he replies, and runs across the cobbled square until he has caught up with them. For a moment, for the briefest moment, he feels a sense of *déjà vu* and wonders why. Then he realizes: it is because, for the first time in years, he feels part of a family again. Though he knows the feeling is illusory, it is unsettling.

That evening they camp by a river, on a grassy verge under some old oak trees. The sun that had eluded them in the mountains is now setting, red and magnificent as it tumbles down the horizon. They have eaten well, a meal of fried rice and vegetables, which Anna prepared while Steve put up the two tents, his tiny one and Anna and Sophie's larger, more cumbersome one. Sophie followed

Steve around as he worked, handing him the pegs, holding up the canvas.

How quickly we fall into established patterns, Anna thought as she chopped up vegetables on her small round wooden board. But still she was relieved that Steve was handling with such dexterity the old, awkward tent, still wet from the rain the night before; relieved that she could get on with preparing a meal while he hammered and lifted and made their shelter for the night.

Now, dry and replete and slightly fuzzy from the Rioja they are drinking, Steve and Anna watch Sophie wandering up the shallow riverbank with a makeshift rod, trying to catch the small trout scurrying about in the clear water.

'How contented she is,' Anna says. 'She has this amazing capacity for happiness.'

'Most children do,' Steve replies, thinking of Sam.

'Sophie's not like most children.'

Steve says nothing to this. There are questions he wants to ask but he knows he will have the answers faster if he does not press.

Anna, liberated by the wine, by Steve's reticence, says, 'Sophie's father died when she was a year old. Killed when his home-made boat went down in a storm. He was trying to cross the Bristol Channel single-handed.'

Still Steve does not speak. In the distance they can hear Sophie's voice teasingly cajoling the fish to play fair and be caught.

'Sophie thinks he's a hero.' Anna stares at the water, remembering Richard. Remembering her short marriage, remembering how she loved him.

'But you don't,' Steve says. 'Think he's a hero.'

Anna looks at him, startled. This is too perceptive, as if he has stepped inside her. Years ago Richard walked into the deep spaces inside her with that same kind of perception, filling them with light and sweetness, and where was all that now: where was *he* now?

24

She says, shortly, 'No. I don't think he was a hero. I think he was a coward: I think he was running away.'

Before Steve can answer she is up and walking along the river towards Sophie, whose delighted laughter at the quicksilver fish tumbles along the water and reaches Anna, reaches Steve, making both their hearts ache for reasons not quite so entirely different. As Anna reaches her daughter she decides that the quicker they cross the Pyrenees and reach France the better. Sophie and she can find sea and sand and sun, and Steve can find his way – alone – back to England.

But in the morning Sophie isn't well. She has one of the fevers that plague her at times, one of those inexplicable high rises in temperature that the doctors can't account for. Although the morning sun is hot and welcoming through the window of the tent, Sophie wants only to turn and go back to sleep. Anna gives her tablets to try to reduce the fever; she insists Sophie drinks some of the peach juice she so loves. Sophie, restless and understandably irritable, says she just wants to sleep, and turns over and does so. Anna, as usual, is outwardly calm and efficient, and inwardly frantic. She can never get used to it, though she has lived with it for years; the fear crawling around in the pit of herself like some icy bloodless creature: the panic, the helplessness. She closes her eyes and tries to take some deep breaths before she quietly leaves Sophie asleep and walks out of the tent.

Steve is downstream, washing his face in the river. He waves at Anna and she slowly walks towards him. He is wearing only jeans: his body is very lean but nice, sinewy. His dark hair is soft and curly after its soaking of the day before and his moustache is bushy and dark. Yesterday, wet with rain, he looked fragile, vulnerable, and it registers somewhere in Anna's mind that he uses his hair and the fuzz on his face as some kind of protection, some kind of armour, against the more hostile elements of the world he lives in. These thoughts go through her mind quickly, automatically, on the periphery of her consciousness. Her only concern now, as always, is for Sophie.

'Morning, Anna. What a day, eh? Our tents are dry already.' He picks up a faded red towel lying on the grass and rubs his face and arms with it.

'I'm afraid Sophie's not well. I can't move her today so I'll have to stay here another night. I'm sorry about that but you'll have to go on to England without us. I'm sure you'll have no problem getting a lift.'

Without looking at him Anna kneels on the grassy bank of the river and splashes water on her face. Wordlessly Steve hands her his damp towel. She dries her face quickly and says, lightly, 'If you get an early start you'll be over the Pyrenees and into France by this evening.' She smiles at him perfunctorily, as if remembering her manners; then turns and paddles into the water. She is wearing dark shorts and her legs look long and white underneath them. She obviously doesn't tan very well, Steve thinks irrelevantly.

Anna goes out further into the river. The water feels good to her, warm and friendly, more like a great overgrown bumbling stream than a river. She strides through the current, her back to Steve, wishing he would go, and go quickly, so that she can have a good cry in this gentle burbling water before pulling herself together and willing Sophie through this latest crisis.

But Steve has waded in beside her, not even bothering to roll up his jeans which are now being soaked thoroughly to the knees by the swirling water. He takes her arm, turns her around so that she is facing him.

'Just like that, eh?' he says, not unkindly, but there is a hint of anger there also. 'Just like that you change your mind, and goodbye Steve.'

'Look, I'm sorry, okay? There are things you can't understand – '

26

'Why don't you try me?'

Anna looks at him hopelessly. 'People don't want to know. They don't want to get involved. Just go, okay? Sophie and I are fine.' She turns away from him again and walks up the river towards the tents.

Steve stands where he is, the water gently caressing his jeans and says, to her back, 'Well, isn't that just great? Don't you think you're being a bit unfair? We decided yesterday, the three of us, when you nearly ran me over on the road, that we would travel together to France. Well, we're not there yet.'

'Things change,' Anna shouts, not looking back. 'I'm sorry.'

'Oh great. Things change but you're not going to tell me what. Look, maybe I can help.'

He has caught up with her again and Anna stops, turns to him. 'Steve, leave it. No one can help, okay?' Then, more gently, 'We're all right, Sophie and me. I'm used to her being ill, I can handle it. She has a fever, her temperature is quite high, but she's had this before – she'll be better by tomorrow or the day after. I just don't want to move her now and there's no reason for you to stay as well.'

Anna comes out of the water, followed closely by Steve. The grass feels warm, comforting, on their bare feet. On a slate-grey rock, a brown-green grass snake suns itself peacefully.

Steve says, reasonably, 'Anna, listen to me. We are miles from the nearest village, on a little-travelled road in a foreign country. We haven't much food: if you remember we said we'd go shopping today, so we only have enough for break-fast. You cannot leave Sophie alone while you drive around looking for provisions. I'll stay until she can travel again, then we can all go on to France as we planned.'

The relief Anna feels at this sensible decision is so over-whelming it makes her feel weak, so she sits down on the stone that the snake, disturbed by their approach, has just vacated. For a moment she feels a pure, uncomplicated human emotion – gratitude – and then, just as suddenly, the mood changes, slithers away like the snake from the rock, and she feels despair, anger, hopelessness, even jealousy. 'Oh God,' she moans, putting her head in her hands.

Steve, sitting on the grass beside her, says, 'Anna, what's wrong? There's something terribly wrong and if you don't want to talk about it, fair enough. But if I'm going to stay around, maybe I can help – '

The emotions whirling around her mingle, mix and inevitably combust, as they do so often these days. 'Help?' she whispers, trembling. 'Why? Do you feel sorry for us? I don't want any more heroes, thank you.'

The injustice of this makes Steve stiffen, draw away. And then Anna is crying, harsh ugly tears that bring no relief but only more chaos. Steve's arm is around her and she cries and cries, tears of relief now that she is being comforted, tears of anger that she needs comfort and can't do this thing on her own, tears of jealousy because she cannot be all things to Sophie.

And then suddenly Steve stands up and rushes to the door of the tent where Sophie is standing wobbly, flushed and crying. As Anna leaps up to go to her she sees her daughter stumble, sees Steve hold her. Then Anna is there and together they carry her to the air mattress, give her the drink she is craving, and tuck her into the sleeping bag. Anna looks at her knees; they are swollen, they look painful; that was why she stumbled. Anna gives her a tablet to ease the water retention, holds her hand and strokes her forehead until her shivering stops. For, despite the fever and the heat of the morning, she feels cold, clammy.

When Sophie is finally more relaxed and settled she gives Anna and Steve a sweet smile and says, sadly, 'I'm sorry I'm spoiling the holiday.'

'You're not spoiling anything, love,' Anna says. 'This is a

beautiful spot, the sun is shining, and we'll just stay here until you're better.'

'Steve too?' she asks sleepily.

'Yes,' her mother replies unhesitatingly. 'Steve too.'

Steve looks at Anna and nods his head. Suddenly, she is glad he is here, grateful he is here. Together they wait until Sophie falls into a deep, peaceful sleep: then and only then do they leave the tent. Anna looks at Steve, at his troubled face, the perplexed look in his eyes, and takes a deep breath. He has been tactful and sensitive, not asking many questions, not pushing her for explanations. It is time, now, to tell him everything.

Chapter Three

THE sun outside the dark tent hits them like a fire-bomb: hot, dazzling. They have camped in an idyllic spot: far enough from the road to be well away from the infrequent car that goes by, hidden by the grassy, tree-crammed verge. The only signs of life are some birds chattering in the nearby trees and the sound of a moorhen on the other side of the narrow river. 'Steve,' Anna says, tentatively and rather formally, 'I feel I owe you an explanation.'

'Breakfast first,' Steve says firmly. 'We have all day to talk.'

He lifts the camp stove and frying pan out of the tent and on to the grass. 'You sit in the sun, rest a bit. I'll cook. I do a mean breakfast.'

They have a feast: eggs, sausages, fried chunks of ham. 'This was to be Sophie's treat,' Anna says sadly. 'She loves big breakfasts on holiday. We never eat like this at home.'

'I'll cook her another one tomorrow: hopefully she'll be better by then. I'll go and find a village and do some shopping this morning while you stay with Sophie. Will she be hungry later? What would she like to eat?'

'Nothing while she has this high temperature. You can buy some more fruit juice, she especially loves the peach juice they have here.'

Steve nods, pours them both a third cup of tea from the old teapot. 'And you say the fever will go down in a day or two? She'll be okay?'

Anna hesitates. She hates explaining about Sophie, she doesn't know what she fears most: an instinctive withdrawal, or compassion. Both are hard to deal with.

'The temperature should go down in a day or so, it always does, and she'll be better, yes, and ready to travel.'

Steve rolls a cigarette. He knows that's not all, he knows Anna hasn't finished. So he waits. He takes a drag on his cigarette, looks at Anna. She is staring at the moorhen on the edge of the river, staring as if mesmerized. The moorhen, as if aware that it is being scrutinized, makes a sudden move, disappears into the long grass.

Anna reluctantly looks back up at Steve. 'Sophie will never get better,' she says starkly. 'She was born with a rare genetic liver defect. The doctors said she wouldn't live more than a year or two, but we've proved them wrong so far.'

Steve pulls a few blades of grass, stares at the bright green in the palm of his hand as he assimilates all this. His thoughts riot: in his head he sees his own son, Sam, sturdy and healthy; then Sophie, stumbling in his arms this morning as he half-carried her to the tent. Finally he says, 'Is there anything that can be done?'

Anna shrugs, avoiding his eyes. Too much compassion there: she can't handle it. At least he's not shutting off, preparing to run. People do that too; they feel so sorry for her they get embarrassed, can't handle their feelings, can't cope with her and with Sophie. In the end no one can cope – not even Richard, Anna thinks, not even Sophie's father, much as he loved her. Richard couldn't take it either, he ran away and killed himself.

Steve is looking at her again. At least he's braver than most, she thinks dispassionately, at least he's looking at me in the face now. She says, flatly, 'The only thing that can save Sophie is a liver transplant, the doctors say. When the liver starts to fail irrevocably, they want to transplant.'

'Is that what you want?'

In the hot Spanish sun Anna is starting to feel rage again, irrational, overwhelming. 'I want what Sophie wants, that's all. I want her alive and healthy. I want her skin pink and not tinged with yellow so that she hates to go out because she's embarrassed at the way people stare. I want her to be able to run instead of limping along on swollen ankles. I want – ' She breaks off, her anger gone. 'I want her to live,' she says finally, quietly.

Steve doesn't say anything for a moment or two. Then he asks, 'Won't all this happen if Sophie has a liver transplant?'

'I don't know. It's a dangerous operation: the success rate isn't high. It's a difficult organ to transplant successfully. But I don't want to think about it until the time comes. Until I have to.'

Steve says, gently, 'And when will that be?'

Anna looks out at the little river babbling incoherently to itself as it scurries over pebbles and rocks, and wishes she could dissolve into the cool water and cascade unthinkingly for miles until she reached the dark oblivion of the sea. 'When the liver starts to fail,' she says slowly. 'When it is no longer capable of keeping her alive. That's when we'll have to face it.'

Steve is silent, distressed. He is thinking of Sam, only a year younger than Sophie, living with his mother in the same city as Anna and her daughter. Anna knows about Sam; Steve told her during the long drive yesterday. She knows he is thinking of his son and she is quiet also, giving him space. She knows this reaction well, the reaction every parent has unthinkingly when they hear about Sophie: it could have been my child. There but for the grace of God go I.

When Steve speaks again he says, 'How will you know, Anna? That the liver is failing?'

Anna looks at him, tries to stem the hopelessness welling up into her voice, her heart, as she says, 'Her skin will become very yellow, so will the whites of her eyes. Her abdomen will swell, her ankles and knees as well, as she retains more water. They're all symptoms of the liver breaking down.'

Steve says, 'Oh, Anna!' Awkwardly he puts his hand on her shoulder in an instinctive gesture of compassion and she surprises them both by turning to him and letting him take her in his arms in a wordless, empathetic embrace. They sit together like this for several moments, listening to the manic voice of the river becoming louder and louder in their silence, as if it was trying to tell them something, as if it knew the answer.

Finally Anna breaks away, stands up awkwardly. She fumbles in the pocket of her shorts for a tissue and for her huge round glasses which she puts on her reddened nose, peering vulnerably at him from behind them. 'I'll make a list for you, is that all right? You can take the car, buy the provisions, and I'll stay with Sophie.' She smiles tentatively at him, as if she's not quite sure of him. 'Another bottle of wine would be nice too, don't you think, I've got some pesetas; I want to get rid of them before we leave Spain . . . '

She trails off, uncertain. Under the harsh bright sun she looks gawky, too tall, too skinny, her hair rioting all over her head like a wheat field gone crazy and her glasses magnifying her round dark eyes so they look like cows' eyes, abnormally large for her thin face. Steve smiles back reassuringly, though what he wants to do is take her in his arms and kiss her. Her vulnerability invokes such a tenderness in him that he has a hard time keeping himself from touching her again. Suddenly she seems the loveliest creature he has ever seen, and the thought confuses him. 'Maybe two or three bottles of wine,' he says hurriedly, for she is waiting for him to speak. 'I think we could use it, don't you? I've got some pesetas left too.'

She nods, and goes into the tent to check on Sophie. Thoughtfully Steve gathers up the breakfast plates and slowly takes them down to the river to wash.

The next day Sophie is much better, her temperature is back to normal and she is out exploring the river bank before Steve has even emerged from his tent. Her knees are slightly less swollen but still a bit painful, so Anna gives her the diuretics and the painkillers and she seems lively enough. In the sunlight Anna thinks her skin is not as yellow; perhaps she had been mistaken, perhaps it is not happening; not yet, not yet.

It's again such a beautiful day that the three of them decide there is no hurry to move on, and dawdle by the river's edge, reading, relaxing. Sophie fishes, paddles, has a nap, talks a great deal to Steve who tells her all about his son, Sam.

'Isn't it funny? His name is like my cat's; Samantha and Sam,' she giggles. 'Can I meet him, Steve?' And then, sadly: 'I've always wanted a brother.'

'He lives in Bristol, you know, like you and your mum. I'm sure he'd like to meet you. He doesn't have any brothers or sisters either.' And just as well, Steve thinks ruefully, or I'd have lost them too. He and Tess had wanted several children to start with, but after Sam, Tess realized how a child can bind and restrict you, and by then she was totally committed to her job, her work. She knew she was going places: she was also wise enough to realize she couldn't handle the high-powered career she wanted with more than one child. Steve saw her point, but was still saddened.

'Don't you miss Sam?' Sophie asks. 'Don't you wish you lived with him?'

This is so near the knuckle that it takes Steve's breath away. They are fishing together on the edge of the river with a net Steve bought for her in the village. Sophie catches a tiny irridescent fish, looks at it for a moment, then puts her net back in the water, lets it escape. 'Yes, I miss him a lot,' Steve says, finally, skimming a stone across the water. 'But Devon isn't too far away. I go up often and bring him down to stay with me.'

Nearby, lying on the grass on an old tartan blanket, Anna is trying to read a novel by Gabriel García Márquez. But really she is listening, dismayed. She hates it when Sophie latches on to a kind voice, a sympathetic presence, especially when it is a man. She feels consumed with guilt because she has never given Sophie another father; she feels fear for her daughter, because invariably the man shies away, unable to cope. She has learned from bitter experience not to let anyone new into her life; she has ample friends, a supportive family, and as for lovers, she doesn't need, doesn't want, the emotional toll they take; all she has is spent on Sophie. Besides, she knows that anyone who takes her on takes Sophie as well, and she's never met a man who could handle that. Not even the child's father.

But she says nothing. Sophie is so happy, paddling about in old denim shorts, her thick coarse hair tangling down her shoulders, her eyes bright with fun, with excitement. And so the day passes: then another, and another. They are all loath to move, the weather is perfect, their spot ideal. They take the 2CV on little excursions into the neighbouring villages where Sophie is quick to make friends with the old women in the shops, the little children playing bull-and-bullfighter in the dusty square. Anna, who did a Spanish degree, has taught her daughter the language, and Steve watches with admiration as the two communicate with the villagers.

And then, unanimously, they decide to move on. One morning clouds are hiding the sun and suddenly they want to pack up, move on, go to France, find the sea. This they do at once, laughing jubilantly at their abandon, their recklessness. Somehow it has been understood that Steve will stay with them until England, and the thought no longer threatens Anna. She has immersed herself into a sea of unreality, brought on by Sophie's illness and the strangeness of the holiday. For the moment she is content to float unthinkingly from hour to hour, from day to day.

They sing much of the way from Spain into France. They play, over and over again, Sophie's favourite tape, *The Travelling Wilburys*, and sing along while Steve, when he's not driving, mimes playing a guitar, or takes out the harmonica he has travelled with since his college days. 'You're nooooot a-lone, you're nooooot a-lone, you're nooooot a-lone anymore,' they sing along with Roy Orbison on the tape as the hills of the Pyrenees whizz by. Sophie is looking much better; her colour is definitely not so yellow, her abdomen less swollen. As usual, Anna starts to hope again. Sometimes hope is more dangerous than despair, but she doesn't dwell on that.

They cross the tiny Pyrenean border town into France, still singing, their mood not dampened by being stopped for hours, the car thoroughly emptied and searched by the customs officials. 'It's you,' Anna says laughingly to Steve. 'You look like Che Guevera. You look like a Basque terrorist. Look at that wild hair; far too long! Look at your sweet innocent smile; what could be more mendacious?'

'It's you, it's the 2CV!' Steve retorts. 'Who but an impecunious drug-smuggler, fallen upon hard times, would drive such a car?'

'I love this car!' Sophie says indignantly. 'Don't you say a word against it.'

'It's your mother, then, not the dear old 2CV. She looks wilder and far more dangerous than me, don't you think?'

Sophie, always protective, throws herself in her mother's arms and says, 'Don't you joke about my mum. She's beautiful!'

But Anna, who has been laughing along with Steve, suddenly looks serious, serious and unsure. 'I suppose I must look pretty wild. I can hardly run a comb through my hair.' She fumbles in the pocket of her dungarees for her glasses, putting them on hurriedly.

Steve, also serious, says, 'I think you look beautiful.'

They stare at each other, stunned. Then Sophie, looking from one to the other, grins. 'Isn't this fun?' she says happily. 'Aren't holidays fun?'

They are on such a high now that they decide to drive straight to the sea, even though it will take all night. Sophie is content to sleep in the moving car, she is used to travelling. In the past Anna had been determined to treat her daughter as a normal child, taking her on numerous holidays when their finances allowed, camping in Cornwall, in the Lake District; later, all over France. Sophie loves it, as her father did.

They reach the sea, find a campsite in the early morning, and collapse on a pebbly beach sprinkled with the silted-up remains of old oyster beds. They stay a few days here, a few days there, until slowly they have worked their way up the coast to Brittany, where the sun is still warm and brilliant. Near Carnac, they find a campsite on a dune-covered beach where they set their tents on the rough grass growing sparsely over the sand. Sophie loves it here; there is a friendly green sea and a sandy shore that goes on for miles.

They remain where they are for over a week, until it is time to go home. Mostly they amble around the beach, gathering shells, swimming, building great sand-castles. Sometimes they go looking for the menhirs, the ancient standing stones coaxed into place by some unknown primitive people thousands of years ago. They find them hidden in dusty pine forests, or suddenly alongside the coastal road, tall and grey and forbiddingly stern.

So metimes they shop, driving in to Carnac, or, further afield, to the city of Lorient, where they eat galettes in tiny crêperies. Sophie loves shopping; she adores trinkets, though is not anxious to possess them. Rather she prefers to look, to touch gently, to feel the textures, assimilate the colours. She says she is feeling better, but her skin is still stubbornly coloured with yellow, and more and more often she has to sit down, rest, for her knees and ankles are painful. Sometimes in the evening Steve has to carry her back up from the beach when they have walked too far along the shore. Also, she has intermittent temperatures. Luckily, they never last more than a day, but they are becoming more frequent.

'Shouldn't you get her back to England, to your doctor?' Steve asks one night when he and Anna are sitting on the sand dunes, lazily watching a full bloated moon hanging over the sea. Sophie is behind them, sleeping in the tent, too far away to hear their whispers, but not so far that Anna cannot hear her if she calls.

'She's had these temperatures all her life, and the swollen joints. It happens when the liver is below par. The doctors can do nothing more than I can – they give her painkillers and diuretics.'

Steve accepts this, but he's still uneasy. He knows Sophie's swollen knees are not something sporadic; he knows Anna is fooling herself when a strange trick of the light convinces her Sophie's skin is no longer yellow. But he is not her father; he is not anything to this child, and so he cannot say anything.

'Shouldn't you be back in England?' Anna asks him now. 'What about your guitars, what about your motorbike, what about your woman?'

'This is my holiday,' he says enigmatically. 'My motorbike, is, I hope, back in Devon. I hope Kim has cooled down enough to bring it back to my place. My woman, as you call her, is no doubt finished with me, which is just as well because our relationship was going nowhere. My guitars can wait. They'll be there when I get back.'

And so the days float by, like a drifting raft on a languid sea. And then suddenly it is time to go: suddenly, it is their last day in France.

Steve insists on taking them out for a meal, and they find a tiny dark cavern of a place alight with candles, and gorge themselves on cold meats and pâtés, on chicken and rice and mushrooms, on Breton gâteau and rich runny cream. Sophie has dug out her favourite dress for the occasion, a striped red and white cotton, and Anna has pulled her daughter's hair back in a long pony-tail tied with a red ribbon. Anna herself wears a long white cotton skirt printed with innumerable flowers, with a pale yellow jumper, and Steve has actually put on a shirt of faded blue plaid instead of one of his ubiquitous T-shirts. They feel quite dressy and festive, and admire each other effusively before they set out.

The evening is a success, and after it is over, Sophie, exhausted but happy, is far too excited to go to bed. So they sit outside for a while, making a circle around the thin glow of the gas light. The night is warm, muggy, dark; there are clouds hiding the stars.

'The weather's changing, now that we're going home,' Sophie says. She's wrapped in the tartan blanket and her eyes are huge, luminous in the dark.

'Bed, Sophie,' Anna says. 'We have to make an early start tomorrow; it's a long drive to Roscoff.'

'Can I have a song, please, Steve, before I go inside?'

'We'll wake the whole campsite.'

'No, we won't. We're far away from everyone else; there's no one near us. Besides, it's not even eleven o'clock yet.'

Steve, relenting, takes out his harmonica and begins to play softly 'Morning has Broken', a favourite of Sophie's. Anna, tunelessly, begins to hum; Sophie, to sing in her young girl's voice. Steve goes through all of Sophie's favourites: 'Streets of London', 'Yellow Submarine'. He makes them both laugh with a mournful rendition of 'You're noooot a-lone . . . ', and when at last he finishes, he kisses Sophie lightly and Anna says, 'Bed, love, okay?'

Sophie goes. Anna follows her inside, tucks her in, and within minutes the child is sound asleep.

'Fancy a walk on the beach?' Steve asks Anna when she comes out of the tent.

'I think that's where I came in,' she says lightly. 'The first night I met you, remember?'

'You wouldn't go with me, though.'

'Because of Sophie.'

Steve's face lights up suddenly in the dark night as he strikes a match for his roll-up. 'What about tonight, then?'

Anna says, gently, 'There's still Sophie.'

'We're practically on the beach, Anna. We won't let the tent out of our sight. We needn't go far.'

Anna hesitates, then agrees. They wander along the shore silently: they seem to be the only people on the whole beach. The sea is dark, ominous, without moonlight. A mist is rising, hovering over it. 'Ghosts,' Anna says with a shudder. And then, 'I'm going back to check on Sophie.'

Steve walks part of the way back to the tents but then stops, in the hollow of the sand dune where they had talked earlier in the week. 'I don't want to go in just yet,' he says.

Anna looks in the tent; Sophie is sleeping deeply, calmly. She hesitates; then, quietly, goes back out into the night.

Steve is waiting for her, in a narrow crevice between two sand dunes. Soundlessly she goes to him, and he pulls her gently down on the soft sand and kisses her, again and again. She responds as he had hoped she would: passionately, compulsively. She hesitates only once, when his hand slips under her skirt, under the thin elastic of her pants, but only briefly, only for a few seconds. Then she is with him, then she cannot stop any more than he can, then she becomes as damp and as sweaty and as mysterious as the night as they make love, as they lay entwined and sandy on the quiet dunes.

When they have finished neither one of them speaks, neither of them moves. Then Steve, gently, begins kissing Anna's face, her hair, her eyes. 'I've wanted to do that since Spain,' he says at last.

'Why didn't you?'

'I don't know. I kind of had a feeling you'd bite my head off.'

Anna sits up, pulls on her jumper.

'You're covered in sand,' Steve says, nuzzling her back.

She stands up, finds her discarded skirt and knickers and struggles into them. Steve sits up slowly. 'Hey, what's the rush?' he says gently.

'I've got to check Sophie.'

41

'We can see the tent from here, and we can hear her if she calls. Besides, you checked her only a short time ago.' He grins. 'We were both pretty quick, you know. Didn't waste much time.'

Anna, trying to shake the sand out of her hair, says, distractedly, 'I've got to go in, Steve. I'm tired, okay? Thank you for a lovely evening, it was great. All of it.' She kisses him politely on the cheek and is gone.

Steve watches, with a mixture of hurt, anger, and frustration, as she runs silently to the tent, unzips the flap, goes inside. He lays back down on the sand and watches the mist now swirling in fat ghostly patterns above him. An hour goes by before he finally gets up and goes into his own small tent.

Anna, still awake, hears him. It is a long time since she has made love, three years as a matter of fact. Not since Jake left, not since that dreadful time when she vowed that that side of her life would be dormant, at least till Sophie grew up.

She knows she will regret it. She knows how the heart is inextricably woven in with the body; she knows how the body betrays; she knows that after tonight, she will want this again: she will want Steve again.

And the holiday is over. Tomorrow, they will be back in England. Turning away from Sophie so that her daughter will not hear, Anna weeps into her sleeping bag.

The night-ferry delivers them safely to Plymouth in the early morning and they drive the twenty odd miles or so to Steve's house in a predictable drizzle.

Sophie, tired and grizzly after all the travelling, perks up when she sees the house, tucked outside a tiny Dartmoor village. It's a story-book cottage complete with thatched roof and a garden as old as the moor itself, stuffed with gnarled pear and apple trees, a big, fat clematis crawling up the front wall, and in the back a tiny pond with ducks running frantically about trying to find food for their young.

'Oh Steve, ducks!' Sophie says, entranced.

In front of the house stands a motorbike. 'Well, she's brought it back,' is all Steve says.

They go into the house which is all beams and cob and stone with tiny small-framed wooden windows opening out on to the garden outside. It is small but intriguing, with odd-shaped rooms, with dark tiny corridors which seem to go nowhere. 'It was my parents',' Steve says. 'My dad died and my mother went to Australia, to visit my brother and his brood. She liked it, decided to stay, so I bought her out.'

'How long have you been here?'

'Only a year. When my marriage broke up, three years ago, I stuck it out in Bristol for a while but – ' He shrugs. 'I had to get out,' he says finally, not wanting to say any more, though he sees Anna is looking at him quizzically. It still, to his dismay, pains him, how he was unable to let Tess go, how even after she remarried, he would walk the streets of Bristol gravitating towards her house, knowing full well the torment it would cause him to see her, but unable to stay away.

'Anyway, I grew up in Devon, still have mates here,' Steve continues, for both Anna and Sophie are waiting for him to go on. 'I needed more space too, for the guitars. Want to see the workshop?'

Anna and Sophie follow Steve back outside through the misty rain, across the cobbled farmyard and into the old barn. 'Oh, Steve, this is lovely,' Anna says spontaneously as they step inside. The workshop is large, light, with a huge bow window looking out to the garden. A massive oak beam holds up the ceiling and more beams curve on the white-painted walls. There are shelves everywhere, smooth wooden shelves full of tools and about four or five half-finished guitars. On the deep window seat a huge spider plant spreads its glossy green legs and on the opposite wall there is a large colourful Toulouse-Lautrec poster.

Steve takes down a sleek, bright blue guitar with wild black geometric designs covering it. 'Look, Sophie, see this?

43

Some man rang me up from London, said he wanted a flash blue and black guitar for his son. After I made it he rang up again, said his son had changed his mind, wanted a bright red one with great yellow streaks.'

'So what did you do?' Sophie asks, laughing. She is holding the guitar and Steve is showing her where to place her fingers. She is caressing it as she caresses her favourite doll.

'I told him to sod off,' Steve said. 'You get nuts like that sometimes. A shop in London is taking this guitar; I'm going up there with a couple more as well.'

Sophie is trying to strum some chords, but all that comes out is discord and she looks as if she's going to burst into tears. Steve notices and gently re-arranges her fingers on the strings. 'You have to press down as hard as you can,' he says. 'Now try.'

She does, and something very like a proper chord vibrates through the little workshop and she giggles. It takes so little to make Sophie happy, Anna thinks. She has a tremendous capacity for enjoying life, loving it, in spite of what life has done to her.

'I'll make some tea,' Anna says, leaving them to it and crossing the yard back to the house. She doesn't notice the old black car parked behind the house so she is stunned to find a young woman in a red leather miniskirt standing in the kitchen spooning out instant coffee from a jar and putting it into a brown ceramic mug.

She hears Anna and turns. Anna immediately recognizes her, recognizes the pale spiky hair, like a toothbrush gone out of control. It's the woman Steve was with: Anna had seen her briefly when they arrived at the Spanish campsite.

'You're Kim?' she asks hesitantly.

'Uh huh. Where's Steve?'

'In his workshop.'

'Christ, he's only just got home and already he's making his bleeding guitars.

'Do you, uh, live here?'

'God, no. Do you think Steve would let a woman move in? There's no room with all those fucking guitars.'

There is nothing to say to this so Anna plugs in the electric kettle, opens a cupboard to look for tea. Kim watches her, then says, 'Oh, shit. Sorry, I'm a bit slow. Are you his latest woman? God he works fast.'

'Look, I'm not – '

'But then he always has, hasn't he? Two hours after we met we were in bed together. Couldn't keep our hands off each other! What a weekend – it was that festival down in Cornwall, it – '

'I'll call Steve,' Anna interrupts, making quickly for the door, not wanting to hear this but unable to stop the woman from continuing.

'Don't bother,' Kim says, shutting the kitchen door with an angry kick and running her long thin fingers distractedly through her scrubbing-brush hair. 'Jesus, I don't know why I'm upset or even surprised; we agreed from the start it was a no-strings relationship. It's just that after eight or nine months you begin to want more, y'know?'

Anna knows, but she is not about to listen to any more appalling revelations. Just as she is about to open the door, leave the kitchen, find Steve, he comes inside and says, calmly, with only the slightest trace of irony, 'Well, hello, Kim. So nice of you to return my bike.'

Kim sees him and her face softens. Oh God, Anna thinks, she still cares for him, still wants him. She suddenly wants to go; England and the rain and now the presence of this woman are setting up the barriers that the holiday had knocked down. She can feel Steve receding from her like the lights of France as they watched it last night from the back of the ferry, becoming smaller and smaller before finally disappearing completely.

'I've got to go,' Anna says, moving towards Sophie who has come in behind Steve and is staring wide-eyed at Kim. 'My parents are expecting me.'

'Have a cup of tea first,' Steve says.

'I can't.'

'Look,' Kim says to Steve. 'I'm sorry about the bike, I was in a temper.'

'Didn't it occur to you that you were leaving me a bit stranded?'

'Uh, Steve, Sophie and I have got to go.'

'Yeah, but by then I was on the ferry. Look, I said I'm sorry.'

Anna gives up and gently steers Sophie towards the door. She can't bear to see the worry in the woman's eyes, can't bear to hear her pleading. Anna doesn't want to see this, doesn't want to know. She is beginning to feel superfluous with this young woman here, and hurt, and rejected, which doesn't make sense because she has already decided she isn't going to see Steve again. There is no way she can get involved, not with Sophie; there's no room for anything more in her life. She has tried it before, with Jake, and on a lesser scale, with others; it has never worked.

Suddenly a fierce loneliness attacks her, so viciously that she feels frightened. Grabbing Sophie she flies from the house, calling over her shoulder that she must be off, and rushes out into the drizzle, into the rain. She is as weepy as the magnolia tree dripping in the yard: the holiday is over, and reality is too grim to be bearable. The sun has gone; Sophie is – she cannot pretend any longer – getting worse: and there will be no Steve around to help set up tents against the storms that lie ahead. Wallowing in unaccustomed self-pity Anna opens the back of the 2CV and motions Sophie to get in.

But then Steve is there, and Sophie is hugging him, saying goodbye. 'Please, Steve, come see us in Bristol. Soon.'

He helps her into the car. 'I promise, Sophie. Soon.'

Steve collects his rucksack, his jacket, out of the car, then puts his arms around Anna, kisses her. 'See you in Bristol,' he says. Anna wonders if Kim is watching out the window, wonders if she will stay with Steve tonight. The thought fills her with dismay and she pulls away from him, distancing herself. 'I don't know,' she says, 'I don't know if we'll have time to see Steve, Sophie, what with my work, and your school – '

'Mum!' Sophie shrieks from the back of the car. 'Mum, he promised!' and of course Anna relents and says, 'Right, Steve, see you in Bristol.'

And then the three of them laugh and Anna thinks: well, you never know. Maybe. And a sudden sharp shaft of joy pricks and bursts in the bubble of her despair and she thinks God, Anna, you're a bloody manic depressive, that's what you are.

The last thing Anna sees as the 2CV bumps along the narrow dirt track away from the house is Steve standing and waving, waving, waving, until they turn a corner and drive out of sight.

Chapter Four

'Y OU'RE late.' Stuart Gallington views his daughter and
granddaughter with a mixture of pity, despair and
annoyance. They look damp, dishevelled, dirty, as well as
incredibly tired.

'Dad, we've just come from France. It's hard to be exactly
on time for a luncheon engagement when you've been on a
ferry all night.'

He relents, and kisses them both.

'Sophie, Anna!' Eleanor cries as she rushes to meet them.
She embraces them warmly, then: 'Oh, dear. You look
rather crumpled. Come upstairs and have a good wash, a
shower if you like. Then you can change into clean clothes.'

'We don't have any clean clothes,' Sophie giggles. 'After
three weeks of camping, Mum gave up hand-washing the
last few days. The water on the campsite was too cold,
anyway.'

Anna whisks Sophie upstairs to the guest bathroom,
which seems unspeakably, wickedly, luxurious with the
plush grey carpet, soft white towels, scented, unused soaps.
The two wallow in it for as long as possible, giggling secretly
together.

'Lunch is ready,' Eleanor calls, and they all go into the
dining-room, where all meals, even the simplest, are eaten.
The long oak table is set elegantly for four and the air is
scented with perfume from the magnolias in the centre.

'It took you long enough to get here from Plymouth,'
Stuart says as he cuts great slices of fresh ham straight from
the bone.

Anna doesn't mention her detour to Steve's place, and
Sophie, concentrating fully on her food, doesn't either. As a

49

matter of fact they stopped at a Little Chef soon after leaving Steve: Sophie was hungry and already missing Steve and wanted a comforting English teacake, and Anna too felt she needed to stop and pull herself together before facing her parents.

Sophie is hungry again; she is always hungry, for her body, not digesting properly, needs more and more food to stoke up her energy. Now she piles Eleanor's special potato salad on her plate, and fresh tomatoes which she loves, and lettuce and raw green peppers and great chunks of Stilton on granary bread. She sets into her lunch with the same gratified relish she gives to most things in her everyday life: it makes Anna smile, and Eleanor sad.

'And how was your holiday?' Stuart asks, secretly hoping, now they are safe at home, that it was not as successful as the cosseted holiday he had planned for them.

Sophie looks up from her lunch and says, glowingly, 'Oh, brilliant. We had rain in Spain and the tent leaked so we had to pack up quick because we were soaking wet and freezing cold. Then we saw this man Steve hitchhiking along an empty road and when Mum stopped to pick him up she went smack into a ditch and couldn't get out.' She turns placidly to her potato salad. 'But after that things settled down,' she finishes.

No one speaks for a few moments after this. Then Stuart says, 'Eleanor, what's for dessert? I hope it is your delicious apple pie. Sophie, did you know your grandmother makes the best apple pie in England?'

'Yes, I know,' Sophie agrees solemnly, and smiles innocently at her mother.

After lunch Sophie and Anna go upstairs for a sleep, neither of them slept much on the ferry. After the evening meal they both excuse themselves and go back to bed, though Anna knows her father is displeased, knows he is ready for their obligatory talk about the future. But she is far too tired to face it tonight.

'What a fun holiday,' Sophie says as she snuggles into the clean sheets, the fresh fluffy duvet.

'It was good, wasn't it.' Anna kisses her goodnight.

Sophie, half asleep, giggles to herself. 'I'm not too sure Grandpa approves of our picking up Steve,' she says mischievously. 'Grandma looked shocked too.'

Anna says nothing, thinking how quick she was to notice their reactions.

'Don't worry, Mum. When they get to know him, they'll quite like him.'

Anna refuses to comment, and goes off thoughtfully to her own bath and bed.

The next day there is no getting away. The rain has stopped and though it is still grey, threatening, Stuart suggests a walk on the Cob around the harbour and everyone obediently agrees, though Eleanor would rather be contemplating her rhododendrons, and Sophie and Anna out looking for fossils on the huge beach a few miles out of town. However, the Cob is pleasant enough and an easy walk for Sophie, for they have taken the car to the sea-front. Stuart and Eleanor are still enchanted with the town though they have been here already seven years, moving from Leeds when Stuart retired as an obstetrician: Stuart to fulfill some long simmering dream about living in the West Country, and Eleanor to minister to him as she has done for the forty-two years of their marriage.

The walk is pleasant; the sun is beginning to beat back most of the clouds and the day is suddenly more promising. Anna looks across the water, marvelling that France is out there somewhere; it seems years since the holiday. They leave the Cob to walk Ollie, the Border Terrier, along the sand but Eleanor says, as if on cue, 'Sophie, why don't we look in the fossil shop again, just you and I? I know you love to look at all the stones and things.'

So this is it, Anna thinks: The Talk. Resigned, she

watches her daughter walk off with her mother, noticing how tall the child is becoming, how she is growing. Before they cross over out of sight they both turn, simultaneously, and wave, Eleanor all beige and tan in her cord skirt, sensible walking shoes, cotton jacket, and Sophie like the sun in bright yellow jumper and trousers.

Stuart and Anna turn back to the sand and the dog, crazed with delight, paddles like a maniac in the shallow water, retrieving the sticks that Stuart throws. Anna notices her father's limp is much worse; he has an arthritic hip but wouldn't dream of having a replacement operation, not now that most of his medical colleagues have retired. Stuart has an unspoken but deep-seated conviction that the medical profession is not what it used to be and there is no one quite good enough to operate on his hip. Anna's brother, Mike, a GP in Bristol, laughs at this, but Anna cannot; she finds her father insufferably irritating, as well as suffocatingly interfering. The fact that he means well, and that she loves him, only slightly softens her feelings towards him.

Now, without preliminary, Stuart, staring at the green-grey sea, says, 'Sophie's liver has deteriorated; you can tell just by looking at her. You never should have taken her on that holiday.'

This of course maddens Anna. Her father knows as well as she does that Sophie's condition is not dependent on outward circumstances, that if there is a deterioration it would have happened regardless. 'Are you saying I don't do what's best for Sophie?' she asks dangerously. 'Are you trying to fill me with guilt now; is that what today's talk is all about?'

Stuart retreats. 'You went so far away,' he says. 'What if Sophie had needed a doctor in a hurry?'

'You put too much faith in your profession,' Anna says wearily. 'I know what the doctors do when Sophie's knees swell, when she's in pain, when she has a fever. They give her drugs, that's all. They give them to me to administer to her.'

Stuart bends stiffly, picks up another stick, and throws it to the dog. 'All the same,' he says, softening, 'I think it's different this time. I think you'd better take her to the hospital when you get to Bristol.'

Anna says nothing, for she knows her father is right. She's noticed it too: a slight, almost imperceptible worsening of Sophie's condition over the last few months. She had already planned to take her daughter back to the hospital for the battery of tests she knows is inevitable – that was why she was so adamant about the camping holiday. One last fling before facing an uncertain future.

That night Anna has two whiskies. Sophie has eaten early and gone to bed, she wants to leave first thing in the morning for home, she whispered to Anna, tactfully when her grandparents were out of earshot. She is eager to see her cat, her schoolfriends, Madge who lives next door, her little bedroom.

'Surely you're not letting her go back to school?' Stuart asks as Eleanor brings him his second whisky.

'Of course I am,' Anna says crossly, taking a large sip of her own drink. 'Sophie loves school. The only reason she agreed to take her holiday during term time was because she hates the summer crowds. You know how they upset her.'

'Your mother and I have been talking,' Stuart says and Anna's heart sinks. She knows it is more likely Stuart has been talking, and Eleanor listening.

'Yes?' she says warily.

'Why don't you and Sophie come to live with us? We have plenty of room, and it would be so much easier for you. You can't do this alone.'

This doesn't surprise Anna; it comes regularly, this suggestion, once a year or so. She says, lightly, 'I have so far, haven't I? Since Richard died I've lived alone, except for Sophie.' Except for Jake, she thinks silently, but that was only for a few months. That was all he could take, and when Anna is honest with herself she knows that was all she could take as well. Sophie, as usual, was the one who suffered most from Anna's involvement: she had liked Jake, liked having a man around. And besides, she told Anna after he had gone, he made her laugh.

Eleanor also is having a second whisky; they must be distraught, Anna thinks. Do I have this effect on everyone, she wonders despairingly? She suddenly feels tremendous pity for her parents, saddled with a stubborn, wilful, widowed daughter and a granddaughter everyone expects to die.

'Anna,' Eleanor is saying, 'I know we have discussed this before, but you must remember it will be different now. Harder.'

As usual, they have talked; as usual, Eleanor knows all about the conversation on the beach that morning. 'I know, Mum,' Anna says harshly, and hopes her mother realizes the harshness is not directed at her. 'But I need to be alone, with Sophie. We need our life together; we need to feel normal.'

Eleanor understands. Unlike Stuart, who takes these rejections personally, who is threatened and undermined by them, Eleanor has always understood her daughter, and has great admiration for her, though she would be embarrassed to say so. Raised in a strict military family, taught from an early age all about stiff upper-lips and the vulgarity of emotions, Eleanor was never able to respond to her daughter's longing for intimacy, and it is too late now: she accepts this, albeit at times sorrowfully. Sometimes, in her more lonely moments, she blames Stuart, then is horrified at herself, for she loves him. Yet she cannot help remembering the time shortly after Sophie's illness was diagnosed, how Anna telephoned her in shock and in tears, how she had wanted to drop everything and go to her daughter.

Stuart prevented her. 'Did she ask you to go?' he asked, as distressed as she was, but always rational, always in control.

'No, but – I want to, Stuart.'

54

'She has Richard. You mustn't interfere in their private grief.'

She listened to him, for that's what the women had always done in her family, listened and obeyed their men. She had listened to Stuart during Anna's adolescence, when the girl had locked herself in her room as teenagers often do and spent hours anguishing to music, or weeping, or reading *Wuthering Heights* for the third or fourth time. 'Leave her,' he had ordered. 'It's only a phase, she'll get over it. I'm not going to pamper her moods, nor are you, Eleanor.'

Eleanor, though troubled, was secretly relieved: though instinct was hurrying her towards her daughter, the years of burying her own emotions, hiding them as if they were some shameful secret, were driving her in the other direction: she was, in truth, slightly afraid of the overwhelming love she felt towards both her children.

When Richard died, there might have been one last chance for mother and daughter to attain the closeness that had always eluded them, but it never occurred because Stuart, burdened with what he saw as a sudden grave responsibility towards Anna and her child, began at once in his usual unsubtle way to try to take them both over. Anna, of course, resisted, and Eleanor unfortunately became the casualty in the subsequent war of wills between them.

Now Eleanor sits sipping her whisky and listens to the two people she loves totally misunderstand each other, Stuart arguing dispassionately why Anna and Sophie should move in with them, and Anna emotionally pleading why they cannot. Finally Eleanor leaves the room, goes into the kitchen to clear away one or two glasses, take out the half-empty rubbish bag. A moment later Anna joins her briefly, kisses her quickly, and says, 'I'm having an early night, I'm still tired from the holiday. Goodnight, Mum.' She is off before Eleanor can respond, before she can say – but what *can* she say? And once again the moment is gone, lost, unrecognized.

The next day in the car, driving to Bristol, Anna asks Sophie, 'Have you ever thought what it would be like living with Grandpa and Grandma? You and me, I mean. They have lots of room, and often say we should move in with them.'

Sophie is horrified. 'Leave Bristol, leave our dear little house, leave my school? Oh Mum, you're joking!'

Anna assures her that it is only a thought, that she has no intention of moving. She expected Sophie's response, but the fact that she felt she must ask makes her suspect some crisis of confidence in her own instincts. Oh Richard, she thinks desolately, why did you die, why did you leave us, why aren't you here to help me decide what's best for our child?

The motorway stretches endlessly on. Anna switches on the tape. 'You're noooot a-lone, you're noooot a-lone, you're nooooot alone any – more . . . ' croons the disembodied voice.

'Don't you believe it,' Anna mutters: and, to her horror, feels the prickle of tears gathering behind her eyes.

The house in Bristol feels cold, musty. It is one of a Victorian terrace of high ceilings, tall windows, and a walled garden, about the size of Stuart and Eleanor's main bath-room. As Anna leaves her parents' home her next-door neighbour, Madge Tyler, lets herself into the empty house and lights the fire in the tiny marble grate, for it is cloudy and cold once again in spite of the month. The house is damp, but the fire will soon warm the small living-room with its old patterned rugs, the sparse but comfortable fur-niture, the odd assortment of plants that Madge has been diligently watering.

She is glad Anna and Sophie are on their way home; she's

missed them. She has lived in the house next door for twenty years, since she was twenty-five and she and Ron, already married for five years and with two infants, moved in. She remembers very vividly the day Richard and Anna and their three-month-old baby arrived; she thought Richard gentle and kind, and Anna bemused and bewildered.

And so she should have been, Madge thinks now as she bustles about, airing the place, giving it a quick dust and hoover. Sophie's illness had just been diagnosed and both parents were in a state of shock. They had been living in rented accommodation, not far from the university where Richard was a lecturer, and they had planned, in another year or so, to move on, go abroad, travel the world, as it were, while Sophie was still young enough to be resilient. Her illness, of course, shattered everything, and they quickly bought the only house they could afford so that they could stay put, be settled near a good hospital. The house was convenient: in the centre of the city, in the Montpelier area, a part of Bristol that had a slightly seedy charm, as if it weren't sure whether it would decline into complete sleaze and poverty, or become trendy and upmarket. In the years Anna and Sophie lived there, it remained indecisive, and still hovered, even now, on the brink.

Madge and Anna became friends at once. By the time they met Madge had four children, all sons, most of whom still lived with her now, as did numerous of their friends when they were jobless/homeless/motherless or whatever. The only person who didn't live with her was her husband, Ron, who had left five years ago on the day Madge turned forty.

'Madge, we have to talk,' Ron had said to her that evening after all the guests from her party had gone home.

'Sure, honey,' Madge said, taking off her large looped gypsy earrings. 'Oh boy, what a party, what a goddamned crazy party.' She laughed her hot rumbling laugh that seemed to erupt like lava over anyone within earshot, scalding them to attention. 'Oh boy, oh boy, oh boy,' she chuckled, collapsing on to the sofa in simulated exhaustion.

Madge was an addict of American television, and watched all the old movies on video, as well as taped re-runs of the *I Love Lucy* and Jackie Gleason shows. Over the years her speech had surreptitiously – and unconsciously – acquired much of the slang and a good deal of the rhythm of the other side of the Atlantic, and even her clothes seemed a hybrid throw-back of California in the sixties mixed with Southern suburbia. She had a huge collection of love-beads and wild, shoulder-length earrings which she wore indiscriminately, but she also leaned to cotton trousers (which she called slacks) in dusty pastel colours worn with matching sweatshirts. She had valid claims on the States: her formative years were spent there, her father working as an engineer on a huge dam on the West Coast until the family separated and her mother returned alone with Madge to England.

'What a night,' Madge repeated. 'What a way to turn forty!'

Ron loosened his red bow tie, the one that lit up when you pressed a secret button in his pocket. He had a chunky face and manly rough hair; he was not unattractive except for times like these, more and more often lately, when his face was blotchy with drink, his eyes puffy with excess. 'Hmm,' he muttered distractedly, struggling to undo his top shirt button which was feeling uncomfortably tight.

Madge fondly helped him take off his bow tie, loosen his collar. She was wide awake and bouncy now, looking forward to a good romp in their soft lumpy double bed that night: the combination of alcohol and the open admiration of her male friends had made her flushed and lusty.

'Coffee, cutie?' she said seductively, wiggling with anticipation as she unbuttoned his shirt.

'What?' Ron sat up and looked at her strangely. 'Yes – no

– I don't know. Look, Madge, we have to talk,' he said again pushing her hand rather insensitively away.

Offended, Madge was silent. 'Well?' she said.

'This is hard, Madge. This is bloody hard.'

'Is it? What is?'

Ron looked at her despairingly. 'It's just that . . . you're forty, for God's sake.'

'You're real slow sometimes, aren't you?' she said, not unkindly. 'We've been planning my fortieth birthday party for months.'

'I know. I've been brooding about it for months.'

'On *what*, goddamn it?'

'On your fortieth birthday.'

Madge sighed, and slipped off her strappy, high-heeled sandals, and rubbed the callouses on her toes. 'Look, Ron, I'm tired. I guess I thought we'd have some coffee and a post-mortem on the party, then go up to bed and, you know, celebrate with an orgy for two up there for a while.'

Ron groaned. 'I can't.'

Madge rolled her eyes, grinned ruefully, and said with a sigh, 'Okay, sweetheart. We'll make it tomorrow. I guess you sure had a lot to drink, and so did I come to think of it. I just thought, because it's kind of a special birthday – '

'Jesus, Madge, don't you listen to a thing I'm saying? *You're forty.*'

'So?'

'How do you think I feel, married to a forty-year-old?'

Madge looked at him blankly. 'Ron, I don't think I'm hearing you.'

He moaned softly, brimming with his own distress. 'I've got to go,' he said, not looking at her. 'I've got to get out. I can't stick it any more, I just can't. I've been thinking and thinking about it for weeks. I'm young, I *feel* young, I only stopped playing rugby two years ago. I'll go under, Madge, I can feel it, married to a forty-year-old.'

59

There was a deadly, viperous silence. Then Madge said, with a sharp little hiss, 'You're forty-one, Ron.'

He bent double as if wounded, and looked at Madge reproachfully. 'I know, I know,' he said, tortured. 'Don't remind me.'

'You're older than me, Ron.'

'God, will you stop saying that. That's the whole point – I don't feel it, I don't look it. Don't you see? You remind me of it all the time, how old we are, how old we've grown. Every time I look at you I see zimmer frames and plastic glasses of grisly false teeth – '

'Oh, for – '

'And it's too soon, Madge. I'm just not ready for it so soon.'

There was another ominous pause. 'I thought I looked pretty young for my age,' Madge finally said, because she was too stunned to say anything else.

'That's not the point.' Ron, not looking at her, dropped his face wearily into his square chunky hands. 'I'm sorry, Madge. I've got to go, okay? I've just got to get out of here.'

Madge sighs, remembering. She lost her anger years ago; she didn't have much time for it, raising her kids. Tom, the baby, was only thirteen when Ron left, and the others, though older, were all still at home. Anna was the one who helped out: Anna, who had lost a husband herself, knew what it was all about. Anna was the one who held her hand in the early days when she woke up at five every morning, no matter what time she had gone to sleep, and knew she couldn't go on: Anna was the one who supplied brandy during those long winter evenings when Madge thought she would die with the love, with the loss. For she loved him still, Madge did; she knew he was a swine, knew he was worthless, but she loved him still as the months, and then the years, moved relentlessly on.

Madge had helped Anna also, helped her during those

nightmare weeks after Richard had taken his boat, the boat he had made himself, into the Channel during the stormy season, no doubt (Anna thought) hoping the right wave would hit the boat at the right time, sending him speedily into oblivion. He was successful almost immediately, and it was Madge who sat day and night with Anna for days before his boat was finally washed up miles away on a sandy cove.

God, we've gone through some hell together, Madge thinks grimly as she opens the fridge, checks on the fresh tomatoes, cheese, and other goodies she has bought to welcome Anna and Sophie home. She is just starting to water the kitchen plants when the door bursts open and she is hugged tightly, kissed warmly, and pelted with words:

'Madge, we're back!'

'A fire, how lovely.'

'I brought you a present from Spain!'

'How have you been? We've missed you.'

Sophie goes upstairs to find Samantha, her white cat, and to check out her bedroom, her dolls and her books and her story-tapes. Madge has made coffee, and bought fresh croissants from the bakery on the corner. 'Thought you'd be missing the taste of the Continent,' she says with a grin as the two women sit at the kitchen table.

The kitchen is small but pleasant, with an old gas cooker, pine shelves and cupboards that Richard made when they first moved in, and a rather shabby wooden door leading to a miniscule garden surrounded by a high brick wall. A wobbly sun tries to find its way in but is thwarted by sudden black clouds; there is a strong wind, much too cold for late May.

'Well honey,' Madge says when they are alone. 'How was it?'

Anna looks at her friend warmly, yet she hesitates before speaking. There are no secrets between them, but she just doesn't know what to say, how to describe the past few weeks, with its strange juxtaposition of despair and contentment, fear and calm.

61

'Tell me about Sophie,' Madge says, when Anna does not speak. She knows Anna, she can sense that there is much to tell. She knows Sophie also, and so is able to say, baldly, 'She's not that great, is she? Her skin . . . ' she trails off: there is no need to say any more.

Anna nods her head. 'I phoned Mike, he's coming out this afternoon to give her a check-up.' She tells Madge, briefly, about the acceleration of Sophie's condition. Madge is not surprised; she too has seen the signs.

When they have finished talking about Sophie, Madge says, 'So what else, honey? What else haven't you told Auntie Madge?'

Anna rolls her eyes, shakes her head. There is no one looking less like an auntie, she thinks, eyeing Madge fondly. Though the woman is ten years older than her, she has much more life and energy. She is fair, with fine straight hair feathering her great circle of a face which is as round and pale as the full moon in the small hours of the morning. Her smile, which stretches broadly from ear to ear, turns it all about, makes the moon new and crescent: promising. She is slightly plump, which looks right and natural with her wide-open face, and men adore her. Since Ron left men have been falling in love with her all over the place, much to the amusement of her adult children.

Anna begins, hesitantly, because she herself is unsure of what happened in Spain and in France. Madge listens well and intently, and when Anna finishes, says, 'Those are the facts, sweetheart. Now tell me how you feel, what this man means to you.'

'How can he mean anything? We've known each other less than three weeks; we made love once, only once.'

Madge grins. 'Was it good?'

Anna grins too, then nods. 'Brief, but I'm not complaining. It rather took me by surprise, though looking back I guess we had been building up to it since the day we met.'

'You're not made of stone, Anna. So admit you need a bit of loving now and again, it's no big deal.'

'You make it sound so uncomplicated.'

Madge takes Anna's hand, gives it a big squeeze, and says, 'It sounds like this is more than a quick roll on a sand dune. Look, it's okay, Anna, it really is okay, to fall in love, let yourself be loved.'

'Oh God. Why, what for, what's the point? They leave in the end, because I love Sophie too much, or they can't cope with her, or I can't give them what they want because I don't trust anyone any more, can't love anyone any more, not properly – '

'Hey, Anna, I didn't realize you've got it this bad – '

'Oh God.' Anna gets up, pours herself more coffee, finds her hands are shaking. 'Oh God,' she says again, looking at Madge with dismay, 'I didn't realize it either.'

A sudden imperious banging on the front door interrupts them. Madge goes to answer it while Anna goes upstairs to check on Sophie, who seems feverish but looks quite happy lying on her bed, stroking Samantha, and listening to her story-tape of *Heidi*. Anna kisses her, covers her with a blanket, and returns to the kitchen, to find Madge's estranged husband Ron eating all the leftover croissants and scolding Madge with his mouth full.

'Oh hi, Anna,' Ron says. 'Holiday all right?'

Though Ron has, for all intents and purposes, left Madge, he is a frequent visitor at the house next door, because of the children, he tells Anna and anyone who will listen. Anna believes it is because he cannot quite let Madge go; having rejected her, he cannot accept that other men haven't; that, on the contrary, they find her compellingly attractive. And so he hangs around as if wanting to discover for himself what it is that other men want, in what he has discarded.

'Yes, fine, thanks. I see you have some coffee.'

'Madge got me a cup. Look, I'm glad to find her here

63

with you, Anna; maybe you can talk some sense into her.'

'Holy hell, I don't believe it, my ex is expounding sense.' Madge lapses into the flippant, sardonic tone she always uses with Ron; since he left her, she has made herself brittle in her relations with him, knowing he would only be scornful of tears or tenderness.

'I'm not your ex yet, Madge. We're not divorced.'

'Only because none of your bimbos will marry you.'

Anna, taking her coffee out towards the living-room, says, 'Uh oh, domestic violence coming up; I'm going in the other room.'

Madge stops her. 'No way, honey, I need you. The man looks ugly.'

Ron sneers, rather ineffectually. No doubt he rather likes seeing himself as a macho tough, Anna thinks, all that beer drinking and rugby club veneer he carries around him like a banner. She cannot see why Madge still loves him, she finds his rugged looks slightly repellent, like a middle-aged Action Man, and his behaviour appalling. After he left his wife and family he found a flat not very far away and lives there still, entertaining a series of young women whose age decreases every year, as Ron's increases. He drives a flash sports car and wears trendy leather jackets and his wiry hair, just beginning to grey when he left his wife, has, through the years, darkened suspiciously to a glossy auburn. At the local school, where he is a physical education teacher, a rumour was started by some of his colleagues that he is illiterate, but the truth is far simpler: he is too vain to wear reading glasses. Madge seriously suspects him of toying with the more wanton sixth form girls.

Now he narrows his eyes at Anna, giving her his sexy look, purely out of habit because he has always felt uneasy around her, all that frizzy hair and unconcealed sadness. He says, 'Anna, you won't believe this, you really won't, what Madge has been up to while you've been away.'

Anna raises her eyes at Ron, surreptitiously winks at Madge. Neither woman says anything.

'She's got a lover, that's what.'

Anna opens her mouth, widens her eyes in mock surprise and horror. 'Nooo!' she says theatrically. 'The hussy – you only left her five years ago.'

Ron scowls at her. Madge says, 'Oh, for Christ's sake, Ron, come off it. Who are you to talk?'

He sniffs righteously, narrows his eyes again, this time at Madge. 'Look, I know you're entitled, I know we've split up. I've been pretty tolerant of all the others – '

'You what?'

'But this is different. You've let him move in with you, and don't deny it, the kids have told me.'

'And what about that Italian *au pair* who rowed with her employers . . . and moved in with you for four months, until she found someone younger and took off with all your CDs and your leather jacket?'

'That's beside the point.'

'And the cutie little blonde number who said she was twenty-five but anyone with half a brain could see was pushing forty – didn't she live with you for quite a while, until you realized she was more expensive than me and all your kids put together?'

'Madge, we're not talking about me, and anyway that's all ancient history. The difference here is that it's still half my house that you're entertaining your lovers in – '

Madge swears colourfully, a mixture of English and American, and says, 'He's a lodger, Ron, he's paying me for a room. Which is more than any of the kids do, or their friends. You haven't exactly paid me a fortune to house and feed your children over the past years.'

'God, Madge, except for Tom they're all over twenty, and he's eighteen.'

'They're still your kids, sunshine. None of them have exactly established themselves yet: they're still struggling, either getting educated, or finding themselves . . . '

'Oh shit. Still using you. You're too bloody soft, Madge, always have been.'

Anna, who is used to these scenes, has been busy making Sophie a cheese and tomato sandwich. 'Lunch, Madge?' she asks pointedly.

Ron doesn't take the hint. 'Look, let's get back to the main subject here. This lodger bloke, is he your current lover or not?'

'I guess that's none of your goddamn business, Ron. You left me, remember? Who I have in that great double bed that used to be mine and yours is *my* affair.'

Ron leans over the table, getting croissant crumbs over his black rugby jumper. 'Look,' he says earnestly, 'it's your life, I grant you that; if you want to act cheap and undignified, carrying on in the family house, it's up to you. It's the kids I worry about. It's not a very good example to them, having your lover move in like that.'

The hypocrisy of this is so gross that both Anna and Madge spontaneously giggle, then catch each other's eyes and laugh long and helplessly. Ron, hurt, says, 'Oh sod it, it's no good trying to talk reasonably to you when you're in this mood. I'll speak with you another time, Madge.' He adds caustically, 'When you're alone.' Getting up to go he nods curtly to Anna, throwing her his tough macho sneer which she catches by blowing him a wide-eyed, innocent, little doll-like kiss, which takes him totally by surprise. Not quite sure whether she is flirting with him or not, he stares at her with his hot sexy look and a kind of leer which unfortunately comes across as silly rather than smouldering. Then, suddenly suspecting he is being made a fool of, he stomps out, slamming the door with manly vigour behind him. Anna and Madge collapse in hysterics.

'Oh God!' Madge says when she finally stops laughing.

'Anna, you're wicked. For a moment he thought he had actually made a new conquest.'

'I can't help it, I just can't help trying to deflate that man's incredible ego; he really does think he's God's gift and all that.'

'Hmm,' Madge says, preoccupied, her mood suddenly sombre.

'Hey, look, I don't mean to put him down. I know you still want him back, and if that's what you want –' She breaks off; she has had this conversation before with Madge.

'It's okay, honey. I know him for what he is, and it may not be much, but he's the father of my kids, you know? Anyway let's not talk about him anymore.'

'What's this about your lover moving in? When I left you were off men, hadn't had a partner in six months! Who is he?'

'Would you like to meet him? He's next door now, playing chess with Tom. Thank goodness Ron came straight in here to find me; they haven't met yet.' She leaves to fetch her new man while Anna goes upstairs to take Sophie her sandwich, chat to her for a few minutes. When she returns to the kitchen she sees Madge wrapped in an erotic embrace with what looks, from the back, like a young boy, in dark track suit bottoms, a colourful tie-dyed granddad shirt, and a red headband holding back shoulder-length black hair, as shiny and flowing and straight as an elegant inky waterfall.

'Oh, uh, Anna, sorry, thought you were upstairs.' Madge disentangles herself and Anna sees the boy is a young man with lugubrious black eyes and incredibly high cheek bones. 'This is Juan Carlos,' Madge goes on. 'He's from Chile, studying engineering at college here.' Seeing Anna's face she adds, with her wide half-moon grin, 'He's a mature student, honey, don't you worry.'

Anna smiles: the lad is surely not a day over twenty-five. '*Encantada de conocerte. ¿Cómo te parece nuestro país?*' she says.

Juan Carlos grabs her hand, shakes it passionately, replies in Spanish how wonderful it is she speaks his language. '*Fenomenal. Hablas castellano.* How fluent you are.'

'I've always wanted to go to your country,' Anna says. 'It was . . . our dream,' she finishes weakly.

Juan Carlos nods sympathetically; Madge has told him all about Anna and Richard and Sophie. They talk about Chile for a few moments, until Madge says, 'Juan Carlos is supposed to be practising English, you know, though he's quite good.'

'It is the writing I find difficult, the writing and the grammar. Reading too is sometimes a problem for me, the – how do you say it, the idiom, yes? So hard, you know.' He shakes his head despondently, and his silky hair ruffles gently, like water stirred by a soft breeze. He looks so sad and troubled that Anna can understand why Madge feels moved to run her fingers through that cascade of hair, letting them linger in the flow before resting them lightly on his strong young arm.

'Well, he *would* try and start with Dickens,' she says fondly, giving his arm a little squeeze to which he responds by taking her hand and lightly kissing the fingertips in a gesture as natural and easy as a smile or a shrug.

'It is the writer I was told was most well-respected and famous in your country,' Juan Carlos explains. 'I did not want to begin with anything less.' He looks so solemn and serious that Madge is moved to take his arm again, and he winds his fingers through hers like a vine.

'I found him in the library,' she says fondly, as if referring to a stray puppy or a mislaid fountain pen. 'He was struggling with *Bleak House* and I was trying to get everyone out to lock up.'

'I was depressed and discouraged. My translation made no sense; my English was rubbish.'

'He looked pretty gloomy,' Madge agreed. 'When I found out he didn't even *have* to read Dickens, he was just doing it to improve his English, I gave him some modern novels and a collection of Spanish poetry in both languages.'

Juan Carlos smiles at her, and his mournful eyes look slightly less tragic. 'Lorca, Neruda . . . in an English library, what joy, what bliss!'

'I guess it was, baby doll, after Dickens! Anyway, he looked hungry as well as depressed, so I took him home, and here we are!' She presses his hand, still entwined in hers, and adds, rather enigmatically, 'It's amazing what some good home-cooking can do.' They look as if they are about to start nuzzling each other, like puppies or adolescents, but then Anna volunteers to help Juan Carlos with some English lessons and they turn to her eagerly.

'I am afraid I cannot pay you,' he remembers suddenly, in great distress, his enthusiasm of a moment ago shattered. 'I have a poultry grant and that is all.'

They look at him in some confusion. 'You know,' he explains. 'Not very much. Trifling. Poultry.'

'I think you mean "paltry",' Anna says, and then to Madge: 'Thank God you've weaned him from Dickens.' She tells him she'd be happy to help Juan Carlos as a favour to Madge, who has helped her so often in the past. And besides, she rather likes this young man with the soulful eyes and the erratic temperament, plunging from joy to despair in the midst of sentences and hovering over Madge like a dark bee over a pale plump flower. It will be a change from her usual students wanting a crash course before a holiday in Majorca or a package tour to the Costa del Sol. Anna is a Spanish teacher and has been for years; she earns her living doing private teaching, some supply work when available, and the odd translations. She needs to be flexible because of Sophie and this mixture of several part-time jobs suits her well.

Juan Carlos is so grateful he is almost delirious, and in a sparky, ebullient mood entertains the two women with outlandish stories about his childhood in Chile. He is witty and fun, and Anna asks them to stay for lunch, making another pot of coffee and some sandwiches, checking first on Sophie who has fallen asleep upstairs with the cat curled snugly on her belly. The indecisive sun has finally penetrated the clouds and the high brick wall and is shining in the tiny garden, so they take their sandwiches outside, pulling out the kitchen chairs to sit on. Juan Carlos places his chair close to Madge's and as they eat he rests his leg so that it is touching hers, as if he cannot be without that contact, not even for a moment. Anna, noticing, feels oddly bereft, as if the warm spring sun has somehow missed her, leaving her permanently in shadow.

When the doorbell rings she feels a spasm of relief. Enjoyable as she is finding the company of Madge and Juan Carlos, there is an energy, a charge, she finds disconcerting, unsettling, as if it is forcing something inside *her* to stir, grow, come alive, something she'd rather remained dormant. Thoughtfully, she opens the door and a large woolly man grabs and embraces her. It is her brother Mike, whom she both loves and likes enormously. He has come to look at Sophie, and the faith and trust and hope in her face as she kisses him, telling him how grateful and relieved she is that he came so quickly, pains him, for he would do anything for Anna and knows that the one thing that would bring her peace and happiness is the one thing he cannot give her: Sophie's health. Sadly, he follows her into the house, determined at least to do all in his power to protect her, to shield her with his great clumsy love in whatever way he can, at whatever cost to himself. He has done this all his life anyway, since the day Anna was five and some school bullies took her glasses, which she had to wear all the time then, and hid them amongst the frog-spawn behind what the primary school teachers called the Science Room. Mike found her at break time curled like a foetus in a corner of the room, her astigmatic eyes black with shock and damp with unshed tears which finally flowed in a copious torrent when she saw her brother. The mixture of unbearable tenderness and a righteous, blazing rage that overwhelmed him then was to return time and time again, whenever Anna was hurt, suffering, in pain.

He feels it now, feels it as he follows her up the stairs to Sophie's bedroom, despairing that protecting his sister now will never be as easy as finding the two thugs who had bullied her, threatening them in his potent anger until they were only too glad to apologize and retrieve the glasses from the murky science pond. He hadn't realized then, in his euphoria over his success and Anna's vociferous gratitude, that that victory was the most simple, the most satisfying. The torment and the anguish she was to suffer later, he would not be able to protect her from; and yet he was never to stop trying.

'There she is, she's asleep,' Anna says now at the door to Sophie's bedroom.

'Let her sleep. I'm not in a hurry.'

'Oh Mike! I'm so glad you're here!' The relief surging from Anna stirs his own helplessness. 'I don't know what I'd do without you. I'm hoping you'll say I've been imagining it all, that she just has a virus, or measles or whatever.'

Mike is too churned to answer. *If only I could*, he thinks hopelessly. *If only I could*. Drowning in his own impotence, he walks slowly over to Sophie.

Chapter Five

SOPHIE does not wake as Mike sits down on the bed, and after a moment he leaves her, telling Anna she is sleeping so peacefully it would be a shame to disturb her. Downstairs, Mike is introduced to Juan Carlos, and shortly afterwards he and Madge leave. Whether this is tact or lust, Anna is not quite sure.

When they are alone Mike says, 'The old man phoned after you left Lyme Regis, told me about Sophie.'

'He would. Didn't he think I was capable of telling you her symptoms myself?'

'You know what he's like. This was strictly professional, one medical man to another.'

Anna has to laugh. 'It's only when it suits him that he considers you in the same profession.'

Mike smiles, and his whole shaggy brown-grey beard wiggles and squirms like some furry animal just waking up. He is four years older than Anna, and looks ten years older. He is a GP in the toughest, poorest section of Bristol: he is there by choice, has been for years, and only now has their father become resigned to the fact that his son is not going to specialize.

Mike says, 'I'll give Sophie a good check over when she wakes up; then we'll decide what to do. In the meantime, tell me all about your holiday. But before you do, be warned: our father wants me to find out, discreetly of course, who this Steve is, that Sophie so indiscreetly mentioned.'

'Oh God. Tell them no one, tell them he's just someone who helped us out when the tent leaked, someone we met casually.'

Mike twinkles at her, the eyes of an inquisitive bushy wood creature. 'I don't want to know, you know. Not until you want to talk about it. And I certainly won't tell them, when you do.'

Before Anna can answer she hears Sophie moving about upstairs. 'She's awake, why don't you go up? She'll be delighted to see you.'

He does, and Anna can hear Sophie squealing with delight, can hear Mike teasing her as he always does. 'Goodness! Look at those knees: sausages, that's what they are, sausages!' he exclaims. Anna knows he is feeling them, testing them, but Sophie thinks he's tickling and laughs happily. She never knows when his playing and teasing has stopped and the serious medical examination has begun, so intertwined are the two when Mike is examining her. No wonder there are people queuing to be on his list, Anna thinks.

They come downstairs together, hand in hand, half an hour later. Sophie has shown him all her souvenirs from Spain and France: a tiny paper fan for Alice, her favourite doll, an embroidered collar for Samantha, a shell from the beach with the sand dunes. Anna gives her a drink of orange juice then puts the telly on for her in the living-room. There is an old Hollywood musical on; like Madge, Sophie loves the old films.

Mike and Anna go into the kitchen, shut the door. 'Well?' Anna says, watching her brother's face closely. 'No measles?' she says ruefully, miserably trying to be light. Then: 'She's not that good, I can tell myself. I'd better take her back to the children's hospital, let Miles Jordan look at her again.'

Mike takes a deep breath, looks out the open kitchen door into the tiny garden still grasping the sunlight. 'Look, after Dad phoned this morning, I rang Miles. You only saw him a few weeks ago, remember; he did some tests on Sophie, a day or so before you left for Spain.'

'Yes, I know. Routine tests; Sophie has them regularly.

So what did he say?' But as Anna says this, she knows what
he said. Miles Jordan, and her father, and Mike, have been
preparing her for this for years. Time suddenly stops still:
there are noises outside of people talking, the sound of an
engine revving, but they are not of this moment, they are
detached and floating, the moment itself has frozen: there is
nothing but this: all that has gone before has led only to this.

Mike says, 'You okay, love?' and when Anna nods, he
begins to speak. 'Miles said that the deterioration of
Sophie's liver since the last tests are alarming; it's probably
the spurt of growth she's having as she nears puberty.
He said that the prognosis is not hopeful unless she has a
transplant.'

Anna digests this information which Mike has delivered
quickly, professionally, though he has gently put his arm
around her shoulders, as if he could protect her from the
deluge of anguish and despair flooding her as she assimilates
this new information. Reggae music floats from the pub
behind the house over the high brick wall and from far away
Anna can hear laughter. Her world has cracked and there is
still laughter: she cannot understand this.

She says, shaking her head as if trying to clear it, trying
to understand something incomprehensible and slightly
repellent, 'You know I haven't decided yet about a transplant. It's dangerous, they often don't work. Or if they do
maybe it's for a few months, a year, then the patient dies
anyway. And then there are the drugs, all those awful drugs
they give which cause other problems, terrible problems.
I can't do it, can't let her go through it.'

The tears are rolling down her cheeks but she doesn't
even notice them, she is looking at Mike pleadingly, and it
breaks his heart. 'Anna, listen to me,' he says forcibly.
'Anna, every day there is progress made on transplants, new
safer drugs to counter rejection, new techniques to match
organs. You've got to give it a try.'

'You sound like our father.'

'Sometimes he makes sense, you know.' He takes a large red, rumpled handkerchief out of his pocket, gives it to Anna. 'Listen, Miles Jordan has phoned the liver transplant unit at the hospital in Birmingham; it's closer for you to get to than London. He's made an appointment for you to go there with Sophie for a few days of tests. At least have the tests, talk to the doctors at the transplant unit. The final decision is still yours, but at least talk to the medical team there before you make it.'

When Anna is silent he says, gently, 'You've got to give Sophie a chance, Anna. She has none at all otherwise.'

Anna nods. She is so shattered emotionally that she doesn't know if she feels relief or anger that suddenly, without her knowledge or consent, things are starting to move for her daughter. 'So when . . . when is this appointment?'

'Tuesday. You'll be in for most of the week. You can stay with her, of course, they've got accommodation.'

Tuesday. Today is Saturday, Anna thinks distractedly then says, brusquely, 'Out of the question. Sophie is looking forward to going back to school on Monday; she must have some time back with her friends. You'll have to postpone it.'

Mike, knowing the stress she is under, takes her hand again and holds it gently. 'Anna, Miles says Sophie will become weaker very quickly now: if there is to be a transplant, it must be done as soon as possible.'

Anna knows he is right. She crashes into reality with a shattering of emotions: shock and grief and terror. *Her child may die.* The thought hammers her almost senseless: she has never really believed it until now.

'You're late.' Mike's wife, Mary, greets him crossly at the door. 'The kids have been waiting to go to the zoo for ages. Some afternoon off this is.'

Mike hugs his three assorted children, all under eight, and kisses his pregnant wife. She was nineteen when she boldly, assertively, asked him to marry her; she was a student, but desperately unsuited to it, as all she wanted was babies. Often he wonders why she chose him as the father; certainly she is not much interested in him as a husband. Her babies are her life, her heart and soul: she loves them with a passion and an intensity she has never felt for Mike, and which sometimes depresses him, though luckily not often. He himself is obsessed by his patients, by their illnesses and vagaries and complaints and terrors, so he understands his wife's obsession with her offspring.

With much clamour and chatter, the children are scurrying into the hallway to find coats and jumpers, hurried along by Mary. 'They've been hanging around my feet for the past hour, waiting for you. I haven't been able to get anything done, I wanted to re-pot the plants in the conservatory.'

Mike sighs. 'You knew I was at Anna's. I told you I might be late.'

'I thought we'd have dinner in the conservatory tomorrow evening, now that the weather has turned mild. You do remember the Johnson-Scotts are coming over? He's the new headmaster at David's school; I thought we should get to know him as all the children will be going there eventually.' She is busy with zips and buttons, with shoe laces and buckles. David, the oldest, is nagging at the others to hurry up but at the same time is surreptitiously unlacing his younger brother's trainers, hoping to trip him up.

'Everyone's temper is frayed,' Mary snaps, insinuating that it is all her husband's fault. 'And Owen has a dreadful cold.' She takes out a handkerchief and wipes her middle child's nose.

Mike says, evenly, 'Anna was distraught. I had to examine Sophie.'

'Always Anna, always Sophie. You spend more time with them than with your own family.'

This is so untrue that Mike doesn't even answer. This is an old familiar argument which he doesn't want to get into now, so he just says, mildly, 'You could have come with me, you and the kids; Anna and Sophie would have liked to see you all. Then we could have gone straight to the zoo from there.'

Mary doesn't answer. Instead, she walks away into the kitchen to collect her wax jacket from a hook behind the door. Mike follows her, but she ignores him as she ties a patterned scarf around her long, lank hair which is pulled back and fastened with a clip. 'We'd better go,' she says shortly. The querulous voices of the children, still arguing in the hallway, filter into the rest of the house.

Suddenly Mike is angry. The emotion is so sharp, so volatile, so unfamiliar, that he is taken aback. 'You haven't even asked about Sophie,' he says, his cheeks, underneath all the hair and fuzz, bright red.

Mary looks fleetingly guilty and says, begrudgingly, 'I've known she's not well for ages, just as you have. I don't like to talk about it, that's all.'

'Jesus. Where are you, Mary? What world do you live in? My niece is probably going to have a life-or-death operation and you don't want to talk about it. What the hell do you want to talk about: what wines we'll serve to our son's head-master tomorrow? Owen's sniffles?'

Mary stiffens, puts her hand to her face in a defensive gesture and says, stubbornly, 'I just don't think we should dwell on it. It doesn't help anything.'

All the anger drains out of Mike like a blocked-up pipe suddenly opened, leaving him empty and weary. He knows why Mary hardly ever goes to see Anna and Sophie, knows why she abruptly, rudely, tries to change the conversation whenever he talks about them. It is because she is frightened. Superstitiously, she feels that the more her children have contact with Sophie, the more chances they have of losing their own robust health and becoming mortal, which she pretends to herself they are not. She doesn't think these things consciously, but they are there, they are there. And so she wounds her husband, antagonizes Anna, and deprives all the children, both Sophie and her own three, of a family bond and companionship they all crave and need. Most of the time she is not even aware she is doing this: she says she is too busy, too tired; she says the children are too busy or too tired.

But today it is Mike who is tired. Even his own children, whom he loves, cannot energize him; for a moment he thinks he will renege on the zoo, tell Mary to go without him.

He doesn't, of course. He is one of those rare things, a genuine carer of others. Composing his worn furry face into some semblance of joyful anticipation he shouts to the children, 'Who's ready, then? Let's go to the zoo!'

During the next few hours, while Mike shepherds his children around the snakes and tigers, Anna balances on the abyss, trying not to look down, trying to stand firm on the edge of normality so that she does not totally collapse. Mike stayed with her for quite some time; when he finally left, on Anna's insistence, he went next door and asked Madge to come over. Madge despatched her eighteen-year-old son, Tom, to take Sophie, who was feeling better after Mike's visit, down the road to Daphne's Café to treat her to a hot chocolate and a Danish pastry. Then she sat Anna down at the kitchen table and listened while Anna talked, around and around in circles, and cried, and despaired. By the time Sophie and Tom came back much later, Anna had smoothed the ragged tatters of her composure and was able to send Madge home to look after her own brood. Then she cooked a meal for Sophie, listened to her excited chatter, her pleasure at being home again, and tucked her up fairly early into bed as she was looking wan again, and febrile.

Now Anna, having wandered around the house in an exhausted daze too tired to even attempt to sort out bags and camping equipment, sits down to watch the ten o'clock news but she cannot concentrate. For her there is no news but the catastrophic one about Sophie: she doesn't give a damn for the rest of the world at this moment. How strange, she thinks detachedly, how appallingly selfish one becomes when in the midst of a personal tragedy.

She is staring at the small coloured screen, wondering how she is going to get through the night, when the telephone rings.

'Anna?' says a familiar voice. 'I'm in Bristol. Can I see you?'

It is Steve, and Anna's first reaction is a sudden longing to see this man again, this man she hardly knows yet knows intimately, having lived with him on holiday for three weeks and made love to him, albeit only once. It is immediate and intense, this craving: and disturbing because although she has thought of him several times, when she was telling Madge about the holiday and, later, watching Madge and Juan Carlos together, she has not thought of him once since Mike left after examining Sophie. It was as if all memory of Steve had been eradicated completely by her telescopic focus on her daughter.

But a second, stronger, reaction supercedes this first one of longing and vulnerability; it is some kind of survival mechanism for she automatically closes herself up, puts up the defences. She cannot, she tells herself, off-load her personal grief on a virtual stranger, especially one for whom she is feeling dangerously fond. When she and Sophie left him at his house in Devon she felt oddly bereft and suddenly lonely, lonelier than she had felt since Richard died. She doesn't need that kind of involvement now, she tells herself: she has Sophie, that's enough. Any crumbs from that cake she gives gladly to her family, to Madge and other friends, but that's all she has left now, after Sophie. Crumbs.

So she says, clutching the telephone tightly, 'Steve, I only got back from my parents today; I'm exhausted, just about to go to bed. Maybe next time you're in Bristol give me a ring.'

A pause. Then, lightly, 'Fine. I'll be in touch.'

He hangs up, and the momentary pang Anna feels is

pushed aside by thoughts of Sophie, as she struggles to come to terms with the idea of a liver transplant for her child. She has always been wary of transplant operations, and now she must decide whether her daughter should have one. Though the medical profession will give her the facts, and her own family and friends advise her, she is still very much aware that the final decision must be hers, as Sophie's only surviving parent.

As usual during moments of stress and panic like these, she thinks of Richard, Sophie's father, unable to help her, unable to share the burden she is carrying now. She remembers their closeness in the early days of their marriage, remembers the light-heartedness they had shared, planning for the future that was never to materialize.

'Travel!' Richard had cried one tipsy evening as they drank cheap bubbly and talked about what they wanted from their life together.

'Children!' Anna said, clinking his glass and settling down on his lap. 'But do they go together?'

'They will in our family. Our kids will be the best back-packers in Europe.'

Flashes of remembered conversation strike Anna at random: unwelcome lightning, illuminating a past she finds too painful to see clearly. 'What do you mean, Anna, sell the tent? Why?'

'We need the money, Richard, and . . . we'll never be able to travel with Sophie, you know that.'

'Ah, Anna, Anna.' An embrace, a reassuring smile, and then: 'When she's older, love, you wait. She'll love camping as much as you do.'

And another time: Sophie with a high temperature, Anna waiting for the doctor, and Richard suddenly home from work, though it was only mid-morning. 'Why have you come back?' Anna asked. 'We agreed there is nothing you can do here; she is no worse than she has been at other times. Look, she's asleep.'

'Have you eaten anything yet, any breakfast? Have you even had a coffee?'

'No, I suppose not, but – '

'I've been worrying about you all morning. I'll stay with Sophie now and you go downstairs. I've bought a loaf of that rye bread you love, it's still fresh and warm . . . '

Remembering, restlessly walking from the high long windows near the door, around the dining-table covered with Sophie's books and drawings, into the kitchen and back out again, Anna begins to feel the growing bitterness, animosity, towards Richard that always spreads like an evil weed inside her when anxiety for Sophie ploughs her under into despair. For in the end he abdicated: having shouldered early on so much of the responsibility for Sophie, he was broken by the intolerable weight. *He should be here*, Anna thinks desperately. *He should be sharing this with me now.* She remembers painfully how she loved him, how she trusted him more than she will ever trust anyone again, and, not for the first time, denounces him in her heart for abandoning her.

An hour passes. Anna paces, sometimes picking up a crayon drawing of Sophie's, sometimes just stopping suddenly and staring into space. And then, shrilly, the doorbell rings. Anna hesitates. It is Saturday night and Richmond Road is, as usual, rowdy with the overflow of the pub around the back. She opens the door cautiously, secure behind the chain, and sees Steve standing there looking apprehensive.

'What about your early night?' he says sheepishly when he is in the house, the door shut behind him, and they are hugging tightly in the middle of the living-room. When he finally tries to pry her loose, for she seems to be sniffling and choking in his arms, he realizes she is crying.

'I feel like a sodden waterfall,' she says at last. 'I've been doing this on and off all afternoon.'

Steve sits her down on the old sofa in front of the fire,

opens a bottle of Rioja that he bought at the bottom of the road 'for old time's sake', he explains with a grin, and after pouring them each a glass settles back to listen, while Anna tells him everything that has happened that day.

'My family will push me into Sophie having a transplant,' she says finally.

'Of course they will, they're in the medical profession. They have to believe in what they are doing, and you'll have to start believing in them too.'

'Oh God, my mind goes round and round – '

'Listen, Anna, there's nothing you can do, nothing at all, until you've been to Birmingham. There are no decisions to be made until then.'

'Where is all this bloody inner strength you're supposed to get when there is a crisis, a tragedy? I feel weak and angry and selfish and stupid.'

Steve kisses her. 'You need food,' he says when the kiss is over.

Anna laughs, for the first time in hours. 'I thought you were going to say: you need a fuck. I'd have hit you.'

He kisses her again. 'Food first,' he says. 'Then a fuck. I bet you haven't eaten since you left your parents.'

Anna hasn't, and Steve makes omelettes, a salad, while Anna just sits and lets herself be taken care of. They eat hungrily, hardly talking, and it is not until they have finished that Anna says, suddenly, 'What are you doing here? I thought I told you on the phone not to come.'

Steve laughs. He's made coffee and they take it into the living-room where they sit comfortably side by side on the big solid sofa. 'I was furious with you after that phone call,' Steve says. 'I thought, the hell with her; and I got on the motorway and headed for home.'

'And you turned back?'

'Yeah, I must have a pretty thick skin, eh? I suddenly wanted to see you, badly, and decided to take a chance that you'd be less off-putting in person.'

'What nerve you have! How did you know I wasn't putting you off because my lover is here?'

'I thought *I* was your lover. That *was* you on the sand dune, wasn't it?'

Anna smiles, and Steve takes her in his arms. '*You* needed to see *me*?' she asks incredulously. 'I thought it was the other way around!'

'You should pay more attention to my body language.' He begins kissing her, slowly. It goes on and on and on, and then his hands are touching, caressing, and then after a time they are on the floor and starting to make love on the old Indian carpet in the middle of the living-room.

Suddenly Anna says, 'We should go up to my bedroom, okay? If Sophie wakes up and finds us . . . '

Steve agrees, and they go upstairs. As they pass Sophie's room they hear her moan restlessly in her sleep. When Anna goes in she wakes: she is feverish, unsettled, and Anna brings her a drink, some tablets. Then she sits with her for a long time, until Sophie finally drifts off into a troubled sleep.

'Sorry about that,' Anna says to Steve, who has taken a shower and is sitting on the edge of Anna's bed leafing through a book of Spanish short stories.

'It's all right,' he says reassuringly and moves towards her, but she says, 'Look, Steve, I'm sorry, but I feel about as sexy now as cold mashed potatoes. It's been a terrible day and I'm exhausted, both physically and emotionally.'

'You look a bit fraught,' he agrees gently. 'Look, you go to sleep; I'll bed down on your sofa downstairs if that's all right.'

'It's okay, you can stay here, this is a huge bed. I'm not sure if I have the energy to dig out the spare blankets for the sofa.'

Anna opens a drawer, takes out a nightshirt, and trails off to the bathroom. 'What I need is a long soak in the bath,' she says. 'Maybe that will revive me.'

But when she returns she is even more drained than before; she looks pale and trembly and fragile. Steve turns back the duvet and covers her up as he would Sophie, and before he himself can get in the bed she is heavily asleep. Thoughtfully he puts out the light, listening to her breathing for a long time before he finally goes to sleep himself.

It is just beginning to get light when they both, simultaneously, awake. They begin to touch: tenuously at first, lightly. Then, as they sense each other's response, their touching becomes surer, stronger, more sensual as they begin to make love. And this time, it is truly making love as opposed to having good sex on a sand dune. Steve is tender, gentle, and Anna clings to him like a snail on a rock, feeling her whole body quivering under her skin and when finally the sun is up and shining through the thin blue curtains she knows she is in love: now when she wants it least, now when she needs to be strong, now when love can only be a hindrance to the things she has to face in the future.

But for the moment, she succumbs. Steve whispers love things in her ear and Anna whispers back; for the moment they are both daft and happy; for the moment there is only this, and each other. She cannot remember losing herself like this since Richard died.

Sophie sleeps late. Anna and Steve are downstairs, dressed and drinking tea, when she finally appears. 'Steve!' she shouts, rushing at him, throwing herself into his arms. 'When did you get here? What are you doing in Bristol?'

'I came up to see my son. He was in the hospital for a couple of days but he's okay, he's home now.'

Anna stares at him. 'You never told me. I just assumed you were here because of work, selling a guitar or something.'

'What happened?' Sophie asks.

'We had a bit of a panic the day we got back from France, a few hours after you left to see your parents in Lyme Regis.

Tess rang to say Sam had been in an accident with his skateboard. He ran straight out into the road in front of a car.'

'Oh, God.'

'He didn't regain consciousness for a bit, so we had a pretty harrowing night on Thursday in the hospital.'

'The poor boy,' Sophie says with motherly concern. 'Are you sure he's all right now?'

'Positive. He came around finally and is miraculously fit, except for concussion. We both stayed at the hospital all day Thursday and Friday and he was sent home yesterday evening.

Sophie commiserates, asks all the questions Anna never did. Anna is strangely silent, until Sophie finishes breakfast, gets dressed, and goes next door to visit Madge. Then she turns to Steve in dismay and says, miserably, 'You never said. I feel so mean and selfish, going on and on about Sophie, and you never told me about Sam.'

'It's okay, Anna. My crisis was over when I got to you. I was lucky, Sam is fine.'

'But I didn't even want you to come; I tried to send you away. I didn't even ask you what you were doing in Bristol at that hour of the night.'

'It's all right, honest.' He tries to hold her, but she breaks away, opens the kitchen door into the garden, letting the cool but bright morning wander inside.

She turns to him. 'You see why I can't get involved?' she says passionately. 'All I care about is Sophie. I'm obsessed about her life, obsessed about her dying. I want nothing else from life but that she live. When she was a few months old, the doctors said there was nothing more they could do for her, just keep her happy; they said, don't worry about what you feed her, how to help her, because there's no help, just let her be.'

'Look, Anna, I know – '

'No you don't, that's the point. They thought she'd die within the year, so what did it matter? But I fought for her,

Steve. When Richard died I loved her enough for both of us, and I read every book I could lay my hands on, on nutrition, and vitamins, and exercise: on medicine and surgery, on the liver and its function. I read everything I could on transplants, and rejected that at first: the liver is such a complicated thing – '

'Anna – '

'Alone, Steve, do you understand? The others tried to help, but I'm the only parent, the only one that really knows Sophie, the one responsible. Look at you and Tess, you've split up, you barely get on now, but when your son is ill, you are together – Tess doesn't want her new man and you don't want me.'

'That's not true, Anna. On Thursday night when I was racing towards Bristol thinking my son would die, might be dead already, I thought of you and wished you could be with me, because you more than anyone would know what I was going through. Then, later, when I knew Sam would be all right, I thought of you again, how you go through this every time Sophie is ill, has a crisis. I don't know how you do it; I know I never could.'

He rubs his hands wearily over his face and they are both silent for a moment. Finally he looks up and says, quietly so that Anna can barely hear, 'I'm not Richard, Anna. I'm not Sophie's father. But I'm father of another child whom I love as much as you love Sophie, and I've known fear, and loss too. I lost my son when Tess and I split up. I know it's not like your loss but it'll have to do, it's all I can offer you.'

Anna closes the kitchen door; it's too cold to leave it open, in spite of the uneasy sunshine. She sits down at the kitchen table and says, woodenly, 'I'm a mess, Steve. I'll drive you away like I drove Jake away. I don't know which he found hardest to handle, Sophie's illness or my constant panics over her.'

'I don't think you panic. Look at that crisis in Spain, you were cool as a cucumber.'

'I pretend, Steve. For Sophie's sake. That's why it's no good letting anyone get close to me, I fall apart. Jake found that out and couldn't take it. He left us after a few months of moving in.'

'That was rough.'

'For Sophie, mostly. To me he was more of a lifeline; looking back I'm not even sure I loved him, though I guess I must have. He was the first man I had a serious relationship with after Richard, and I vowed I'd never do it again.'

'Uh oh,' Steve says with a grin, sitting down facing her. 'Too late.'

'Too late,' Anna agrees. Only she's not smiling: she knows she couldn't take it if this one turns out to be a mistake also.

Steve says, 'Maybe it'll be *you* wanting to get rid of *me* this time; remember I've a bad marriage behind me and one or two disastrous relationships of my own.'

'Kim?' Anna asks. 'I suppose she's still sitting in your kitchen, waiting for you to come back.'

'No way, she's given up on me – though she's buying my motorbike, said she got fond of it on the journey home from Spain. But she's given me up as a loser, said I was too wrapped up in my guitars to form any kind of a relationship. She was right, too: after my marriage turned sour I deliberately avoided any emotional involvement with anyone.'

Now it's Anna's turn to grin. 'Too late,' she says lightly.

Steve touches her hand. 'Yup,' he agrees. 'Too late.'

It seems like a commitment, and suddenly they both feel shy and awkward, and even a little frightened. Neither one of them can think of a thing to say, but that feels all right too. Then the door flies open and Sophie is there, clutching a tape. 'I just got this out of the 2CV, Mum, can I put it on, remind us of Spain?'

Without waiting for an answer she sticks the cassette in the player, presses a button, and out comes the deep voice: 'You're nooot alone, you're nooooot a-lone . . . '

Anna and Steve burst into wild laughter; Sophie, not understanding the joke but not minding, joins in. Loudly over their shared hilarity Roy Orbison sings: 'You're nooot a-lone anymore . . .'

Chapter Six

LATER that day, when Steve has gone off down the Richmond Road to buy bread and the Sunday newspapers, Anna tells Sophie that they are going to Birmingham. She explains to her daughter what the child already knows: that her condition has worsened and that it is necessary for her to have a thorough check-up. Sophie listens. She is not particularly upset – she has been in and out of hospitals since she was born and they have never threatened her.

'But why Birmingham?' she asks. 'Why not Bristol, where I usually go? Or London? I liked it when we went to the hospital in London – the nurses were such fun!'

'There is an excellent liver unit at Birmingham, a transplant unit. They could give you a new liver if they think you need one.'

Sophie is thoughtful. She and Anna have talked about liver transplants before, but only generally. 'I wouldn't mind a new liver, Mum,' she says at last. 'If it meant I could run again. I just can't run any more – I haven't been able to for ages. I wouldn't mind an operation if I could run when it's over.'

Anna has to wait a few moments before she can answer her daughter. 'You'll run, Sophie,' she promises, her voice husky. 'You'll see, you'll run again.'

Sophie smiles radiantly. 'Well, then,' she says grandly. 'Birmingham here we come.'

In the face of such optimism Anna feels a slight rustling of hope stir in her, like leaves in the very faintest of breezes. 'Birmingham here we come!' she echoes. Not for the first time her daughter has given her courage, and when Steve

91

gets back with bread and black olives and hummus for their lunch the whisper of hope has grown, gone wild, lashes at her heart so that for the first time in weeks she feels the sudden lifting of the despair that has been pressing heavily on her.

Anna's mood holds for all that day, and the next as well, especially as Sophie's temperature is down and she seems much brighter. On Monday Sophie insists on going to school, even though it is only for one day. 'I want to see my friends before I go to Birmingham tomorrow, Mum,' she pleads with Anna. 'I want to take my photos from Spain and France, show everyone.'

Anna reluctantly lets her go, knowing that Sophie's schoolfriends are important to her: at home she is almost always surrounded by adults. Anna used to worry about this, until she realized that her daughter actually enjoyed adult company, sought out people like Madge or Mike. It was as if Sophie knew that children were sometimes uneasy around her, especially in a one-to-one situation, sensing her difference from them. And yet Anna knows that she is sometimes wistful for friends her own age and for this reason cannot help feeling bitterness towards her sister-in-law; though Sophie's cousins are younger than she is, they could have provided her with the close, easy everyday companionship she has missed over the years.

And so Sophie, ebullient and excited, clutching her photographs and her lunchbox, waves to them from the school gates. Anna tells herself not to worry; all the teachers know about Sophie and will look after her diligently. After they have watched her disappear into her classroom Steve says, 'What a gorgeous day it is! Shall we go to Bath? It's not far and I've never been there.'

'I shouldn't,' Anna says reluctantly. 'I need to be near the phone, in case Sophie gets taken ill.'

Steve ushers her into the car, gets in himself. 'Sophie's

teacher knows her condition. You told me the school has your brother's phone number, both home and at his surgery, and Madge's as well. Let's go to Bath.'

And so they do. Feeling like a truant, Anna lets herself go, and they do the day properly, beginning with coffee in the Pump Room next to the Roman baths. Steve, in faded jeans and multi-coloured hand-knit jumper, winks at Anna as a waiter in a dinner jacket shows them to a table adorned with fresh daisies on an immaculate white tablecloth. Nearby is a raised platform where a pianist, a cellist, and a violinist are playing something from Gilbert and Sullivan.

'Makes a change from rock 'n' roll,' Steve grins, biting into the Bath buns they ordered.

'Shouldn't you be home, working?'

'I'll go tomorrow, when you go to Birmingham.'

Anna suddenly goes quiet. Steve says, 'Look love, I said I'd go with you to the hospital.'

'It's okay, we're better on our own, Sophie and me. Lots of people have volunteered to come – my parents, Mike, Madge – but I'd rather be alone with Sophie.'

Steve shrugs, says nothing.

'Besides,' Anna continues lightly, 'you've got to start making guitars again. I thought you were a workaholic.'

'Yeah, so did I.' He wipes the butter off his fingers with a clean white linen napkin and reaches across the table to take Anna's hand. 'I don't know what I'm doing here.'

He is teasing but Anna is serious, unsmiling. 'I don't know either.'

Steve narrows his eyes, strokes his droopy moustache with his free hand, and hisses theatrically, 'Sex.' At that moment the music stops playing and two smartly-dressed matrons at the next table look surreptitiously at them. Giggling, they pay their bill and leave the tea-room.

The day continues easily, happily. They wander through the Roman baths, the Abbey, the American museum; they find a tiny wine bar and have a hearty lunch. When at last they meet Sophie, chattering and laughing with a group of friends at the school gate, Anna feels refreshed, calmer. Sophie too has had a good day, and although tired, seems content.

That evening, when Sophie is in bed, Anna's brother comes over. He is surprised to see a strange man cooking spaghetti bolognese on his sister's old cooker and after Anna has introduced them, he watches Steve warily, notes his familiarity with the house, with Anna herself. He finds Steve easy, reposeful, but that doesn't make him less vigilant.

'Look, I want to go with you to Birmingham,' Mike says when they are all sitting together in the living-room. 'I've arranged to get a locum in for a few days.'

'What about Mary?' Anna asks.

Mike is silent. When he had returned home from work that day he had asked Mary to come with him to see Anna and Sophie. 'The kids would enjoy it, and we could pick up some Indian takeaway or something on the way.'

Mary, wiping mashed banana off the face of Annabel, the youngest, said, 'You know the children can't eat spicy foods.'

'The food's not the point, they can have peanut butter or something. I thought it would be a nice idea to call in, spur of the moment, that sort of thing. We are family after all.'

Annabel squealed, 'Dadadadadadad,' and Mike plucked her out of the high chair. 'On a school night?' Mary said, writing down 'bananas' on a blackboard hanging by the fridge. 'Not a good idea. Besides we have masses of leftovers from last night. Wasn't the *salsa* a big hit with the Johnson-Scotts? Thank God for that new Italian deli! Wasn't that olive bread amazing?'

'Look – '

'Roland is rather interesting, don't you think? He was very impressed with David's academic record.'

'David is eight years old, Mary. I would hardly think he has an academic record.'

'I didn't think much of his wife. Pity she's on the school committee.'

Mike, still carrying Annabel, hitched her up to his shoulders and walked out of the room, joining his sons in front of the television, where he stayed until Mary called them all in to dinner. Later, after he had helped with the washing-up, looked at David's school project on trees, listened to Owen reading, he quietly left the house, got into the car, and drove the short distance to Montpelier.

Anna knows how Mary feels, knows why Mike cannot answer her question, knows that Mary would consider it a gross betrayal if Mike accompanies them to the hospital in Birmingham. He is too loyal to speak of these things and Anna does not press him. 'It doesn't matter,' she says gently. 'You can tell your wife not to worry: I don't want you to come. I don't want anyone to come.'

Steve says quickly, 'I volunteered as well. I'd like to be with Anna and Sophie.'

Mike looks at him doubtfully. This strange man has come into his sister's life too quickly to usurp the role of brother, protector. He would like to say something to establish his claim on Anna, his self-imposed role as guardian, but his thoughts are too slow to formulate. Instead Anna says forcefully, 'We've been through all this. I don't want to talk about it any more. I want to go to Birmingham alone, all right? If there are any decisions to be made I want to make them alone, as Sophie's parent. Mike, you'll bombard me with medical facts until I'm more confused than ever; and Steve, I'm sorry, but you'll just distract me. I'm grateful to you both for offering, but please, please, please – just let me be, okay?'

They understand she is emotionally exhausted and forgive her, but secretly both men are hurt. Mike leaves soon afterwards. He thinks he could like Steve, but admits this to himself grudgingly. Having seen Anna wounded and cornered, he is afraid for her, afraid this man will damage her also. Thoughtfully, he drives home. At least Mary will be pleased to hear of this new man in his sister's life, he thinks: but the thought brings him no comfort.

The next few days Anna finds surreal. Outside, Birmingham is grey and gloomy, but inside the hospital everything is bright, cheery, positive. Sophie undergoes one test after another: the countless blood chemistry tests, and a liver biopsy which is painful and distressing.

'There, what a girl!' The biopsy is over and Sophie is being comforted by a nurse with a smooth calm face thatched by deep red hair.

'Oh, Belinda,' Sophie says weakly. 'I hate those biopsies. Why do they have to hurt so much?'

Why indeed, Belinda thinks grimly, but she says, 'You're a brave little thing, Sophie.'

'Not so little,' Sophie grins. 'I'm almost as tall as you and I'm not even twelve yet.'

Belinda laughs, and settles herself on the edge of Sophie's bed to make small talk for a few minutes. Anna, watching, takes advantage of the nurse's presence to go to her little room nearby and flop on the bed for a moment. The room is austere, but Anna is grateful for it. Beside the bed is a small table with a manuscript of a book in Spanish – Anna is supposed to be translating it. It is another source of income for her, the translations, especially valuable in times like these when she can do no supply teaching, when she has to put off her evening students for an indefinite period.

But she has not opened the manuscript. She has done nothing but be with Sophie, talk to the various doctors and surgeons who have given her their scrupulous attention. One of them, a Mr Harold Wright, is particularly keen to do a transplant on Sophie if the tests prove that she is a suitable candidate.

The week drags by. Sophie, usually so good in hospitals, treating them like holiday homes, becomes restless, wanting to return to Bristol. Her normal lively cheerfulness has been dampened by the illness that is dragging her down, beginning to depress her.

'Oh God!' Belinda exclaims in the canteen to one of the student doctors, a rotund young man called Jim Winters. 'That poor child, she's such a trooper but it's all getting too much for her. I wish they'd finish the bloody tests and send her home.'

One morning after a particularly painful liver biopsy, Sophie bursts into tears and says she is not staying in hospital another moment. When Anna tries to reason with her, the child becomes frantic and has what almost amounts to a temper tantrum, something she has never had before. When finally Anna calms her she finds that she herself is shaking, and so, leaving her daughter with Belinda, races to Marvin Templeton's office.

Marvin is the transplant coordinator, the person that Anna was told she must turn to if there were any particular problems that needed to be talked through or clarified. Anna, without preamble, says, 'I'm taking Sophie home. She's had enough.'

Marvin, getting up from his cluttered desk, is obviously used to distraught relatives, for he hardly raises an eyebrow. Motioning for Anna to sit down he says, calmly, 'Why is that?'

'We've been here almost a week. Sophie's been very good, very patient, but she wants to go home now.'

As Anna speaks she is aware of how foolish she sounds, how petulant she is making Sophie appear. Marvin, trained to be diplomatic, watches Anna patiently – no doubt remembering every word, Anna thinks bitterly, so that he can write 'hysterical mother' on Sophie's medical record.

She breathes deeply and tells herself not to be irritated at Marvin's professional caring attitude. It's his job to soothe

97

the frantic relatives of ill and dying patients; he can't help watching her, judging her. Anna looks at his pointed face with the trim, salient black beard and the incongruous white eyebrows and wishes suddenly that Steve were here.

'Look,' she says slowly, determined to be articulate. 'My daughter usually likes hospitals. Oddly enough, she's had some good experiences in them. She's usually quite patient and resigned when she's been in other hospitals, enjoying the friendliness of the staff, all that care and attention.'

'Hasn't that been the case here?'

'Yes, everyone has been fine. But . . . the biopsy was painful, so painful that she's terrified of them now. Then she had to have a second, because the first was inconclusive. And all this waiting, and no one telling us when we can go home . . . ' Anna trails away dismally.

'It's necessary, my dear. You know that. It is all necessary so that we can help Sophie.' It is a slight admonition, as to a bright but naughty child.

And now Anna feels caught, trapped. As Marvin kindly and patiently explains to her why her daughter must be carefully monitored, why these things cannot be hurried, she feels foolish, in the wrong. 'It's a matter of life and death, Anna,' Marvin finishes. 'You can't whisk Sophie away because of a burst of tears.'

She leaves the office chastened. Checking on Sophie, who is calm now and talking to Belinda, Anna goes to the pay phone. She is tempted to ring Mike, ask him to come up: she knows he would drop everything and be here at once. Even her parents would be better than this void, this desolation. She doesn't let herself even consider Steve: it is not his child, not his life.

But she can't ring Mike, nor anyone. It is something to do with Richard, with the husband who gave her a child, and then abandoned her. Richard was the only other person in the world who could have felt as Anna is feeling now, and because he is gone, she cannot ask anyone else to stand in for him. If he can't be with her in Birmingham, no one can.

The next day two people sit in a dark blue car in the hospital car park, talking quietly.

'Do you want me to go in with you?' Peter Allison says to the woman in the passenger's seat.

'I'd rather not.' She studies his face, sees that he is hurt. 'You will meet Anna and Sophie one day,' she promises. 'But not in these circumstances.'

'I've been part of your life for six years, yet I still haven't met your granddaughter. Nor your daughter-in-law.'

Rosamund Beer looks fondly at the man, at his sparse sandy hair, his fine, thin face. She has known him for twenty years, meeting him when they were both married to other people. They were friends for fourteen of them, and six years ago became lovers.

Peter has loved Rosamund for twenty years, fourteen of them silently. His marriage, loveless and childless, ended in divorce several years before Rosamund's husband died. After the funeral he bided his time, knowing that to rush her would be counter-productive, though he did invite her to visit him at his house in France occasionally which she willingly accepted. It took Peter over a year to convince Rosamund she could love him too, and when it happened, he knew the wait was worth every second.

They have just returned from France now. Peter is an estate agent dealing mostly with properties abroad, and so spends most of his time there. He would like Rosamund to live with him in his house in France, or in his flat in Malvern where he stays when he is in England, but she insists they live separately, for obscure reasons Peter can never quite fathom.

Sometimes Rosamund cannot fathom them either. She has no doubt that she loves Peter, but she also knows she wants him separate from the reality of her life, which is her small house on the outskirts of Malvern, and her workshop where she makes the bold, chunky pottery for which she is known throughout the country. Reality is also her beloved grandchild, Sophie, the daughter of her dead son Richard, and her daughter-in-law Anna, whom she loves dearly. This is her life, these are the passions in it. Whilst being intensely fond of Peter, she still tries to keep him in some kind of perspective: it makes her feel more in control of the relationship.

'What will you do while I'm inside?' Rosamund asks now. 'It's rather dreary to be walking around Birmingham.'

'I'll find somewhere for a coffee, buy a newspaper, read.'

'I'll want at least a couple of hours with Anna and Sophie. I haven't seen them for weeks and weeks, and now this – '

Peter looks at her pale face, etched with lines in the grey daylight, and is moved to kiss her. 'I'll come back here in two hours, but don't hurry. I'm good at waiting for you, remember. I've done it before.'

Gratefully, she takes his hand, holds it tightly for a few moments. Then she is striding quickly towards the main entrance, holding her head down against the damp wind, a slight figure with thick, straight silver hair which blows across her eyes and nearly obscures her face as she turns and waves briefly at him.

Sophie sees her first. 'Grandma!' she calls, jumping out of bed and going to her, embracing her warmly, tightly.

Anna is right behind her daughter. She too kisses Rosamund affectionately, eagerly. 'Did my parents tell you where we were? When did you get back from France? How sophisticated you always look when you return from there!' She admires her mother-in-law's new dangling silver earrings, and the long cranberry-coloured skirt with small elegant buttons all the way down the front.

'We were in France, too,' Sophie says. 'We thought of surprising you, calling in to see you, but we weren't anywhere near.'

Rosamund smiles, thinking of the surprise it would have been for them if they *had* dropped in, found her there with a strange man.

Anna says, 'I didn't get in touch; I didn't think there was any point writing to you in France, especially as we're not sure yet what is happening.'

'I may be getting a new liver!' Sophie exclaims cheerfully.

'So your other grandmother told me,' Rosamund says. 'How splendid!'

'Nothing is definite yet,' Anna says cautiously.

At that moment Belinda walks by and Sophie stops her, insisting on introducing her favourite nurse to her favourite grandparent. 'Why don't you sit in the day room?' Belinda says. 'It's empty now. Would you like coffee?'

In the small staff kitchen she finds Jim Winters boiling the kettle. 'Want a cup?' he asks.

'Not for myself, no. I'm making one for Sophie's grand-mother; she's driven out from Malvern to see her.'

'That's nice for Sophie. Maybe it'll cheer the poor kid up a bit.'

'It has already. She's obviously dotty about her grand-mother. Not much good for the grandmother, though – she looked shattered, watching Sophie. That same bloody haunted look that her mother has.'

'Belinda – '

'I know, I know. Professional detachment.' She takes the tray and storms out, slamming the door with a purposeful kick.

Three hours later Peter watches Rosamund walking towards him in the car park. Her head is bowed as before, but not against the wind this time for the day has grown still and quiet. Her hair is no longer blowing wildly but is smoothed behind her ears, the silver fringe thick and shiny and reaching to her large, troubled blue eyes, dark and smudged with strain and tension.

She doesn't say much on the way home, only: 'Sophie will

have to have a transplant. It's the only thing that will save her.'

Peter nods, takes a hand off the steering wheel to put it over Rosamund's. 'Will you stay with me tonight?' she asks suddenly.

He is moved. It is only in France, when she is visiting, that they share a bed for the entire night. No matter how late he stays at her house in England, she always insists that he leave before morning.

So he says, 'Of course I will. I would like – '

'Just for tonight,' she says firmly.

He nods again, and holds her hand tighter as he drives steadily with one hand along the dual carriageway.

A few days later Sophie and Anna are in the 2CV with the top down – for the weather has suddenly turned warm and sunny – on their way home. Sophie is playing her favourite tape and they are both singing along, euphoric at being let out at last.

Sophie is to have her liver transplant; it has been decided. The tests all indicate that the operation should be success-ful, and mother and daughter are buzzing with hope and excitement. 'Mum, I know!' Sophie shouts above the noise of the 2CV, the music. 'Let's not go home, let's go to Steve's.'

'But Sophie, I thought you wanted to see Uncle Mike, your cat, your friends – '

Sophie is thoughtful. 'I do, Mum. But . . . it's going to be hard, not going to school. I'll miss everybody.'

'We can invite your friends to the house, you know.'

'I know,' she says half-heartedly. 'It's not the same, though.'

Anna is silent, knowing she is right. However much Sophie's classmates are willing, they understandably find it difficult when her illness prevents her from sharing many of their games, their outings, their interests. They try to be compassionate but cannot sustain it: their healthy rough and tumble world is too compelling to allow them to be drawn for long into Sophie's orbit.

Sophie is preoccupied, thinking about school, about the hamster in her classroom, and the goldfish, and the funny tiny prickly cactus plants which her teacher, Miss Hanson, lets her water sometimes. 'I wish I could go back,' she says sadly, 'but I know I can't, I know I'm not that strong any more. Just before we went to Birmingham, that last day, remember, when Steve was here? I wanted to go so badly, and then I felt so awful by lunchtime that I went into the loo and cried.'

'Oh, Sophie!' Anna is horrified. 'You never told me.'

'I didn't tell anyone, not even Miss Hanson. It's okay, don't look so worried. I felt much better after lunch.'

They drive along without speaking for a few moments, then Sophie says, 'That's why I thought it would be fun to go to Steve's for a few days: I wouldn't miss school so much, wouldn't be just hanging about waiting to go back to the hospital.'

Why not? Anna thinks. Devon is where she would like to be too. She and Steve have talked on the phone every night while she was in Birmingham: she misses him, and misses him badly.

And so a few hours later they are on Dartmoor, driving through Steve's village, then a half-mile out of it to the house itself. As soon as the car stops Sophie runs into the workshop. Anna, more cautiously, follows, wondering if this is a good idea, suprising Steve like this. He will be working, and the interruption may be unwelcome. It is with trepidation that Anna opens the door, looks in, but already Sophie is in Steve's arms and he is holding her as if he could hold her forever, as if she were his own child.

All the tears that Anna held back in Birmingham fill her eyes now like potholes after rain, until Steve sees her, adds her to the embrace. Suddenly, he rushes with Sophie out of the workshop and into the house, then promptly out again carrying handfuls of bread, and the two disappear down the garden towards the duck pond.

Anna is grateful for this respite. All the euphoria she felt at leaving the hospital has gone, leaving her drained and exhausted. She goes into the kitchen, lays her head down on the table, and cries.

Steve finds her there, about five minutes later. Cradling her in his arms he rocks her like baby, soothes her. 'I'm so glad you've come,' he says, over and over.

Finally she is able to say, 'Where's Sophie?'

'At the pond, feeding the ducks. Lying on the grass in the sun and looking amazingly happy.'

'She is. The doctors have convinced her that she'll be a healthy, normal child when she has this transplant.'

'You don't sound so convinced.'

'Oh, Steve! It's a dangerous operation, and Sophie's in a weakened condition – '

'It's her only chance. Talking to Sophie out there with the ducks, listening to her bubbling on about all the things she's going to do after the operation, I was impressed by how she believes in her future. You must too.'

Anna shakes her head, too weary to talk any more. Then Sophie comes in, full of enthusiasm for the ducklings and plans for the new enlarged pond she and Steve have decided is necessary for the extended family. Anna watches her, her cheeks flushed with excitement over its usual yellow tint, her dark hair dishevelled, unruly. She looks taller: she is growing, Anna thinks with sudden pride; my daughter is growing up. She thinks of the fine young woman Sophie could, *will* be, and, like a lifeline, clings to that thought.

That night Sophie goes to sleep in a tiny attic bedroom over-looking the duck pond, where she can keep an eye on the growing family. The room has a bed, a small roll-top desk in which she places her books, her sketch pads, her drawing materials; and an empty old oak chest which she fills with her clothes. She seems as if settled there forever, which makes Anna worry whether Steve will think it all a dreadful imposition. In his bedroom, a large room with low, beamed ceilings and a huge brass bed, she tries to explain.

'We won't be here long; it's just that Sophie wanted to see you.'

'Uh huh,' Steve murmurs, kissing her neck and undoing the buttons of her striped blue and green shirt.

'I ordinarily wouldn't do this, arriving without any warning at all.'

'Hmm, you have the softest skin just there, right around your nipples. Lovely.'

'I know you have your work and your privacy and I respect them both – '

'Help me undo this zip. There, that's better.'

'And I would never interfere with your guitars. I know they are your life.'

'Anna. Dear Anna. Would you please shut up so that I can kiss you?' He does, and she does. They are on the bed, totally preoccupied, when the phone rings.

'Oh God, Steve. You'd better answer it.'

'Let it ring. It's almost midnight.'

'It'll be the hospital. I gave them this number.'

'They wouldn't phone; they gave you that bleeper for emergencies.'

'You never know. Please, Steve, answer it.'

'Shit. Okay.' Steve, naked and erect, rushes off to the phone. A moment later he calls upstairs, 'Anna, it's for you.'

Now Anna runs to the phone. She is sure it's the hospital: there is a liver for Sophie – oh God, not yet! *Not yet.* 'Hello, yes?' she says.

It is her father, his voice cold and indignant. 'Your mother and I have been frantic. You telephoned us this morning to say you were leaving the hospital, going home. I have been ringing Bristol all evening.'

105

'Oh. Sorry. We changed our plans.'

'Luckily your brother suggested you might be here, and kindly looked up this strange man's number for us. Don't you think you could have had the courtesy to tell us where you were?'

Feeling both cold and foolish standing in the corridor half-naked, Anna says, caustically, 'Dad, I'm thirty-five years old. Surely you don't seriously expect me to report all my comings and goings to you?'

Stuart is deeply injured by this, and says so. 'This is not a normal situation, Anna,' he concludes. 'Sophie is seriously ill, the two of you are on your own, your mother and I worry. In these circumstances perhaps it would not be too much to ask if we could be aware of your plans and where-abouts?'

Anna relents. 'We're staying with a friend for a few days, Dad. I'll let you know when we go back to Bristol.'

There is a pause. 'Hardly a friend, Anna. You only met him a few weeks ago.'

'Dad – ' Anna begins warningly.

'I think, since you are so fond of him that you choose to go there for a few days, instead of visiting your mother and me, that perhaps it is time we met him. Since you are in Devon, you can bring him to Lyme Regis for lunch tomorrow or the next day.'

'I don't know, Dad. Look, it's late. I'll phone you in the morning, all right?'

She goes back upstairs thoughtfully. 'See, I told you it wasn't the hospital,' Steve says, pulling her down on the bed and stroking her gently, sensuously.

'It was my father. He wants us to go to lunch.'

'Fine. Now, where were we? I think we were about here . . .'

'I don't think it's a good idea. What's the point in you get-ting involved with my family so soon? Everything might fall apart and then all that hassle would have been pointless.'

'Anna. God. I'm trying to make love to you. *What* would have been pointless? What are you talking about?'

'Our relationship, that's what. It happens all the time; they fall apart.'

Steve groans, sits up. 'They do, yes. But one does usually begin in hope. One doesn't begin a relationship anticipating the end.'

'This is different.'

'I don't see how.'

Anna, tensing, sits up also. 'Because of Sophie,' she says impatiently. 'How can I have a normal relationship with anyone, with Sophie?'

'Oh Christ, Anna. What the hell *is* a normal relationship? You have a seriously ill child; I've lost custody of my son whom I love dearly. Other people have other encumbrances. No one comes into a relationship at our age without a load of baggage on their backs.'

'You don't understand. With Sophie it isn't just her being ill, it's every day, every moment, expecting her to die, wrestling with life and death constantly. It's emotionally killing, but I'm her mother, I have to go through with it. Why should *you*, why should anyone?'

'What about if I love you? Isn't that a good reason?'

Anna shakes her head sadly, pulls the duvet up around her shoulders. 'Love isn't always enough. It wasn't enough for Richard, and he was Sophie's father. He left us in the end.'

Steve gets out of bed, walks to the window. The curtains are open and the night is clear, still. Stars flicker over the empty moor spreading behind the house and somewhere an owl hoots. Finally Steve says, without turning, 'Stop blaming Richard for dying.'

'I can't.'

'It was an accident, Anna. Let the poor man rest in peace.'

And now Anna stands up, fumbles for her shirt, puts it on. 'It wasn't an accident,' she says harshly, slumping on a

107

wooden rocking-chair near the bed. 'We knew Sophie was seriously ill almost as soon as she was born, but she was a few months old before we were told what it was. The doctors said she wouldn't live very long, but they weren't sure just how long she had. It was about then that Richard started building his catamaran.'

She leans back in the rocker, closes her eyes, begins rocking back and forth slowly, monotonously. 'Richard became obsessed by this thing, this boat, and worked on it every evening, all weekends and during all the school holidays. He built it in a shed belonging to the father of one of his students, down near the harbour.

'Oddly, I didn't mind that much, the time he spent away from Sophie and me, working on that catamaran. I knew he loved Sophie, loved us both, and the building of that boat was therapy for him. I had Madge right next door, and my brother Mike, but Richard was always very solitary. He only had us, and I guess I wasn't much help to him, because I was as full of despair and confusion as he was.'

She stops talking and opens her eyes, still rocking slowly in the old chair. Steve has turned from the window and is looking at her, not interrupting the words that are tumbling from her mouth like apples from a broken sack.

'He maybe loved Sophie too much,' she finally goes on, and there is anger now in her voice. 'As she didn't die, as she turned into a lively, endearing child of two, three, she became for her father a constant source of agony, of terror. Every slight illness was a crisis, every headache, stomach pain, was perhaps the beginning of her death which was, so they told us, inevitable. Finally, when the catamaran was finished, when Sophie was just three years old, Richard decided to sail it across the Bristol Channel over to Wales.'

She doesn't go on now, but sits quiet and motionless in the chair, the rocking stopped. She is looking beyond Steve, out of the window and at the stars, and she is far away from him. He waits a long time for her to return and when still she remains silent, he asks gently, 'Is that when the accident happened? On the way to Wales?'

She stirs, looks at him. 'That's when he died, yes. But it wasn't an accident. He chose to go during autumn half-term, in October, when the weather is particularly unpredictable. And he insisted on going on his own, when the mate he was going with backed out. He never made it. A westerly gale came up when the tides were going out – the tides in the Bristol Channel are treacherous – and the sea was so great he never made it.' She pauses. Then, dully: 'Apparently he tried to shelter in Lundy Island, but it didn't work. His boat was found wrecked a few days later on the North Devon coast. His body was never found.'

'Oh God. Anna.'

'First I went mad with grief. Then a terrible anger. I didn't want him to go; I asked him not to, but he was adamant. As my anger grew I began to hate him, hate my dead husband whom I had loved so much. He couldn't cope with loving Sophie, couldn't cope with knowing he might have to watch her die. So he chose to go first – I'm sure he went into that sea hoping to die. I've never forgiven him for deserting us.'

She is finally finished. Steve waits a few moments and then says quietly, 'You don't know for sure, Anna. People who do dangerous things do them for many different reasons, not necessarily because they have a death wish. Maybe he thought he could forget, for a time, his fear and despair over Sophie by building that boat, sailing it alone across the channel. Maybe his own death was the furthest thing from his mind. Can't you give him the benefit of the doubt?'

Anna looks at him, then away. 'He left us,' she says tonelessly. 'Whatever happened, and for whatever reasons, he left us. It's hard to trust anyone after that.'

Steve goes to her, takes her hands, draws her up until she is standing facing him. 'You'll have to start somewhere,' he says. 'It may as well be now, and it may as well be me.'

He takes her back to bed, begins making love to her all over again. It is hard for her to relax now, hard for her to let go, and the sex is not good for either of them but the making of love is. When Anna finally falls asleep in Steve's arms the last thing she feels is an overwhelming tenderness towards him, and the first tenuous budding of trust. He lies awake for another hour, holding her as if afraid she will drift away if he closes his eyes for even one moment.

Chapter Seven

NEITHER Sophie nor Anna want to leave Steve's place. It is as if they are somewhere separate from the real world of cold rain and antiseptic hospitals; it is as if nothing mattered or existed outside the heat of the sun, the cool oak-beamed house, the greening of the new leaves on the trees around them.

The three of them venture from their insular nest for a few hours to go to lunch at Lyme Regis. While Eleanor fusses over the food and urges everyone to eat more and more, Stuart brusquely interrogates Steve. Anna, feeling the habitual tightening of her chest that means anger is not very far away, is prevented from making a scene by the slight pressure of Steve's hand on her thigh underneath the table. 'It's all right,' he says later. 'Your father doesn't mean to come on heavy – he's just worried about you. I am after all a strange hitchhiker you picked up in Spain.'

That done, they settle into an easy routine which the idyllic weather, the bovine countryside, accommodates. Sophie, fascinated by the old English cottage garden with its ancient fruit trees, scented magnolia, shrubs and flowers growing seemingly at random, makes up games along the almost hidden stone path that weaves in and out of the foliage. When she tires of this she lies on a blanket in the sun by the pond and watches the ducks, reads, sometimes draws, sometimes dozes.

Steve and Anna work. He has a guitar he must finish, and she begins the translation of the Spanish text. 'You don't mind?' Steve asks, incredulously.

'Mind what?'

'All the time I spend in the workshop.'

'Of course not.'

'You're the first woman since Tess who hasn't minded.'

Anna is silent, wanting to hear more, for Steve has not said much about his ex-wife. But he doesn't volunteer any more information, and Anna doesn't ask. She doesn't know that Steve is refusing to think about Tess, to think about what she means to him now. He knows he is beginning to love Anna, but he hasn't worked out what this has done to his feelings for Tess. He is glad he has a couple of rush orders; when he works, his mind and emotions concentrate on only one thing, the guitar he is making.

Then, a few days later, Steve comes out of his workshop early one morning and says abruptly, 'That was Tess on the phone. Her husband has to go away on one of his innumerable business trips again, only this time it's Paris and Tess insisted on going with him. She had arranged for her child-minder to move in for the week and look after Sam but the woman is in hospital with a broken leg.'

Anna looks at him questioningly. Rather agitatedly, he continues, 'Tess is putting Sam on a train to Plymouth. He'll be arriving at two o'clock this afternoon.' He slumps at the kitchen table, puts his head in his hands.

The breakfast is cooking on the wood-burning Rayburn: fresh farm eggs, scrambled in butter; granary toast, coffee, home-made marmalade that Anna bought from a jumble sale in the village down the road. Sophie is still asleep and Steve has been up and working for two hours already.

Stirring the eggs Anna says, 'I'll leave, of course. Sophie and I will go back to Bristol. We only came for a few days anyway.'

'I don't want you to go. I'd like you to meet Sam. Sophie too. I want them to get to know each other.'

'Whatever you want, we're easy. I can stay as long as you like – I can't start teaching again with Sophie home, and there's no point starting my private lessons when any day now we might be back in hospital – ' She breaks off when she sees Steve is not listening. 'Steve? What's wrong?'

112

'Fuck the woman,' he says, and his fist pounds the kitchen table in one swift hard blow.

'Don't you . . . want Sam here?'

'Oh God. Jesus. *Want him?* I want Sam with me just about every hour of my life. Why the hell do you think I used to spend every waking moment of the day working, why, until you, was I never able to form a stable relationship with another woman? I was, I am, besotted with Sam. Since the day, the moment, he was born, I lost myself in him. Maybe all parents do, who knows: all I know is that some core in me, the thing that made me free and unique, had gone, and that from then on my life, my happiness, would depend on the welfare and happiness of that tiny ball of flesh I was holding for the very first time.'

There is silence for several moments. The eggs are burning and Anna takes them off the hot plate, puts them aside. She understands Steve perfectly; there is nothing she can say. Finally he goes on, more mildly, 'Of course I want to see Sam. But it's that woman, what she does to me. She controls me, controls my life, because she has the custody of my son. If I ever want to see him during non-allotted times, she always refuses, no matter what the reason. I can beg and plead and she doesn't give a shit; and then, like today, she suddenly rings and knows I'll drop everything, help her out, because I want, I need, to see my son.'

He gets up and starts to walk out of the kitchen. 'Where are you going?' Anna asks.

'Look, I'm sorry, but I need to get out. I'm taking a walk up on the moor, okay? I'll be back in a couple of hours.' He is gone before Anna has time to reply.

She looks at the eggs, at the toast getting cold beside the Rayburn. She wishes she were in Spain or in France, cooking on a camp stove out in the open air. She wishes she were in Bristol and that Sophie was well and in school and she herself sedately teaching Spanish to an eager class of sixth-formers. She wishes she were her dead husband,

and so beyond all wishes, beyond all pain and loss and grief.

Numbly she throws out the eggs, the toast, and sits aimlessly at the kitchen table for almost an hour, until Sophie finally wakes up and she has, at last, something purposeful to do.

Steve walks for over two hours. He climbs the hill behind the house and through the woodland to the open moor where he first follows the river, then a sheep track across the soft springy grass. The day is bright and still, and the outline of each granite rock on the distant tor is clear, defined, like a drawing in a child's colouring book.

Steve's anger over Tess's manipulation is beginning to dissipate with the joy he is feeling over seeing Sam again. He missed seeing the boy at half-term because he was on a camping trip with a schoolmate and his parents, and Tess felt that this was no reason for Steve to be granted an extra weekend. Tess doles Sam out like pennies, one at a time, making sure there is a good reason for letting him out of her pocket. She likes the control this gives her, a control she never had when she and Steve were married.

He married her because she was vibrant, confident, knew what she wanted from life, and she married him because he was laid-back, restful, and obviously adored her. He was attracted to her at first for the same reasons nearly everyone was: she was quite stunningly beautiful, and full of spark and vitality. 'Come on,' she'd beguile, waking Steve at dawn on a Sunday morning after a late night, 'have you seen the sunrise, can you imagine what the sea will be like now?' She would laughingly, cajolingly, drag him out of bed, bundle him into the car, and when they at last got there she would always be right: the moment would be perfect, the early morning bright and luminous, the sea iridescent and magical.

He loved this energy, this decisiveness in her, the ability to grab exactly what she wanted from life and wring every drop from it. He loved the way she knew what she wanted at all times, and went for it. 'I may be only a shop assistant now,' she'd tell him earnestly, 'but it's just the first step, you'll see.'

'You'll own the shop next,' Steve would laugh.

'Maybe. Who knows. If I want to I will.' She always said this seriously, as if reciting a litany: *If I want to I will*, and Steve knew she would, whatever it turned out to be, and in those early days he was fascinated by this solemn, whole-hearted tenacity.

Tess in turn loved the way Steve wafted though life, making his guitars without hassling over the future. He was happy to plug into her own future, her own plans, to get whatever buzz he needed, having apparently no major needs of his own. He had Tess, he had his work, and soon he had Sam: he wanted not one thing more. But after a time, what had initially attracted her began to irritate. As she grew even more dynamic and ambitious herself, she felt Steve should also be this way, and the fact that he was content to make his guitars and earn enough merely to subsist, and not want anything more, was suddenly not enough for her. Understanding that his guitars were good, that he was beginning to make a name for himself with established musicians and rock groups, she could not comprehend why he did not want to push himself to achieve the recognition, and financial reward, he deserved.

'Have you finished work already?' she asked incredulously one afternoon when she had come home from the shop early, ill with a rare cold. Steve was on the kitchen floor playing with Sam while the *au pair* watched television in the living-room. 'Yep, I delivered that jazz guitar at long last and didn't feel like going back to the workshop to start anything new, so I thought I'd take Sam out somewhere. Do you think he'd like the zoo? It's a lovely day.'

Tess said nothing that time, but brooded on it. By then

she was working long hours as a fashion buyer in one of the prestigious department stores; because her own career was soaring, she couldn't understand why Steve's wasn't. It was all right being married to an appealing but feckless guitar maker when she herself was only a shop assistant, but wasn't it time now that they grew up, became responsible? Steve worked, of course, but it wasn't enough. 'You've got to push yourself,' Tess told him again and again. 'Sell yourself and your guitars. No one else will.'

'Why?' Steve would ask, genuinely perplexed. 'We're making enough money, we have what we need, we're not in debt.'

'But you're *good*, you *should* be making more, it's a question of worth. And anyway it might be enough now, but it won't be later when Sam gets older. With a bit of push and some good PR you could make Dunstan Guitars a big name in the business.'

At this point Steve would always switch off, go back to his workshop or seek out Sam, play trains with him or read him a storybook. As the months went by Tess inaugurated the same conversation over and over again, sometimes approaching it obliquely, sometimes winsomely, and then, more and more, angrily. She could not understand how her easy, pliable husband could be so stubborn: she felt his unwillingness to expand the business, invest in high-powered advertising, hire an assistant so he could spend more time on self-promotion, was a deliberate affront to her. Steve in turn couldn't understand what all the fuss was about: he was happy the way she carried on her own career, why couldn't she leave him in peace about his?

And so, finally, Tess left. She knew what she wanted in a husband now, and though there was a residue of nostalgic regret that it wasn't Steve, she was determined to have it in someone else. By that time she was no longer in love with Steve, or, rather, had convinced herself that he was not worth loving. She felt he had failed her, and blamed him for being wilful, for thwarting her marvellous plans for him and, in consequence, holding *her* down. And so she left him for the director and principal shareholder of a chain of fashionable boutiques.

'I'm going, and Sam's coming with me,' she told a shocked and disbelieving Steve late one evening when she came in from a meeting at work. She coolly, calmly, told him about the man she had met, the man she was going to divorce him for and marry.

'You're not taking Sam,' Steve had said, when he could think clearly enough to speak. 'I'll fight you all the way.'

'Fight as much as you like,' Tess said casually, walking away from him and into the bathroom to run a bath. 'I'll win, you know. Children are rarely taken from their mothers, and I'm offering Sam a much better life. Carl has a house in Clifton, a much safer and salubrious neighbourhood than this one. He has a responsible job, money, prestige, security: the court will certainly approve.'

'I'm Sam's father, for God's sake.' Steve, running after her, understood at that moment how it was possible to hit a woman.

Tess, throwing bath salts into the hot running water, said contemptuously, 'It's not enough, Steve. What are you, anyway? A two-bit craftsman, an ex-musician, a worn-out hippie still thinking that life is nothing more than a couple of guitars and a bottle of cheap plonk with your friends.'

This was so untrue and so unfair that Steve, knowing he *would* hit her if he stayed, walked out of the house and into the night. Later, he thought that if Sam had been home (the boy was spending the weekend with Tess's parents), he would have taken him too, and perhaps the outcome of the whole sordid mess would have been different.

But Sam was away, and Steve crazy with rage and anguish and disbelief. For two days he drank without stopping at the home of friends. Then, for the next three, he was violently

117

ill and unable to move from the spare bedroom. By the time he was physically well enough to go home, Tess – and Sam – had gone.

Even now, all these years later, Steve silently condemns himself for not fighting Tess for the custody of Sam. Perhaps he would have lost, but at least he would have tried. Walking steadily up the rock face of the looming grey tor, wet with sweat and burning in the hot June sun, Steve wishes he *had* tried. But then, advised by well-meaning friends, a solicitor whom he had consulted several times, Steve knew he couldn't do it. He would not have had much of a chance, for in no way had Tess been a bad mother, and Sam loved her as he loved his father. Especially, Steve couldn't do it to Sam, couldn't drag his child through a court case that was sure to be vicious and nasty.

At the top of the tor Steve collapses in a hollow between the rocks, closes his eyes to the sun. Slowly the long-ago pain and anger evaporate, and he lets himself be filled with a clean, simple love and longing for his son. In a few hours he will see Sam, have the boy for almost a week. It is a surprise gift, an unexpected joy, and he lets himself savour it.

As he walks back slowly down the tor Steve realizes that for the first time since the divorce, he has talked to Tess without being achingly and despairingly in love with her, as he has been despite all she has done to him. Overwhelmed by this great revelation, he begins to run, and runs all the way home, falling at Anna's feet in the garden in a sweaty, smelly heap. On his face in the warm sweet grass, spread-eagled on the ground, he says, panting, 'Oh, God. Anna. Oh, hell. I just have to say . . . shit, I can't breathe. Whew, that's better . . . look, I love you. No, I mean *really*. I LOVE YOU ANNA BEER.'

The effort of shouting these last five words undoes him, and he lies gasping for breath in the hot sun at Anna's feet. Sophie, who has been watching all this with interest, says, 'My. What fun. Wait until I tell Uncle Mike and

118

Madge.' She begins to giggle, as does Anna, and in a second or two the jerky shaking of Steve's prostrate body tells them that he too, as he rasps for breath, is joining in their laughter.

Sam, a slight boy with hair the same rough texture as Steve's only cut short and smoothed straight over his ears, is shy at first, as is Sophie. For the first hour or so he clings to his father and watches Sophie and Anna warily, unsure of whether to be angry because he no longer has Steve to himself, or delighted because there is someone more or less his own age to play with. By evening he has succumbed to delight, for Sophie, inordinately pleased about this young newcomer to their Devon family, has let him beat her at Monopoly, shared with him her favourite story-tapes, and halved a bar of white chocolate that she was saving for a special occasion.

'One more hurdle over,' Steve smiles at Anna when the children are at last asleep. 'They seem to like each other.'

'He's a sweet boy,' Anna says. 'He looks like you, too.'

'Handsome? Sexy? Devastating?'

'Well . . . sort of cute, as Madge would say. Small pert nose, good bones – '

'Enough. I can't bear such excessive flattery.' He hands her a cup of tea he has made and sits beside her on the sofa. 'It's great that they're getting on so well. It feels almost like a family now, don't you think?'

'Steady on.'

'Oh Anna, Anna. Why is it that every time I say anything, however light-heartedly, about our being together, you run a mile? Don't you feel how good this is, how good we are together?'

'It's early days yet.'

'I know, I know. God, will I be glad when we're old and have been together forty years or so. Then maybe you'll believe I'm not going to run out on you.'

119

This soothes Anna unreasonably. Oh, if only . . . ! For a moment she lets herself hope, lets herself dream . . .

The dream darkens somewhat back in Bristol. As if scripted in a formula play, the sun disappears a week later when Anna and Sophie are home, and there is torrential rain, thunderstorms. Sophie is in pain again, and feverish, and spends much of the day lying on the living-room sofa watching television. She misses Sam, for the two children were firm friends by the time they returned to the city. Thrown together in such close contact, Sam quickly adjusted to Sophie's illness: her strange colouring, her inability to run and play energetic games, her sudden brief temperatures, her need to rest. Sophie in turn was drawn to this slight restless boy with the round glasses and perpetually-skinned knees, fussing over him when he tore his jeans climbing through hedgerows, or succumbed to the young stinging nettles at the side of the pond as he searched for a missing duckling. Sam rather enjoyed being fussed over: his mum did it when she was at home, but that was seldom, and the woman who looked after him when he wasn't at school treated him like a rather backward adult whom it was better to ignore as much as possible.

Anna had offered to drive Sam back to his home in Bristol, saving him the train journey, and when they arrived she met Tess for the first time. She was unprepared for how beautiful Steve's ex-wife was. Rich brown hair, like the most expensive dark chocolate. Pale violet eyes with the obligatory full black lashes. Oval face, good skin, wonderful body – the lot, Anna thought with dismay. She was also pleasant and charming, inviting Anna and Sophie in for a drink after their drive from Devon. Anna said she was sorry, but her daughter was tired and wanted to go home. Tess quite understood. 'And how is Steve?' she asked. 'He was looking tired when last I saw him.'

'Fine. Working hard.' Anna found this awkward, talking about her lover to his ex-wife.

For a moment the expression on Tess's face changed, became slightly annoyed, even bitter. 'Yes, so I hear. Ironic, isn't it? He's doing now what I begged him to do all those wasted years of marriage, becoming ambitious at last and making something of himself.'

'I don't think it's exactly ambition. I think he just likes making guitars.'

'Obviously you don't know him. He liked them well enough before, but he never worked at it, the way he does now. I hear from old friends that he's selling guitars to some very famous rock groups, that a Steve Dunstan guitar is becoming one of the most prestigious – and expensive – instrument you can buy.'

Anna shrugged, hating this conversation. 'I'm sorry, but Sophie's in the car, waiting for me. I must go.' She looked around for Sam, to say goodbye, but the boy had disappeared.

But Tess would not be deflected. 'He's doing it to score off me, you know. To pay me back for leaving him all those years ago.'

Anna stared at the woman. This was so outlandish that she wanted to shake her. She had missed the whole point. Steve had not suddenly become ambitious, seeking prestige and recognition, but was only doing what he had always done, making the finest guitars possible. The only difference was that when he lost his son and his marriage, he made a great many more guitars, spending whole days and nights in his workshop because it was the only way he knew to keep his sanity. The result, ironically, was the success he had never wanted, but that Tess had craved.

'Oh, hell,' Anna sighs now, thinking of that meeting as she prepares a meal for herself and Sophie and Madge, who is upstairs now reading to the child.

'What's wrong, sugar?' Madge comes into the kitchen and gives her friend a quick hug. 'You look real down, like you're feeling lousy. You okay?'

'Yes. No. Missing Steve like mad.'

'I know. I miss Juan Carlos too.' He is away for a few days and Madge is restless, spending most of her evenings next door with Anna and Sophie. During the days she works in the local library, as she has done for years, but she is finding the friendly noise and chaos of her house overwhelming these late spring evenings without Juan Carlos to distract her.

'Are all your sons still at home?' Anna asks, putting long thin spaghetti into boiling water.

'Yep. Every one. Tom has a mate with him who has nowhere to live for the moment, and Larry's latest young woman also seems to have moved in.' Larry is Madge's eldest son, now in his early twenties.

'Do you mind?'

'It doesn't usually bother me. I like having them around. It's just that sometimes I can't hear myself think. I can't remember when I've sat quietly and read a book.'

'They must be sleeping all over the woodwork. I hope they're paying you rent.'

'Hah.'

Anna shakes her head. She thinks her friend is incredibly tolerant, and says so. Madge shrugs. 'I love my kids. Besides, they fill the gap that Ron left. Gives me something to love.'

'Oh, Madge! How can you say that? You've had men all over the place falling in love with you. And what about Juan Carlos?'

Madge's moon face softens. 'Hmm, Juan Carlos. He's such a cutie, isn't he? And some lover, let me tell you. I'd forgotten what young men were like.'

'There, you see? How can you still be pining for Ron when you have someone like that?'

Madge thinks carefully for a few moments then says, 'You're talking about different things here, Anna. Juan Carlos is all sex and fun and passion and laughter. Ron is . . . my husband. Even though he's left me, he's still my husband, and you're talking about twenty years we had before he went. You're talking about babies, having them together and raising them. Cleaning up sick and getting up in the night, sharing all that. Sharing too getting older, the aches and fears . . . We have a shared past, we have our history. That's love, honey. That's what I want.'

Because she has known Madge a long time, Anna can say, though she says it gently, 'It's not what Ron wants, love. You know that. It can only work if you both want it.'

'Then I'll wait until he comes to his senses.'

Anna doesn't say (though Madge is waiting for it): 'And what if he never does? What then?' Instead, she says, 'Things change, Madge. Life changes. You're holding on to a past that is gone; you're not looking towards the future. You're going to miss out on some good moments, you know, unless you can stop grieving over things that are finished, things that are sadly over.'

Madge looks at her strangely. 'Remember that, Anna, okay? Just remember you said that.'

Late that night Juan Carlos returns, silently letting himself in with his key and not putting on any lights so as not to waken the rest of the household. As he creeps through the living-room towards the stairs he steps on something soft and feathery yet hard underneath, which starts to groan and then to swear. 'Oh, uh, I am so sorry. I had no idea someone is sleeping here,' Juan Carlos stammers.

The sleeping bag thrashes a bit and mutters, 'S'okay, I'm a friend of Tom's,' and then all goes quiet except for a peaceful snore. The room reeks of beer and musty sleep, and Juan Carlos hugs the wall as he makes again for the stairs and inches up them stealthily. As he reaches the landing there is an almighty shriek, the slamming of doors. 'Jesus, mate, what's the idea, slinking around like a hired assassin? You scared the shit out of Kate, she was just on the way to the loo.'

Juan Carlos looks sheepish. 'Sorry, Larry. I did not want to be a bother and wake someone.'

'It's okay, I'm just glad it's you. I'd better go and let Kate know she's not going to be murdered in her bed. See you in the morning.'

Everything goes dark and quiet again and it is with great relief that Juan Carlos opens the door to Madge's bedroom and creeps like a man come home into her bed. She is deeply asleep, able to shut herself off from the noises of the household, and he begins to make love to her wordlessly, soundlessly. Dozy from a pleasant dream she responds languidly then sensuously.

'Hmm, ten out of ten,' she says afterwards as they lie breathless and sweaty on top of the covers. 'So what are you doing coming back tonight? I thought it was tomorrow.'

He strokes her plump shoulders fondly, kissing them as he speaks, using his lips rather like explanation marks. 'I couldn't wait to see you. To make love to you. Like this, so!' Little kisses explode like crackers down her body and Madge laughs and squirms. 'That tickles!'

Juan Carlos, taking her round face between his long brown fingers, stares into her eyes with his tragic black ones and says passionately, 'All the time when I was away, talking to my countrymen, exiles in London who are planning to return to Chile now that Pinochet has lost his power – all I can think of as they talk is how I am going to make love to you.' He kisses her lips to emphasize his point.

'Some revolutionary you'd make,' Madge gasps when her lips are free for speaking.

'Madge, I love you!'

'No, you don't. Believe me, honey, you don't.'

Juan Carlos sits up in bed and glares down at Madge. 'Do not tell me you are old enough to be my mother! What is age, what does it matter?'

'You're sitting on me, that hurts – stop bouncing around! I wasn't going to say anything of the sort as a matter of fact;

124

I would prefer to forget entirely that I am old enough to be your mother. Stop reminding me.'

'Age is nothing. *Nothing.* I want to marry you.'

'*What?*'

'Take you back to Chile. To meet my mother, father, brothers, sisters. To see my godfather, ask his blessings – '

'Uh, hang on, honey – '

'To see the land where I was born. The lakes, the mountains, the desert – '

'All in one place?'

'You joke. I tell you my dreams and you joke.' Juan Carlos looks so crestfallen that Madge reaches up and tenderly touches his mournful stoic face.

'I'm sorry, baby doll,' she says gently. 'I wasn't making fun of you. You're a real sweet kid, but – '

He rises indignantly from the bedsheets, suddenly tumescent, muscles twitching powerfully as he squares his shoulders, kneeling above her. 'I am not a *kid*, I am a man! Have I not just proved it tonight?'

'Oh, God . . . '

'Shall I prove it again? Is this what you want?'

'Look, will you just relax? Of course you're a man, you're a wonderful man!'

He looks slightly mollified and starts to smother her with kisses again when she says in a muffled voice, 'All this marriage stuff, it's just . . . a bit sudden.'

'Sudden? I do not understand. I have adored you from the first day I saw you standing over Charles Dickens in the library.'

'Sweetie, that wasn't all that long ago,' Madge says kindly.

'A lifetime, *mi amor*. I was born on that day, over the Charles Dickens.'

'Sure, sweetheart,' Madge murmurs placatingly. She is suddenly feeling incredibly sleepy. 'Look, why don't you come down off your knees and come under the quilt with me? It's getting chilly.'

'You will marry me, Madge?'

'Let me think about it, okay, angel face? A woman doesn't like to be rushed.'

Juan Carlos dives under the duvet and wraps his sturdy young limbs around Madge's plump, womanly body. 'I understand. I will be patient, for I love you. *Luz de mi vida*, you are my woman. *Mi amor, mi corazon*. There is time. I will wait.'

'Uh, good. Good,' she says drowsily, rolling over away from him, hoping to get some sleep before going to work in a few hours. But already he is kissing the back of her neck, already he is hard and pressing against her. Wondering fleetingly if having such a young lover is after all a good idea, Madge resigns herself and turns to face him. After a while, when Juan Carlos has found erogenous zones in her body she never dreamed existed, she decides maybe it is a good idea after all.

The next day is Saturday, and Sophie is restless, unable to settle to anything Anna suggests. 'I want to see Sam,' she says plaintively. 'I haven't seen him all week.'

'He's been at school, Sophie. He had to miss a lot when he joined us in Devon.'

'I miss school. I miss Sam. Steve as well. How long do we have to wait for this stupid liver anyway?'

Anna's hand goes to the pocket of the khaki shirt she is wearing over jeans. Inside is the bleeper she must have with her day and night. When a liver becomes available for her daughter, she will be bleeped by the hospital and must then rush to Birmingham as quickly as she can. Their necessary belongings have been packed and ready since the last time they were there.

'Listen,' Anna says coaxingly, 'why don't I phone Sam's mother and see if he would like to come out for the day? Would you like that?'

Sophie is pleased. On the telephone Tess is breezy and

casual, and says that she will drop Sam off at once because she has been invited somewhere for lunch. 'I've been at my wits' end looking for a child-minder for today. You know mine is still laid up, and this wretched new woman doesn't like working on Saturdays. Carl is away as usual, so this suits me fine.'

Anna and Sophie are both glad to see Sam. Tess appears briefly at the door to make sure she has the right house but doesn't come in. 'How odd. When Steve and I were married we lived not far from here. Just around the corner as a matter of fact.' She is too polite to say she would not for the world live in the neighbourhood again, but it is implied.

When she goes Sam relaxes and lets Anna and Sophie kiss and hug him warmly. 'Where's your mum going?' Sophie wants to know. 'She looks all dressed up.'

Tess had been wearing a deep blue silk dress, and her chocolate hair was hanging loosely to her shoulders. 'She's ever so pretty,' Sophie goes on.

Sam is not much interested. 'I don't know where she's going. Out to lunch somewhere. She's always going out to lunch. She has this important job, you see, and customers are always taking her places.'

'Where's your dad?'

'You know. Devon.'

'Silly, I don't mean Steve. Sorry, I should have said your step-dad.'

Sam looks thoughtful. 'He probably won't even be that for too much longer. He and Mum are always fighting. He's always got to go away on business and she doesn't like it much, because she has to go to important dinner parties and things alone.'

'She could take you,' Sophie says seriously.

'I've offered to go,' Sam replies, equally serious. 'She gets really cross with Carl, keeps telling him she's going to leave him. I wish she would, I don't like him much. Mum is much more fun without him.'

127

The children both lose interest in this topic and run upstairs to find some games in Sophie's room. Anna, who overheard this conversation, finds she is disconcerted. She wonders if Steve knows that Tess's marriage is shaky, wonders if and how the knowledge will affect him.

She decides to phone Devon. It will please Steve to know his son is with them, if only for the day. After he has talked to Sam she will mention the boy's comment about his step-father. After all, Steve has a right to know what is happening in his son's home.

She begins dialling the number. But before she has finished there is an ugly, unfamiliar sound: it drums in her ears, beats around her head. Dropping the phone she stands like granite while the strange piercing noise goes on and on and on.

It takes another few seconds for her to register what is happening. It is the bleeper, of course. Stricken, she cannot even shut it off; then, an even louder sound confuses her. It is the noise of her heart, pounding with such terror and insistency that it muffles even the relentless bleeping which is filling the whole house with its sickening, ominous, summons.

Chapter Eight

WITHIN half an hour Anna and Sophie are on their way to Birmingham. Madge is in the house in Bristol looking after a bewildered Sam and making phone calls to Anna's parents, her brother; to Rosamund and Steve. Anna rang the hospital and Marvin Templeton told her briskly and economically that there was a liver available for Sophie and she was to get the child there as soon as possible.

There was a moment when Anna thought Sophie would resist. Clinging to her mother she said, tearfully, 'I don't think I want to go now, Mum. Do I have to? Can't I keep my old liver for a bit longer?'

It was Sam who rescued Sophie. 'Oh, go on,' he said persuasively. 'Maybe a new liver will help you win at Monopoly.'

This made Sophie giggle through her tears and she went upstairs with Anna to get their bags. 'I'd better take Alice,' she said, holding on to the old rag doll with the freckly face that Richard had given her all those years ago. 'You never know when we'll be back.' She looked at Anna and tried to smile. 'Or even if we will be back.'

Anna held her tightly. 'We'll be back, love.'

Sophie, gently and not unkindly, pushed her mother slightly away. 'People die during operations,' she said softly.

Anna took her hands, held them tightly. 'You won't, Sophie,' she said, meaning every word. 'I promise you won't.'

Now, in the car and approaching Birmingham, they are silent. As they drive into the car park Anna says, 'What a lovely day it is today, Sophie. It's the longest day, did you know that?'

Sophie rolls her eyes. 'That's for sure!' she exclaims, making a face combining fear, despair and wry amusement, and Anna marvels how this child, throughout everything, rarely loses her laughter, her sense of humour.

'I think it's an omen, you know. The longest day, the beginning of summer.' The car stops, and Anna opens the door.

'Poor Mum. It'll be much longer for you. I'll be asleep through most of it.' She takes her doll from the back seat and tucks it under her arm. She kisses Anna, takes her hand, and they walk into the hospital together.

The longest day has begun.

The moment they walk through the hospital doors, Anna loses Sophie, loses her to modern medicine and technology and the expertise of a dozen people who hardly know her daughter, but who know everything about the human liver, about transplant operations, about human biology, about medicine, surgery, drugs. Anna watches, helpless, as Sophie is quickly, expertly, made ready for the operation. Marvin Templeton is on hand for her benefit, to soothe and reassure; to bring her coffee in clean white mugs; to tell her she mustn't worry, that all is proceeding normally, efficiently. Anna watches it all with shocked eyes; everything seems clear, outlined, sharper: the white of the sheet on Sophie's bed, the pale blue of Harold Wright's eyes as the surgeon briefly bends over Sophie for a pre-op word. And then suddenly there is quiet, suddenly there is space, for everyone seems to have gone. Anna is on her own.

She goes slowly to her room, the same one she had during the last hospital visit. Marvin offered to be with her during the operation so that she need not be alone, but she refused. He was surprised and disapproving that she was on her own and offered to phone her brother, her parents. 'I'm all right,' she insisted. 'I'd rather be alone.'

Lying on the bed in the small room, staring at the white

ceiling, wondering how she is going to survive the next seven or eight hours, Anna wishes she were *not* alone. Her body seems to have collapsed, weakened, lost its bone and muscle, and she can do nothing but whimper and shake. And then there is a knock on the door. Suddenly alert she sits up quickly. 'Yes? Come in.'

Someone is holding her. Someone is letting her cry at last and tremble and go to pieces, but it's all right because she knows that she won't fall apart, won't be fragmented. Steve is holding her like glue, will bind her together as she breaks into shards, and as she clings to him and weeps she thinks that love is like glue, is the only thing that can mend us when we shatter and splinter into bits.

'She's being operated on now,' Anna says at last.

'I know, that fellow with the pointy beard told me. When I asked for Sophie they sent him out. He looked rather suspiciously at me, and asked what relationship I was to the family. I told him I was your brother; I couldn't be bothered with long explanations.'

'Steve! How devious. That was Marvin, the transplant coordinator.' She giggles. 'He knows my brother's a doctor, so he'll think I'm in good hands.'

'How's Sophie?'

'She was actually quite cheery at the end, just before they gave her the injection. Her favourite nurse, Belinda, was there, holding her hand, and Sophie told her she couldn't wait to get her new liver. Then she asked Harold Wright how long it would be before she could run.'

'What an amazing kid.'

'I'm glad you're here.'

Steve nods, holds her. He doesn't ask why she didn't phone him herself, why she didn't ask him to be here. He knows she needs to do things her way, needs her little rules which make her feel independent and in control. He understands that she needs these pretences, to help her through the bad times with Sophie.

'I could do with a wash and a shave and a coffee,' he says now. 'I rolled out of bed early this morning and straight into the workshop. I was there when Madge phoned, and just dropped everything, threw some clothes in a knapsack and drove off.'

'You look wonderfully scruffy,' Anna says fondly. 'Your hair gets curlier and curlier when you don't comb it.'

'And yours gets more and more frizzy. Wouldn't we have incredible children? Their hair would be like the nest of wild birds.'

Anna says, warily, 'That's something we'll never know.'

'Never? That's a bit final, don't you think? I'm sure Sophie would love a little brother or sister.'

'Steve, don't go on. I wouldn't have another child. You know Sophie's damaged liver is the result of a genetic defect.'

'But both you and Richard had the same defect. It was such an incredibly tragic thing that you both possessed the same gene – the chances must be so slight of that happening. Anyway, there are tests now, blood tests, to prevent it happening again. You could have a perfectly healthy baby, Anna, and you know all this; you don't need me to tell you.'

'I don't want another child. All I want is Sophie.'

Steve stands, stretches, looks out the window at the hospital grounds, the sculpted hedges, the green lawn. 'Fine,' he says at last. 'If that's what you really want. If you're not kidding yourself. I just wonder why you've never been sterilized. Wouldn't it be a lot safer than the Pill?'

Anna hesitates. Steve has touched something in her, the root of some deep enigma which she has refused to acknowledge, though in honest moments she has recognized its existence. 'I was offered a sterilization,' she tells him at last. 'Right after Sophie's illness was diagnosed. I wanted one, and Richard agreed. But somehow at the last minute I couldn't go through with it. To this day I don't know why because I most emphatically didn't, *don't* want any more children.'

132

'What about later? If you were so sure you didn't want children, why didn't you get sterilized later?'

'I thought about it when I met Jake. But it seemed like such a hassle. Going back on the Pill seemed easier.'

Steve relents, doesn't pursue it. 'You look washed out,' he says compassionately. 'I'll have a shave and we'll go and find coffee.'

An hour later they are still sitting in the small staff kitchen which Marvin said Anna could use. Learning from past experiences in hospitals, Anna has packed tea bags, Nescafé, and an assortment of packets to make instant soup which she somehow finds comforting in stressful situations. Something to do with the nostalgia of childhood, she thinks: the safety of home-made, warming things like her mother's chicken and lentil soup on a cold bleak day.

They are both smoking roll-ups. Anna rarely has a cigarette, and Steve is not a compulsive smoker, but these are exceptional circumstances.

Marvin finds them as they are drinking their second cup of coffee. 'Ah, there you are. Your brother has found you. Good. I'm glad you have family here, Anna; they can be great support.'

'This is Steve Dunstan, a friend of mine,' she says quickly. 'I'm afraid Steve was so anxious to find me that he said he was my brother.'

'I'm sorry about that,' Steve says as Marvin frowns. 'I didn't have time to make explanations. As a matter of fact I'm practically family. I hope to marry Anna before too long.'

Marvin beams. 'Ah, Anna's fiancé. How nice.' He looks relieved: this poor widowed mother has someone to look after her now.

'Any news of Sophie?' Anna asks.

'I've just looked in on her and things are proceeding as expected.' The operation has been in progress for an hour and a half.

133

After Martin has left, Steve asks, 'He doesn't just barge in there every hour or so to see what's happening, does he?'

'No, apparently there is a room with a glass window looking into the theatre. Marvin can check on each stage and report to anxious relatives. It's a long operation.'

'I know.'

'He means she hasn't died on the operating table. That's what he means when he says everything is proceeding as expected. I'm so afraid, Steve. Sophie's in such a weakened condition.'

'It's out of your hands now, Anna. It had to be done.'

'I can't bear this waiting. I thought I could do it alone, but I couldn't have. Thank God you're here.'

'Even though I lied and perjured myself to get near you?' he jokes, to distract her.

She manages a shaky smile. 'You're incorrigible. First my brother, now my fiancé.'

'Well, I thought it would be a lot easier hanging around here and sharing your room if I'm legitimate family. Do you really want to introduce me to all the medical staff as some bloke you picked up in Spain a few weeks ago?'

'I suppose you're right. Being my fiancé gives you some right to be here, I guess.'

'Oh, Anna. Is that what it takes for me to have a right to be in your life? An engagement? Right, let's get engaged. Anna, marry me.'

'Don't be daft.'

'I'm actually being serious. I want to live with you and Sophie. I want you to get to know Sam. I don't want to be separated from you any more, Anna.'

What has started as a joke has suddenly turned serious. Anna begins the usual cliché, that they've only known each other a short time, but as she says it she knows it is rubbish. She's been closer to Steve than she ever was with Jake, closer than any man other than Richard. Stopping in mid-sentence she puts her head in her hands. It is all too much; she is overwhelmed by too many emotions.

'It's all right, love,' Steve says gently. 'It's not the time to talk about this now. We've plenty of time later.'

Anna nods gratefully. 'I'd better phone people. My parents, Mike, Madge, Rosamund.'

'I'll come with you.'

Slowly they leave the kitchen, go down the corridor to the pay phone. The operation has been going on for two hours. There are still hours more to wait.

'We should be there,' Stuart Callington says to his wife in Lyme Regis. 'I have a good mind just to go.'

'It's pointless. Anna has just told us that everything is going as well as can be expected.'

'She has no one with her. She'll be traumatized with all this waiting.'

'She has Steve.' Eleanor opens the sitting-room window, lets in the sun.

'I mean family. My God, we're her parents – Sophie's grandparents. We have a right to be there.'

Eleanor looks at him as if she is about to speak, but then turns away. *It is too late,* she would like to say, *we should have gone to her years ago, when Sophie first became ill, before Richard died and Anna tried to assume control of her own life, a life that had suddenly plunged into chaos.* But Stuart had his own peculiar sense of order: one did not interfere between husband and wife; one stayed detached and let them get on with it. Now, with Richard gone, he does not understand why he has not been allowed to take his rightful place as head of Anna's family.

Eleanor goes to him and uncharacteristically puts her hand on his shoulder. 'Anna is right now under a great strain. She doesn't need us, doesn't need to have to play the dutiful daughter when being a mother is just about all she can cope with.'

135

Stuart looks at her sharply. His wife has never been so outspoken about Anna before. He starts to reply; then, noticing the set of her lips, the lifting of her chin, he changes his mind and remains silent.

In Malvern, Rosamund Beer hangs up the telephone and sinks down on a stool in her pottery. She knows she will do no more work today; what she *will* do, she hasn't any idea. For some time she just sits, knowing she should go inside, change her clothes, wash off the residue of clay which is still clinging to her fingers even though she wiped them quickly when the phone rang.

She would like to be at the hospital, but would not consider intruding. Anna sounded desperately afraid, but she said she had that young man with her. Rosamund knows about Steve: when Anna returned from Devon, she drove up to Malvern to tell her about it, leaving Sophie at home with Madge for a few hours. Rosamund knew by that that something important was up: Anna never left Sophie unless it was absolutely necessary. It was a dismal rainy morning, and Rosamund offered coffee and hot bagels from her local bakery which Anna ate voraciously as she had left Bristol early, without breakfast. After she had finished a blueberry bagel, a cinnamon one, and half a sprouted wheat, she began to talk.

'I was going to write to you about Steve. I started, but I tore up the letter.' She seemed tense, on edge.

Rosamund nodded. This was indeed serious. When Jake moved in with Anna and Sophie, it was worth no more than a brief phone call.

'You know a bit about Steve. We met him in Spain, and stayed at his place recently. Sophie sent you a card.'

Rosamund nodded again. Sophie had been quite taken with him after the holiday, had talked about him a great deal that day Rosamund visited her in hospital. Anna had been more reticent, but in that reticence Rosamund recognized a depth of feeling she had not seen in her since Richard. She waited quietly for Anna to go on.

Anna was suddenly confused, not knowing quite what to say. She had come up on impulse, the letter she had started seeming inadequate, yet what could she say about Steve now that she was here? The week in Devon had been some kind of a turning point for them: she knew when she returned that Steve was beginning to fill a place in her life and in her heart that only Richard had before. She needed to share this with Rosamund – why, she couldn't have said. To get her blessing perhaps? Or her forgiveness, for finding someone to take her son's place? Yet no one would ever do that: she wanted Rosamund to know that also.

In the end she said, 'I can't tell you very much about Steve, about his relationship to me and Sophie, because I'm not sure myself. I mean, he's not moving in with us or anything; he's got his workshop in Devon and our life is in Bristol. I'm not even sure if I'd want him to, not yet – and I don't know why I feel like that either.'

Rosamund recognized this, with something of a shock, as what she felt about Peter. 'I can understand that,' she said thoughtfully.

'But I do love him and he has already become an important part of my life. That's why I came up here to tell you. It is nothing like my feelings for Jake, or for anyone else . . . except Richard. I loved Richard too, and I want you to know that.'

Rosamund said, simply, 'I've never doubted that, my dear.'

'And . . . I want to tell you, that loving Steve doesn't cancel that out.'

'I never thought it would.' They were silent for a few moments, thinking of Richard. For a brief, almost imperceptible moment, Rosamund was gripped by a clutch of sharp, sudden emotions, a mixture of despair and grief, bitterness and regret, for the fact that Richard's wife and

Sophie's mother would move on, love again, live again, while Richard was irrevocably gone. And then the moment passed, the emotions lifted and disappeared, and Rosamund felt only love for Anna, and happiness for her, and relief that both she and Sophie had found someone to care for.

'I am as pleased as if you were my own daughter instead of my daughter-in-law,' she said, embracing her. 'He seems a good man, for both you and Sophie.' She held Anna for a long time, feeling her tears, and understanding them.

Later, after Anna had told Rosamund all about Steve, his son and Tess, his guitars, his home, she said, 'And yet I keep pushing him away. I love him, but I stand back when he starts talking about us being a family, that sort of thing. I know why, too, but it doesn't help. I'm afraid to let him come too close because if I lost him, as I lost Richard, I couldn't take it, couldn't survive it a second time.'

Rosamund was too troubled to reply, suddenly seeing the parallels with her relationship to Peter. Is this why she insisted upon compartmentalizing him, why she would not let him seep into the bulk of her life? Shaking her head as if trying to shake away these thoughts, she made herself concentrate on Anna and what she was saying . . .

Standing up and beginning to pace the tiled floor of the pottery, unable to think about anything but Sophie undergoing her operation, Rosamund feels, for the first time in years, a sharp pang of longing for her husband, Tony. He was the child's grandfather: he should be here; they should face this waiting time together. And yet Rosamund knows that if Tony were alive he would be no comfort to her; he would detach himself from the anguish around him by withdrawing deep into himself like a recluse into a cell, as he did when Richard died.

Richard, too, should be here. Her son, Sophie's father, Anna's husband. Yet she knows that if Richard too were alive the pain she would be feeling now would be even more intense, for she would be suffering not only for Sophie but for him, for the agony he would be enduring during this long day.

She never could bear Richard's suffering. Perhaps because he was her only child; perhaps it was just that she found motherhood terribly painful. She simply could not stand Richard being hurt. Whether it was a physical injury – he once broke his arm; another time he had six stitches when he fell off his bicycle – or whether it was an emotional distress, like the death of his puppy, or a brief period of being bullied at school, she suffered a hundred times more than he did.

Richard, fortunately, had been oblivious to his mother's agony, for she had the sense and intelligence not to inflict it upon him. It was something Rosamund kept to herself, not even sharing her self-knowledge with her husband, for Tony had been a rather forbidding man and would have dismissed his wife's excess emotions as an unfortunate by-product of her creativity. Rosamund had loved Tony, but often found him unbending. Richard had shared the same trait, but had learned warmth and flexibility from his mother, and later from Anna, whom he had loved indiscriminately and who had taught him passion.

Now as she wanders out of her pottery and into her conservatory which is dazzling with light and sun, she wonders if perhaps Richard had felt about Sophie as she did about him, unable to cope rationally with even the slightest threat. She hopes not. God, how she hopes he didn't, for the torment he would have suffered during Sophie's early months of life would have been excruciating.

She stops in front of a great bowl of sweet peas, burying her face in them. They smell sweet, heady. First Richard, then Tony. *Please, not Sophie*, she whispers to the multicoloured petals, crushing a flower in her hand without realizing what she is doing.

Suddenly she wants to see Peter, badly, but he returned

to France a few days ago. For the first time she understands that being alone and independent not always strengthens you, but can sometimes work the opposite. The thought dismays her.

In Bristol, Mary Callington says to her husband Mike, 'What do you think of the new uniform Roland Johnson-Scott is introducing to the school for next term? I must say, as a new headmaster, he's not shy about initiating changes.'

'Hmm.'

'David rather likes that new forest green tie. Speaking of David, I think it would be a good idea if you do educational things with him this summer, take him to the science museum, that sort of thing. He has an aptitude for science and I think we should encourage it. Owen would benefit from the outings as well.'

Mike grunts inaudibly, shifts in his chair. Mary glances at him and says, 'Would you stop looking at your watch? It's making me frightfully nervous.'

'Oh. Sorry. It's just that Anna said she'd phone back in a couple of hours, let me know how things are progressing.'

'She only rang a half hour ago.'

'Oh.'

They are in the garden, the phone close to Mike's side. It is a magnificent day; the sun shines as if it has just been polished, and birds twitter all over the city. They have been gardening, Mary weeding and Mike pruning the hedges, but now they are relaxing, drinking lemonade and watching the children splashing about in the paddling pool.

'What a gorgeous day!' Mary cries. 'It's a pity you can't take the children to the sea. Are you sure . . . ?'

'I'm not leaving the telephone. If anything should happen I want to know immediately.'

She sighs. 'Such a pity. An entire Saturday off, wasted.'

'Mary – don't.'

He looks so unapproachable that she becomes petulant. 'You might as well be up there, in Birmingham. I don't know why you're here.'

I don't know why either, he thinks. He says nothing.

'Of course Anna has her new man with her. You've been made redundant, I'm afraid.'

Still Mike doesn't speak. 'Oh, hell!' she cries. 'Are we going to sit around here like this for five or six more hours? How long does this bloody operation go on, anyway?'

Without looking at her Mike gets up, goes inside the house. Mary clenches and unclenches her fists to stop the tears gushing from her eyes like water from a broken pipe. She doesn't know why she says the things she does to Mike, doesn't know why she cannot show compassion to Anna, for in the deep depths of her heart it is there, it is there!

A cry from one of the children alerts her, and she rushes down the garden to mend whatever it is: a stubbed toe, a crushed sibling feeling. *Oh, Anna, Anna. Forgive me, but thank God it is not my child. Thank God.*

On the other side of Bristol, Madge too is sitting by her telephone. Her husband, Ron, has just come and gone, nosing about trying to find out if Juan Carlos lives in the old marital bed or has a room and a mattress of his own. Madge was in no mood for these games and for the first time since he left, told him the house was hers and to get out of it. She feels strangely exhilarated by this. How unimportant Ron suddenly seems, compared to the things she has – her lovely healthy sons, a lusty lover, a friend like Anna whom she loves more than her own sister.

Upstairs her son, Tom, is playing computer games with the boy, Sam, who keeps running downstairs during this long afternoon to ask Madge about Sophie. So far Madge has been able to reassure him that everything is, so far, all right. *And if it isn't?* she asks herself. She shakes the thought from her head, lets it go. Staring at the phone she wills it to ring, wills it to be Anna, saying the operation is over and a success.

In Birmingham it is far from over. 'Aren't you off duty now?' Jim Winters says to Belinda. 'No. Yes. Yes, I guess I am.'

'So why are you hanging around? Not that I mind, of course. You do raise the tone of the place. Refreshing, you could say.'

'I don't exactly have a million things to run home to,' Belinda replies, then is appalled by the bitterness in her voice. Max has been gone almost four months now, though they still see each other occasionally, meeting for dinner in pathetic little attempts to see if they can get back together again. The meetings only highlight what they both already know: that though they still want each other, the stalemate still exists. For Max, there must be children; for Belinda, there must not.

The first time they met after they split up was an accident. They had literally run into each other rounding a corner at the supermarket near Belinda's flat. 'Max . . . you here?' she murmured inanely, taking in his unseasonal tan and the bleached sun streaks in his hair and feeling fresh pain because he had been on holiday without her. 'I thought you lived on the other side of town,' she said, struggling to be casual but secretly hoping wildly that he was on his way to see her.

'Oh, ah, just on my way to have dinner at a friend's. She lives not far from you, actually.'

She, Belinda thought: *dinner*. She noted the bunch of chrysanthemums Max had in his shopping basket, the bottle of Australian Chardonnay, and turned away from him quickly before her eyes filled with tears. At home she cried all evening, imagining Max at that very moment making babies with some other woman just down the road.

Max, distraught at seeing Belinda, unnerved and un-manned by the quiver of tenderness he still felt for her, left the supermarket hastily, greeted his hostess (a young woman he worked with), distractedly, and hardly noticed the *paella* she had so painstakingly prepared. The image of Belinda's vivid red hair, worn slightly longer than he remembered and pushed back behind her sweet vulnerable ears, kept super-imposing itself in front of the young woman in front of him. Finally, at an early hour, he excused himself and went home, pleading a headache and pressures of work.

The second time they saw each other was planned. Max had phoned her, invited her out for an Indian meal to one of their old haunts. Both looked forward to the evening with great anticipation, hoping for a reunion. After a great deal of hand-holding across the chapatas, the conversation got around to children, whereupon they both realized that their position on the subject was unchanged. 'God, you can be so stubborn!' Max said, raising his voice uncharacteristically, causing the tall Indian waiter to frown at him from over at the bar.

'And you have a one-track mind, you can't let up, can you!'

They parted soon after that, and it was a good month before they saw each other again. Each subsequent meeting has been an echo of that first one, beginning with hope and ending in a most unsatisfying manner. But they cannot seem to let each other go.

Belinda, thinking of Max, of her empty flat and the lone-liness she often feels when she comes home from work, has no intention of leaving the hospital now, but for completely different reasons. She says to Jim, 'Actually, I'm hanging around until the operation on Sophie is over. I can't seem to leave until I know she's okay.'

Jim is sensitive enough not to make comments about pro-fessional detachment, not now. 'I'm off soon, too,' he says instead. 'Maybe I'll stick around with you. She's an appeal-ing kid; I hope all goes well. Wait for me and I'll take you down to the cafeteria. We'll need a meal; there's still a lot of time to go.'

143

Belinda nods. She will be glad of the company during this long day.

Steve and Anna are in the cafeteria also. 'Five hours,' Anna says.

'And everything going smoothly.' He looks at his watch. 'I must try and get hold of Sam again; he should be home with Tess now. I want to explain myself what is happening.'

While he goes to telephone, Anna wanders outside into the little courtyard by the entrance to the hospital. The sun is still hot even though it is early evening: how Sophie would have loved this balmy, perfect day! She sits on a wooden bench and imagines her daughter on the operating table: it is an image she can scarcely tolerate. Oh God, she thinks, let this new organ be healthy and strong, let it work, let it be right for Sophie's body!

Then another, insidious thought creeps into her head. *Who was the donor?* For Sophie to live, someone else had to die: *who was it?*

Anna has never let herself think about this before, but now the thought is trapped in her head like a wild bird in a cage, flying around and around without pause or rest. Anguished, distraught, feeling she will never have peace until her question is answered, Anna rushes back inside and goes into Marvin's office. Luckily he is there, rummaging through some papers, a half-finished cup of coffee gathering skin on his cluttered desk.

'Marvin,' she says breathlessly, 'I need to know about the donor.'

He stands and motions her to sit on the armchair opposite the desk. Anna knows that all details about the donor are confidential; patiently, he reminds her of this.

'I don't want a name. Just something, anything. I feel it's so horribly wrong not to even know about him, or her – this person who has died to save my child.'

'Anna, calm down. The donor did *not* die for Sophie. The

144

death came first, the donation because of it. Not the other way around.'

'Please. I need to know. I really need to know.'

Martin is sizing her up, trying to gauge the level of her distress, wondering how much to tell her. It is part of his job, weighing up the hysteria level of frenetic relatives. Anna's must be high, for he says, in his most business-like manner, 'Sophie's donor was French. A girl of ten. She had been on a life-support machine for days after being run down by a motorbike near her home in Normandy.'

He will not say any more, nor does Anna want to hear anything else. She nods gratefully to him, then turns and leaves the office. As she goes looking for Steve the image of a girl, a ten-year-old child who once lived in France but is now somehow irrevocably linked to her daughter, goes around and around in her head. Whoever she was, Anna wills her to give strength to Sophie, share with her own daughter the health and vitality that must have once been hers.

Steve finds her back in the bedroom, sitting on the bed, shivering, though the evening is still warm and tranquil. He sits beside her and holds her for a long, long time.

At last this longest day is over. It is midnight, and Sophie is in the intensive care unit. The operation took eight hours but it has been a success. Anna sits with her daughter, frightened of the tubes and machines and apparatus of modern medical technology surrounding the unconscious child, but she is at peace, marvelling that Sophie is still alive, still breathing. She stays with her for over an hour, then lets Steve take her to their little room where this time she sleeps, white-faced on the narrow bed, while Steve sits beside her, keeping watch. An hour and a half later she is back at Sophie's bedside, and finally, after what seems to Anna a very long time, her daughter regains consciousness, opens her eyes. She cannot speak for she is on a ventilator; a steel

tube goes down her throat as her breathing is being rhyth-
mically, methodically, done for her. She looks ethereal, and
Anna notices she has a strange golden colour unlike anything she has seen before. 'All over, Sophie,' she says as the
child looks at her with bewilderment. 'You've got a new liver
and you're going to be fine.'

Sophie shuts her eyes briefly in what Anna interprets as
relief, then opens them again and focuses on her mother
until finally she sleeps again. Anna sits for another couple of
hours as the child drifts in and out of consciousness.
Sometimes she seems in pain, other times in great distress,
but the staff reassure Anna that her daughter is fine, that
everything is normal. *Normal? This is normal?* she thinks.
These tubes, these machines. This child sliced open and
with an organ of a dead child inside her – this is *normal?*

Later, sitting with Steve in the tiny kitchen making soup
out of a packet, Anna tries to say these things to Steve.
Sophie is in deep oblivion and Marvin sent her away, saying
the child would sleep for hours now and that Anna
needed a break. Feeling slightly dizzy, slightly nauseous,
she agreed.

'You can't think in those terms, Anna,' Steve is saying as
he breaks open a packet of dry tomato soup and pours it
into one of the stark white hospital mugs. 'You can't think,
in a situation like this, about what is normal and what isn't.
Much of modern medicine is totally unnatural if you look at
it that way.'

'Amoral, too. Before last evening, I wouldn't let myself
think about a donor for Sophie, wouldn't face the fact that
Sophie's life depended on another child dying. All I cared
about was *her*, my own child; I had no compassion or even
curiosity for anyone else.'

Steve rolls a cigarette, hands it to Anna, then makes one
for himself. 'You've been in terrible distress, love,' he says
finally. 'Forget about what's normal and not, what's amoral
or not. Everything becomes irrelevant when your child is

146

threatened. The French girl would have died anyway, even if Sophie had never been born. You know that.'

'I know.' She is sad, tired. She watches Steve as he pours boiling water on the dull red powder in the white mugs. 'That looks like blood,' she says sharply; and then, irrationally, 'I can't drink it. I'll get a vegetable soup instead.' She throws the mixture down the sink and watches it for an inordinately long time as it trickles along the grey shiny stainless steel sink and finally down the drain.

Chapter Nine

SOPHIE is in intensive care for several days, as gradually the tubes, or most of them, come out. The golden hue that Anna had noticed right after the operation is gone, leaving her white and fragile. More blood tests are taken, a blood transfusion is given, and a T-tube is inserted to drain the wound and the bile which has to be endlessly checked.

At last, after about a week, Sophie is back in the ward, able to eat and drink normally. Anna is so relieved that it takes her a few days to realize the doctors are not as enthusiastic about her daughter's progress as they were the first day or so.

Ten days after the operation, a broad, sturdy young man with a cherubic face and perpetually raised eyebrows comes to talk to Anna. Conrad Jamison was one of the fourteen doctors, four of whom were surgeons, who assisted at Sophie's operation. Conrad is an expert on the human liver and has been around often since the operation, spending a good deal of time with Sophie and talking to Anna and Steve. 'The blood chemistry is just not coming right,' Conrad says to them now. The three are sitting in the day-room at the end of the ward. From there Anna can see Sophie, sitting up in bed doing a crossword with Belinda.

'You know what that means,' Conrad states flatly.

'Rejection,' Anna says faintly. 'The liver is being rejected.'

Conrad nods. 'For some reason Sophie's body just doesn't want to accept the new organ. It happens sometimes. We're still trying to save it, but it doesn't look too promising.'

Anna is stunned, feels sick, faint: and yet she knew, she knew. She has watched Sophie as her colour changed from that unearthly golden hue to a normal pink and white complexion that only lasted briefly; for slowly, almost imperceptibly, the dreaded yellow tinge began to reappear.

Steve reaches for Anna's hand as he asks quietly, 'What happens now?'

Conrad looks at Steve, then Anna. 'Mr Wright will be speaking to you soon about the possibility of another transplant.'

Anna says slowly and carefully, as if she is speaking under water, 'Tell me about it. Exactly what is happening, what you think will happen. Tell me what you must do to make Sophie well.'

As Conrad talks, she knows they are back in the nightmare.

Harold Wright talks to Anna a few days later. 'Why?' Anna demands. 'Why are you and everyone so sure that a second liver will be accepted by Sophie's body when the first one wasn't?'

'We don't know for sure,' Harold answers honestly, 'but there is every chance that it will. This first one was a fluke. It happens sometimes despite all our efforts. The small tubes in the liver have been damaged by the rejection and once that happens the liver is irretrievably lost. Sophie won't get better now that this has happened. She needs another liver.'

Anna storms into Marvin's office. 'A second transplant – everyone is insisting on it,' she shouts at him. 'How can I let her go through that again?'

'There is every reason to believe this next one will be a success,' he says calmly. 'It is not uncommon for a second transplant to take place when the first is unsuccessful.'

Stuart and Eleanor drive up to the hospital for a day. 'My colleagues in London inform me that despite the best medical attention a liver will, for some reason, simply not be accepted by the body,' he states baldly to his daughter. 'There is no indication that this will happen again.'

150

'They can't save this liver, Anna. If you leave it, it'll fail,' Mike says on one of his visits, hating the desolation in her eyes, the confusion – and even the slight gleam of hope as she talks to him, as if he can help, as if he could be the one to wave the wand and conjure up the happy ending. He is sad that he can no longer make her smile, make her turn on him that fragile sanguine smile that was focused on him when he mended her broken dolls, or found her lost kitten all those years ago. 'You have to give her another chance. You have to let them try another operation.'

Anna listens, and knows there is no choice. Sophie deserves another chance, and she shall have it. Desperately, she agrees to a second transplant.

Anna and Sophie leave hospital on a warm damp day that smells like rain and roses. It is a month since the operation. The doctors wanted Sophie to stay until another liver is found, for they feel she is strong enough now to sustain another transplant. However both Anna and her daughter were so psychologically down that Mike, alarmed on one of his frequent visits, convinced the staff that it would be detrimental for Sophie to stay in hospital, that her mental state would be so poor that it might have dire effects on the coming operation. A compromise was made – they are to stay with Rosamund in Malvern, which is handier to Birmingham, and Anna will have company in her vigil over Sophie. From there the child can return to the hospital for the necessary tests and monitoring while waiting for her new liver, and Anna can be cosseted by her mother-in-law.

Anna drives slowly, bewildered by the world in which she is suddenly let loose. The bleeper sticks out of a deep pocket in her loose canvas trousers. Sophie, though her spirits have lifted considerably since they were let out, is subdued. She is resigned to another operation, but this time she is frightened. The last one with all its after-effects is still fresh in her memory. Mother and daughter are both

151

numb, living from moment to moment, trying only to survive.

Rosamund's house, an old brick farm worker's cottage at the end of a row of newer, more modern dwellings, is a haven after the hospital. A shed outside was, years ago, turned into a workshop, and here Rosamund spends hours making her heavy ceramic vases. Behind the house there is a plum orchard, and next to the pottery there is a wild meadow: a tangle of long grass, thistles with their big blue flowers, goldenrod, docks, and buttercups. The house is square and rather dark, but a small, cosy conservatory transforms it into an interesting dwelling of light and space. Sophie and Anna spend hours here, under the grapevine twining its way around the corners, surrounded by Rosamund's pots and a profusion of geraniums. Sophie reclines on an ancient wicker sofa with deep fat cushions, either dozing or listening to story-tapes on her earphones, while Anna sits at the little table in a corner plodding through her translation. Rosamund disappears for hours into her workshop, then emerges to feed them, pamper them, spoil them as much as Anna will allow. On Sophie's better days, she plays with the twin girls who live next door. The twins are the same age as Sophie, quiet serious girls so self-contained in their relationship with each other that they haven't many friends and don't seem to mind. They were drawn to Sophie from the start, sensing a maturity similar to their own; that, and proximity (the houses practically overlap), and the boredom of a long summer, have combined to forge a satisfying friendship between the three.

The highlight of the stay is a cat Sophie finds, skinny and obviously abandoned in the meadow behind the cottage. It is so tiny and fluffy and soft and grey it looks like a ball of dust when Sophie tenderly brings it into the house. Rosamund's old cat died several months ago so she is delighted to give the new cat a home. Sophie and the twins spend hours playing with Grey, as they have aptly named her, for when the creature is fed and made comfortable, she turns out to be gregarious and mischievous, obviously enjoying the endless games the children devise for her.

Madge visits for a day, as does Mike, and Eleanor and Stuart. Anna and Steve talk on the telephone nearly every night but have not seen each other since Steve left Birmingham, shortly after it had been decided that Sophie would have another transplant.

'Look, I want to see you and Sophie,' he says more than once. 'Why can't I come up, just for the day if I can't stay overnight?'

'I've told you. Rosamund is Richard's mother. She knows about you, but I don't know if she's ready to meet you yet.'

'Have you asked her?'

Anna hesitates. 'We never talk about Richard.'

'Maybe you should. Maybe it's time you did.'

She shakes her head, for herself rather than for Steve who cannot see her, who is miles away. Except that one time recently, when Anna told Rosamund about Steve, she has never talked to her about Richard, not since his death. Rosamund had tried to broach the subject several times, years ago, but Anna never responded, and finally, recognizing something locked and impenetrable in her daughter-in-law, she gave up.

But that night Rosamund, unsettled herself after a telephone call from Peter saying he is not returning to England as soon as he had expected, says, bluntly, 'Why hasn't Steve been to visit you? You two must be missing each other dreadfully.'

Anna, who has just walked downstairs after saying goodnight to Sophie, is disconcerted. 'I don't know,' she finally says lamely.

'I hope it is not me that is putting him off? I should hate that. Sophie misses him too; she told me so the other day.'

For a moment Rosamund fears Anna will not answer her.

Going to the small desk she has been using for her work, she finds her glasses sitting on the Spanish dictionary, carefully wipes them on her T-shirt, and puts them on. At last she looks at Rosamund and says, 'I thought it wouldn't be right. Because of Richard. I thought it would be . . . insensitive, especially right now with Sophie so ill.'

'Oh, my dear, why didn't you just ask me?' Rosamund sighs. 'Richard has been dead a long time. I have already told you how happy I am that you have Steve.'

Something locked in Anna breaks, flies open. 'He can't take Richard's place,' she says harshly. 'He can't really *share*, not the way Richard could. Richard was Sophie's father, he could have helped me make the excruciating decisions I have to face day after day. Big ones, life and death ones, like should Sophie have a second transplant? And then the little ones: sometimes they're the worst. Should Sophie go outside and play with the twins when she seems a bit off-colour? The doctors have all warned me that I must keep her healthy and strong for her next operation. Yet they also said it's vital that she be psychologically ready. Which would be worse: the emotional distress Sophie would feel at not being allowed out to play, or the physical weakening she might develop if she gets overtired? Every day, every hour it sometimes feels, I have to make decisions like those. And Richard's gone, opted out.'

They are both shocked when Anna finishes. The bitterness, the venom, in her voice echoes in the silence around them for a few moments. Anna moves away from Rosamund, walks over to the window and watches the last fragments of a lingering sunset. Finally Rosamund says, gently, 'I never knew that you blamed Richard so vehemently for dying.'

Anna turns to her. 'I'm sorry. I never wanted you to know. I'm terribly strung out, or I would never have said anything.'

'Oh, Anna! Thank God we *are* saying something at last. It's not unnatural to feel anger when someone dies, when we feel abandoned by them. As if they died on purpose somehow.'

'But that is it, you see. I think he did. He went out knowing what could happen, willing it to. As if he wanted to leave us, wanted to – ' She breaks off. In the soft evening light her face looks taut, sombre. 'Anyway,' she goes on finally, 'I don't want to talk about it anymore.'

Anna's words have shocked and distressed Rosamund, but she says firmly, 'I'm sorry, but I do. For too long we have put off this talk, Anna. You think that Richard went out deliberately in that boat to opt out, as you put it? To . . . kill himself?'

Anna turns away, unable to look at her. 'Yes, I do. I'm sorry, I never wanted to tell you this.'

The living-room has darkened as the sun disappears outside, but neither of them bothers to turn on a light. Rosamund moves to an armchair, sits down stiffly. She says slowly, 'I wish you had told me before. I never knew you felt like this.'

'I'm sorry. I didn't mean to hurt you. I've hurt you now, by telling you what I believe.'

'Oh my dear Anna, it's you who are hurt by these things, not me! I wish you had told me years ago because perhaps I could have helped you. You see, I know you are wrong. I know dying was the last thing on my son's mind when he went out in that boat.'

Anna sits down in a chair facing her mother-in-law. She feels, tenuously, the lifting of something that has been pressing hard like a yoke on her shoulders for years. 'Tell me,' she says softly. 'Tell me why you are so convinced.'

In that quiet, darkened room Rosamund begins to talk. 'He wrote me a letter shortly before he died. I tried to give it to you, once, weeks afterwards, but you didn't want to know, didn't want to even speak about Richard. I respected your grief, left you. I wish I had been more persistent now.'

'I couldn't talk about him to anyone. My feelings were too confused. I was crazed with grief, despair – '

'I know, I know.' Her voice is gentle. After a pause she says, 'Can you honestly think, my dear, that Richard would do that deliberately? Cause you such pain – *intentionally* – when he loved you so much?' When Anna is silent she continues, 'You don't doubt that, do you? That he loved you? Or should I tell you how my quiet, uncommunicative son opened out, blossomed, when he met you? His letters to us were such a revelation. For the first time ever he seemed to be able to express himself, articulate what he felt. You, and then Sophie, meant everything to him. He never would have wilfully caused you the suffering his death inflicted on you.'

'I believe he loved me, yes,' Anna says. She lets herself remember, for the first time in years, the good times. How she and Richard met at university, how within weeks they had moved in together, nearly failing their first year because they couldn't tear themselves away from each other to go to lectures.

When Sophie was born and her illness diagnosed, of course their love changed, became less frivolous, ran underground like a river changing course. But though it no longer sparkled lightly in the shallows, it deepened, widened. Richard changed, but so did she. They were no longer the carefree students, the young newly-weds, but then that couldn't have gone on forever even without Sophie. But they changed together, and loved each other more because of it, and even in their worst times were not without dreams, without hopes.

'We made plans,' she whispers now, remembering: Sophie at two, on a good day when she looked like any normal healthy child, picking up stones in the garden and examining them seriously one by one. 'She'll be a scientist,' Richard had laughed. 'Look how thoroughly she is unravelling the mystery of that stone.'

'Shall we get her a microscope for her next birthday?' Anna teased, loving this game because it made her forget, gave her hope, made her believe that the three of them had a long future together.

It was shortly after this that Richard insisted they begin travelling with Sophie. Though they could no longer work abroad, like they had planned, there were the long school holidays.

'Sophie, look!' Richard came in one evening with a huge parcel and Sophie, squealing, tried to grab it and nearly fell over.

'Oh, how delightful!' Anna had cried, for it was a child's cotton sleeping bag decorated with cartoon animals, lion kings, mischievous monkeys and grinning walruses. Inside the bag Sophie found Alice, a rag doll with outrageous red hair and huge brown freckles. 'Oh, pretty, pretty!' she had cried, and had crawled into the bag then and there with the doll and the banana she had been eating.

Anna says now, in a husky voice, 'When she was just over two we took her to France on a camping holiday. It was such fun.' She stares at Rosamund for a long time, but is not seeing her. 'The boat,' she goes on at last. 'Richard finished the boat when Sophie had just come out of a long, particularly bad patch. Richard had been . . . we both were . . . very distressed by it. We had lost our hope, our courage . . . Richard especially, that time.'

'The boat was to regain some of that, Anna,' Rosamund says gently. 'Not to . . . to lose his own life in. It all just went tragically wrong.'

Anna nods. 'I remember now. I've blocked out so much; I've been so angry, so bitter . . . '

We'll sail on it together one day, Anna, the three of us, you and me and Sophie. Maybe next summer we can take it down the coast to Cornwall . . . and when Sophie is older, who knows, maybe even to France!

Anna wipes away tears with the back of her hand. 'He was full of plans, right up to – ' She breaks off, confused.

'Right up until the day he died,' Rosamund finishes.

There is a long silence. 'I have not let myself remember,' Anna says, closing her eyes. 'I have been so unfair to Richard.'

'It is because you were angry with him. Grief makes you crazy, not just with sorrow but with rage. I know.' She thinks of her own madness when Richard died.

'But . . . ' Anna is still struggling with her memories. 'He went off, on his own, during an unpredictable time of year.'

'He went alone because he could find no one else to go with, you know that. And it had to be then. He wanted to try out his boat, and it was half-term. He didn't want to go in winter, and by the Easter holidays he hoped he could take you and Sophie. He wrote to us, you know. I was in France with Tony just before he died, and he wrote to us there. He told us about his planned trip across the Bristol Channel, how this was to be just a trial run before the spring break, to see if the boat was seaworthy enough for you and Sophie. I suppose it was to be a surprise, since I realize now you knew nothing about it.' Rosamund pauses for a moment then goes on: 'It wasn't the sort of thing he would write if he had a death wish, Anna.' When there is no reply she adds, 'I still have the letter. If you want to see it.'

Anna still does not speak; she is too full of an emotion she cannot yet identify. 'Maybe one day,' she says finally. 'I don't really need to now.'

Rosamund is glad that the room is nearly dark, for her own eyes are beginning to fill. 'Richard was a brave man, Anna. You know that. Killing himself would have been the coward's way. All he wanted was to look after Sophie and love you both. It was tragic that he did not live to do so.'

The women sit in silence for a long time, until Grey, asleep until now, jumps suddenly on to Anna's lap. She rouses herself, stands, and goes to Rosamund. 'Thank you,' she says, kissing her. 'Thank you for that.' Upstairs Sophie stirs, cries out in her sleep. As Anna goes to her she feels that for the first time since Richard died she is breathing freely and without restriction at last. As she soothes her restless, sleeping daughter she recognizes that the emotion she is feeling is an intensity of love – deep and translucent and serene – for the father of her beloved child, the father whose features Anna recognizes even now in the sleeping face of her daughter. Her anger has gone, and all that is left is the deep, radiant memory of Richard's love.

When she comes downstairs Rosamund rejoices at the tranquillity she sees in her daughter-in-law's face. It cannot last long, not with another operation looming ahead for Sophie, but perhaps the knowledge that Richard did not deliberately abandon her will give Anna an extra core of strength to face the weeks ahead. At least some ghosts were laid to rest this evening. At least there should be some peace for Anna in that.

Steve comes for the weekend. Rosamund would not hear of his driving all the way from Devon just for a day, so Anna rather reluctantly invites him to stay longer. Steve is delighted, as is Sophie; and as a matter of fact he and Rosamund take an instant liking to each other. With relief, Anna lets herself go, enjoys the weekend. They take Sophie on little outings – into Worcester to buy a new nightie and dressing-gown for hospital; out into the country to a rose-covered tea-room for toasted teacakes. On Sunday morning, the twins come over, and Rosamund insists Steve and Anna go out on their own for a walk on the Malvern hills. It is another glorious day and they walk for over an hour before finally stopping to sit and look at the view. It is all sky and sun and undulating hills, but they scarcely glance at it, so engrossed are they in each other. 'God, I've missed you,' Steve says, taking in her tired eyes, her pale face. 'Sophie too.'

'And me. I wish Sam were here.'

'So do I. We'd be family then.'

They hold hands as they slowly, reluctantly, head downwards.

In September the bleeper sounds again, and the idyll is over. For Anna the next few days are like being in a permanent state of *déjà vu*. Being wiser this second time around, knowing exactly what is happening, does not make things easier for her. On the contrary, anticipation makes her even more fearful.

This time it is Rosamund who sits with her during the long operation, for Steve is in Frankfurt at an important trade show. He goes every year, selling guitars, making vital contacts, and Anna insisted he was not to miss it this year. He went reluctantly, hoping Sophie would not be called into hospital until he returned, and leaving Anna with numerous telephone numbers at which he could be located.

When Rosamund asked if Anna would like her to stay, the younger woman surprised herself by saying, with great relief: 'Oh, yes. Yes, please.' Rosamund drove them to Birmingham, and as Anna sat in the back comforting Sophie she marvelled at how she had done it herself the last time, and wonders why.

Forty-eight hours after the operation, there is a crisis. Sophie is in intensive care and Anna has just returned there, having gone to have a wash, change her clothes. There is bustle, confusion: several doctors are with Sophie and Anna's heart goes cold with terror.

Conrad Jamison takes her aside and says, 'It's all right. Sophie had a slight fit but she's okay.'

Anna tears herself away from him and rushes to her daughter, who seems to be sleeping peacefully. Doctors and nurses are checking machines, tubes, watching Sophie closely. Conrad says, 'The fits were, we think, a reaction caused by one of the anti-rejection drugs. We've lowered the dosage; she should be fine, now.'

Fits? Anna thinks. I thought it was just one? How many? What did they do to her? How will it affect her? Will she have more? The questions shoot out of her and bombard the young doctor. He takes her into the intensive care office and very carefully, meticulously, explains things. Sophie had three small seizures in a row, which are now under control, which should not occur again, which should not affect her at all.

'You must remember,' he continues, 'that Sophie has to be given several potent drugs which, of course, we monitor closely. But it is difficult to predict exactly what reaction each patient will have.'

'You overdosed her,' Anna says frantically.

Conrad looks at her helplessly. 'It happens. I'm sorry, but sometimes we do make mistakes.'

Anna leaves the office and returns to sit with Sophie. Only later does it occur to her to thank Conrad for his honesty in telling her exactly what happened. Coming from a medical family, she knows only too well how closed the professional ranks can be, how secretive when they think it necessary. He's young, she thinks: perhaps later he'll learn how to dissemble. She hopes not.

Later she rings Mike. 'They overdosed her with the anti-rejection drug. She had these seizures. They say there won't be any long-term effects, but I'm worried.'

Her brother is silent for a moment. Then he says, 'You've got to believe him, Anna. They're doing their best. Each patient is different, each drug reacts differently on each one. I wouldn't want to be administering those anti-rejection drugs. If you give too little, the liver is rejected, too much, and there are terrible complications. The trouble is, just what is exactly right is so variable.'

'I'm terrified, Mike. What if they do her permanent damage?'

Mike is silent for so long that Anna begins to wonder if they have been cut off. Finally he says, 'The first liver,

161

Anna. The doctors wouldn't say it outright, but talking to some of them after it began to reject, I know they feel that the dosage of anti-rejection drugs was too low. They want to make sure that doesn't happen again.'

'Oh, God. Is that why her body never took it?'

'I think so. I told you how thin the line is between too much and too little.'

Anna hangs up, hopelessness and despair tangling her like a rank weed, making her immobile. Rosamund, who had been catching up on some sleep during these latest developments, finds her standing aimlessly by the telephone, unable to summon the strength even to return to Sophie. The older woman knows immediately there is something wrong, and takes Anna to a quiet spot to talk about it. Her calm and strength seep into the younger woman like fresh rain into dry earth, and when at last she returns to intensive care she feels hope returning like a recalcitrant child, to sit beside her meekly at Sophie's bedside.

Once again Sophie is back on the ward. She is still fragile but so far she is doing well: so far there has been no sign of rejection.

'Do you think this one will hold?' Belinda mutters to Jim after the two have shared a joke and a laugh with the child.

'It seems much more promising. Everyone has high hopes.'

'We have to live too much on hope in here. I find sometimes my capacity for it is nil.'

'You mean for Sophie? You've given up hoping?'

'God, no. Just the opposite. It's taking up all my energy.'

Jim looks at her appraisingly. 'You mustn't, you know,' he says kindly, 'get so involved.'

'Tell me how not to, okay? Just tell me.'

It is a rhetorical question and Jim knows it. Touching her shoulder briefly he goes to another patient. Belinda stands still for a moment, remembering that Max said almost the same thing to her the last time they had met.

'You're very involved with this Sophie child,' he had murmured disapprovingly as they sat in a wine bar eating a salad and drinking lagers, for it was a hot steamy evening. Sophie had just had her second operation and Belinda had been telling Max all about it.

'She's a child, for heaven's sake!' Belinda had replied defensively. 'How can one be detached from a child?'

Max picked at a green pepper. 'You don't want children of your own yet you become involved with one of your young patients,' he went on stubbornly, knowing he was being totally unreasonable but unable to stop himself.

'What a load of rot. The two things are completely separate.'

'Oh? I don't know about that,' he said enigmatically, because he knew she was right. He realized with some surprise that he was jealous of Belinda's obvious affection for this strange child.

'Well,' he went on, wiping salad dressing from his fingers, 'if you've got that much need in you to worry about every child that comes your way, you might as well have one of your own to worry properly about.'

This is so outrageous that Belinda got up to leave. 'Maybe we should forget about these cosy little let's-still-be-friends evenings we keep having,' she said picking up her bag. 'We can't even seem to talk sensibly to each other.'

'Oh, sit down,' Max said, 'and finish your salad. I promise I won't say another word about children, as long as you don't mention the hospital, all right?'

Belinda hesitated then sat down again. They talked trivialities the rest of the evening, then each went home alone, thoughtfully, to lay awake most of the night brooding.

Now she shakes her head, tries to collect herself before she goes back to her patients. Suddenly the door of the ward opens and what looks like a hundred balloons burst through. 'Hey, Belinda!' the balloons speak. 'Where's Sophie?' She realizes it is Steve behind them, holding the strings, and

163

she smiles with delight and recognition. 'Sophie's been asking for you,' she says.

Steve has spotted the child and is already there, giving her the balloons which are bouncing and bobbing and struggling to get loose so that they can soar right up to the ceiling. 'Oh Steve, they're great!' she laughs. She hugs him and several of the balloons break away. There is a great deal of scurrying around as Steve and Belinda try to catch them.

It is not until a half hour later that Steve finds Anna, dozing in her little bedroom. The night before Sophie had been restless and Anna had sat with her for several hours. Steve is dismayed by the new lines on her face, the unhealthy pallor of her skin.

'Why didn't you ring me, love?' he asks after a time, when Anna has finished telling him about the operation and its aftermath.

'I didn't want to take you away from Frankfurt. There was no need.'

'Jesus Christ, no *need*?' Steve explodes. 'Why in the hell is it always back to square one with you, Anna? I'm involved, remember? I love you, can you vaguely recollect that?'

'Steve, don't.' Anna shakes her head. 'I'm sorry. I honestly felt it would be wrong to drag you away from the trade show. You'd have dropped everything and come, you know you would. I was afraid you'd resent it later.'

Steve groans. 'God, what do I have to do to prove to you – ?'

'It's the same old problem,' Anna cries, interrupting him. 'For years Sophie has been *my* problem, *my* concern, and I can't seem to let anyone else in, not since Richard died.'

'Anna.' Steve pauses, looks at her. 'Anna, tell me honestly: do you want to?'

She is quiet, thinking of the talk she had with Rosamund about Richard. Because she no longer believes that Richard intentionally left her and Sophie, for the first time she can now believe that there are others who might not leave either.

'Yes,' she answers Steve finally. 'Yes, please. I do want to let you in.' She tries to smile. 'Though I think you are already here.'

Steve takes her hands and says, seriously, 'Will you accept that because I love you, I am already involved with you and Sophie? Irrevocably? You both are my problem now, just as I and Sam are yours. It's called taking on responsibility, Anna. When you love someone you take on a responsibility for them.'

Anna nods meekly. 'I accept that now, Steve. I really do.'

'At last,' he says with passion. 'At long last.'

Steve stays with them for a few days, Rosamund having already returned to Malvern shortly before he arrived. Sophie seems to be recovering remarkably well physically, though she is suffering somewhat from memory loss. Her long-term memory seems unimpaired, but often she cannot recall things that happened minutes ago. The doctors say cautiously that this could be a result of the seizures she had, and assure Anna that Sophie's memory will eventually return to normal. Anna, knowing that they are not positive of this, is dismayed, but because her daughter gains in health and strength every day, she counts her blessings and tries to be positive.

But then there is another crisis. One morning Sophie wakes up in an uncharacteristic rage, refusing to wash, threatening to tear out the tube still pumping painkillers into her arm, and shouting at Belinda to leave her alone when she goes over to see what is the matter. Anna tries to calm her and partially succeeds, though Sophie still refuses to eat and throws down the porridge spoon in a tantrum. Leaving the child with Steve and Belinda, Anna rushes off to find Marvin Templeton.

'There's something the matter with Sophie,' she says, confronting him in her office, telling him what has happened. 'She's never acted like that in her life.'

165

'I'm sure it's nothing,' he says reassuringly. 'She is obviously having a psychological reaction to the two operations. I don't need to tell you what a severe mental as well as physical strain she's been under.'

'But she's acting like a spoiled brat. She's never ever behaved that way before.'

'Anna, it's only natural that a child as ill as Sophie should be spoiled a little – we've all done it since she's been in hospital, and it's understandable if you as her mother do it also. She's had, naturally enough, an inordinate amount of attention. It's bound to affect her in some way.'

Anna is outraged. 'Sophie has been pulled about, ordered about, much more than she has been spoiled, as you call it. She's had her moans, her little rebellions, like any other normal child, but she has never reacted like this.'

'She's never had two major operations before.'

'I want a doctor to check Sophie at once. How do I know this is not a result of one of those little seizures you brushed off so lightly?' She leaves in a fury, noting that Marvin is scribbling copiously in a folder. More to add to the medical record about hysterical and neurotic mothers, she thinks. But she is too angry to care.

Conrad examines Sophie shortly afterwards. She has calmed down by then and seems her normal self. The doctor can find no explanation for the child's behaviour and says that she is doing far better after the operation than any of them expected. He too implies, though he is too tactful to say so, that the bouts of temper are nothing more than a display of Sophie's normal behaviour exacerbated by her long stays in hospitals.

However that evening there is a reoccurrence. In the day-room Sophie suddenly begins shouting and angrily throws a magazine across the room, merely because the channel that some other patients are watching is not the one she wants to view. The next day is the same. She refuses to get out of bed so that Belinda can change the sheets, and when the nurse tries to gently manoeuvre her off, Sophie clings to the bed rail and cries and screams.

This goes on for days. Anna knows that many of the staff are beginning to believe that Sophie is merely a spoiled child, indulging herself with scenes now that her physical health is so dramatically improving. Belinda does not feel this way; of all the staff, she has probably spent the most time with Sophie, and knows that the abrupt and wild change in her personality is not normal. One afternoon she finds Anna sitting despondently in the day-room, listlessly staring at a magazine, oblivious to its contents. Sophie is in the ward, sitting up in bed glaring at anyone that comes near her, angrily insisting she is not going to move until she can go home.

Belinda flops into the chair opposite Anna. 'I don't believe it, you know,' she says bluntly. 'That Sophie is usually like this. I got to know her pretty well, before and after the first operation. That's a totally different child out there.'

Anna looks at her gratefully. Tears blur her eyes for a moment, tears of relief that someone else can see this, that she is not mad or biased or blind to what is really happening to Sophie.

'She's a nice kid,' Belinda goes on, for Anna cannot speak. 'She's sweet and sensitive without being cloying and yukkie. She's got such a wonderful sense of humour, too – that alone would prevent her from making such bizarre unpalatable scenes as we've witnessed just lately. There is something seriously amiss.'

'Try telling that to the doctors,' Anna says hoarsely.

'I'm going to. I worked in a children's hospital before I came here, and I've seen kids with all kinds of illnesses, watched their reactions, their behaviour. I can't believe I got Sophie wrong.'

Anna, tears streaming down her face, puts her head in her hands. Belinda, moved by her distress, her fragility that seems at this moment to be as fine as thin glass destined to break into shards at any moment, goes to her, puts her arms around her, holds her while she weeps. *Oh God*, she thinks distractedly: *Is this what being a mother is all about? Is this what Max wants to put me through when he says he loves me?* She holds Anna tightly, as if she could by some osmosis learn what her strength is, the courage that enables her to go on. What Belinda doesn't yet understand is that it is people like her, moments like this one, which are the answer.

The next day not only Conrad, but the surgeon Harold Wright come in the ward to see Sophie, and that afternoon she is given another battery of tests. Later that night, when Sophie is asleep, Conrad comes in again, looking for Anna. 'I think you'll find she will gradually go back to her normal self now,' he says.

'What do you mean? What has happened?'

'We think it's a combination of a couple of the drugs that has caused this personality aberration. We've changed one, altered the dosage of the other.'

Anna groans. 'At last,' she says brokenly. 'At long last.'

'We think the seizures triggered it off, and then the drugs exacerbated it. It will wear off eventually. Hopefully the memory loss will as well.'

Anna shakes her head. 'No one would believe me except Belinda,' she says bitterly. 'No one would believe that Sophie wasn't just having temper tantrums.'

Conrad pats her shoulder. 'The liver has taken, just hold on to that. There is no sign of rejection whatsoever in Sophie's blood chemistry.'

'What a price,' Anna says sadly. 'What a price Sophie has to pay.'

'For life, Anna. The price may be high, but she is getting something special in return.'

She smiles at him gratefully. Her daughter will live, and the thought makes her spirits fly as high as Steve's balloons which are still floating crazily on the ceiling of the ward. She wonders if the price could ever be too much to pay for such a gift: life, with its profundity and banality, its joy and its sorrow. She thinks – she hopes – not.

Contented and sanguine, she goes to her daughter. Sitting next to the sleeping child Anna is convinced that even in the dark she can see the promising bloom of pink on her daughter's cheeks, the strong rhythmic breathing of her healthy lungs. *We've come through*, she thinks with amazement. *Sophie, love, we've made it.* She sits there for a long, long time and Steve, looking for her and spotting her in the darkened ward, leaves her alone. He is content to wait.

Chapter Ten

O<small>N</small> Richmond Road a great banner proclaims: WEL-
COME HOME SOPHIE! It was put up surreptitiously
during the night by Madge's exuberant sons and has not yet
been removed by the local authorities.

Sophie giggles when she sees it. She is in the car with
Steve and Anna, coming home from hospital at last. Tired
from the drive and the excitement, she nonetheless seems
well and happy. Anna cannot stop looking at her.

Madge is there to greet them, hugging everyone warmly.
Sophie's cat Samantha purrs and does all the right things
while Anna settles her daughter on the sofa in front of a
comforting fire. It is early October, but already quite cold.
Steve tucks a duvet around Sophie as she reads the many
cards that have come to the house.

They are not home long before Mike arrives, only this
time he is not alone. With him are Mary and all the
children, plus a baby girl that was born while Sophie was in
hospital. The baby is properly admired and then put down
in a carry cot to sleep. Sophie, pleased by this visit from the
young cousins she sees so rarely, bustles them upstairs to
show them her games and her story-tapes. 'She's been
around adults too long just lately,' Anna comments. 'It's
marvellous for her to play with young people for a change.'

Mary, watching the delight on her children's faces as they
are pounced upon by Sophie, is stricken with guilt, the same
crippling emotion which momentarily assailed her the day
Sophie had her operation and which has been plaguing her
at odd times when she leasts suspects it. She is sure this guilt
brought on her labour early, and though the outcome was
fine, a lovely healthy six-pound baby, Mary can't help but

wonder if some retribution was intended, some warning from the gods, as it were. It is all very upsetting, and so she has decided to try and make amends.

'I'm sorry we haven't seen very much of you and Sophie lately. I'm afraid that's been my fault: I seem to be constantly pregnant or bogged down with my own children. It's all very exhausting, but I shall try to do better in the future.'

'It's okay,' Anna says. 'It really is okay.' The two women look at each other warily, try a tentative smile. Mike, relieved, says quickly, 'I've brought some champagne, shall we have it now? To celebrate Sophie's future. We won't stay long – Sophie musn't overdo it her first day home.'

Before they leave Mary asks, 'Could you come for a meal one evening? With Sophie? If you want,' she adds hastily.

'Sophie would like that,' Anna replies.

In the car Mary says, 'What did she mean, "Sophie would like that"? Was she implying that she would not?'

'Oh, Mary! Stop looking for bones to pick over,' Mike replies. 'I doubt if Anna was implying anything. But you've not made it easy for her. You can't rush things now.'

Chastened, Mary resolves to phone Anna to make a definite date for dinner soon. Perhaps she can learn something from her sister-in-law. Anyone who has gone through what Anna has as a parent surely must have something to impart to other mothers, some lesson in strength or fortitude, she thinks hopefully. Besides, Sophie looks so much better now, her skin a healthy pink and white and not that sickly tinge that used to frighten Mary, made her gather her own children around her protectively. She will see more of Anna, she promises herself. Besides, she couldn't help noticing how docile both Owen and David were around Sophie, and how much they had seemed to actually enjoy being docile. Perhaps an older cousin would be a good influence on them.

That night when the phone has finally stopped ringing, the visitors gone, and Sophie sleeping peacefully in her own room at last, Anna and Steve flop exhausted into Anna's bed. 'I cannot remember when last we were alone together,' he says, turning towards her. Steve stayed at the hospital with Anna and Sophie for a few days after his arrival from Frankfurt, but as Sophie grew stronger he returned to Devon and his own neglected work. This morning he drove to Birmingham to collect them and bring them home.

'How long can you stay in Bristol?' Anna asks as she slides her arms around his body.

'A few days. Until Monday morning. I have Sam this weekend so I thought I'd bring him to you, if that's all right. He's keen to see Sophie.'

'Steve, that's great! A family again, eh?'

He holds her tightly, lovingly. 'You said that without even flinching.'

When he leaves Anna is appalled at the misery she feels. 'God, what a greedy selfish sod I am!' she complains to Rosamund on the telephone. 'I have Sophie home doing so well, getting stronger every day. And here I am pining over some man I've only known six months.'

Rosamund, who is being kissed on the neck by Peter who walked in only ten minutes ago after an unprecedented three months in France, finds it difficult to reply. Shooing him away with her free hand she says, at last, 'It's normal to want adult company, Anna. To want the man that you love with you is not selfish, it's natural.' Peter, listening to this last sentence, opens his mouth in a silent, exaggerated exclamation. 'At your age,' Rosamund adds hastily.

Anna says, 'You must have been lonely at times, after Tony died.'

'Yes . . . there were times.'

'And now?'

Rosamund pauses for a moment. 'I have friends,' she says obliquely. 'Perhaps you can meet some of them one day.'

173

'Was that me?' Peter says when she hangs up the telephone. 'Was I one of the friends you were referring to?'

'How strange,' she muses. 'At sixty-three, I am becoming incredibly soppy. I suddenly want you to meet my family.'

'About bloody time,' he says softly, and this time kisses her on the mouth.

As winter approaches Anna and Sophie fall into a routine which, because of its very normality and superficial dullness, pleases them both after the traumas of the last few months. Sophie has a home tutor now, for she will not be strong enough for school until the new year. Though the temper tantrums and personality alterations are a thing of the past, her memory is still extremely patchy. To her horror Anna realizes that Sophie, once a prolific reader, has almost totally forgotten how to read all but the simplest of story-books. She has also forgotten basic arithmetic, especially multiplication and division. The doctors are vague about the reasons for the memory loss, but the general opinion is that it is a result of the seizures. They say she will have to relearn many of these skills, but she doesn't seem to mind, and looks forward to her daily tuition.

Anna begins gathering her life around her again, taking on more Spanish students, doing the odd bit of supply teaching when one of Madge's sons is around to keep an eye on Sophie, and helping Juan Carlos with his English. She finishes the book translation and is given a play by an up and coming Basque playwright to work on. Steve comes when he can, often taking his weekends with Sam in Bristol so that they can all be together.

One Friday evening when they arrive, Sam announces to everyone, 'Mum is leaving Carl. She doesn't want to be married to him any more.'

There is a rather stunned silence. Then Sophie says, 'Will you miss him?'

Sam looks at her as if she were batty. 'Oh, no. Not at all.'

174

After they have disappeared upstairs to play, Anna looks at Steve in dismay. 'How . . . how do you feel?'

It is a question Steve cannot answer. 'I certainly didn't expect it. I knew from Sam that they've been quarrelling, but I didn't think – ' He stops, shrugs. 'Look, let's have some wine, I've had a long day and the drive from Devon was hell, lots of foggy patches and traffic.' He opens a bottle. 'I've brought some of your favourite red,' he says, handing her a glass. When she doesn't reply, he adds, softly, 'I don't want to waste my weekend with you talking about Tess, okay?'

But on Sunday the subject comes up again. The children are in Sophie's bedroom, playing with Lego, when suddenly she comes downstairs in tears and in distress. 'What is it?' Anna cries. 'Sophie, what's wrong?'

'It's Sam!'

'What has he done?' Steve asks.

Sophie sniffs, brushes her tears away with her hand. 'He said he doesn't want to live with us.'

Anna and Steve exchange glances. Steve says gently, 'I'm sure he would, Sophie, but he's already got a home. His home is with his mother.'

Anna knows how much it costs Steve to say that, and say it without bitterness. 'You know he loves being here with us whenever he can.'

Sophie sniffs again, and Anna hands her a tissue. 'It's not just that,' she goes on. 'He doesn't want Steve to live with us either. He wants Steve to live with his mother again.'

Anna can feel her face go white, numb. Steve says, 'I'd better go talk to him,' and goes upstairs.

Sam is sitting on Sophie's bed, trying to control the trembly feeling he has by leafing through some comics. He knows he has upset Sophie, and vaguely knows why. But he is unrepentant.

Steve sits opposite the boy, waits until he lifts his head and looks at his father. 'Sam,' he says, and the words lay heavy on the air and in his heart, 'you know I can't live with your mother any more. She's married to someone else.'

'She won't be for long.'

'Maybe, maybe not. She might change her mind about Carl.'

'She won't. She told me she didn't want to be with him ever again.'

'Okay. But it doesn't mean she wants to live with me.'

'How do you know?' Sam's voice is belligerent. 'Have you asked her?'

Steve shakes his head, struggling for words. 'I don't have to ask her, Sam. It just didn't work for us before. We couldn't live together, not without fighting and scenes. Neither of us want that kind of a life for you.'

'I want to live with both of you,' Sam says, suddenly pleading and vulnerable. 'I want us all to be together, like we were before.'

The pain these words provoke in Steve make him speak almost brusquely. 'I'm sorry, Sam. I can't tell you how sorry I am. But you want something impossible.'

The afternoon has somehow been diminished. Though Sam and Sophie make it up and are soon playing happily again, Steve is thoughtful, preoccupied. Anna wisely says nothing, but her peace too has grown opaque, a bit blurry around the edges. When Steve takes Sam home he decides to leave for Devon that night rather than early Monday morning as he usually does.

'I'm behind with the guitars, love,' he says to Anna. 'I need a really early start tomorrow.' This is true, but she knows also he needs to be alone for a time. It's his usual reaction when Tess, either directly or indirectly, provokes him in some way. Trying not to resent it, trying not to feel the first rumblings of fear in her belly, she smiles brightly and sends him on his way.

It takes her a long time to fall asleep that night, so when she finally does the pounding and banging that suddenly wakens her both infuriates and frightens her. Lying there, her heart beating, she slowly recognizes the voice shouting in the window of the house next door. 'I know you're there, Madge, you and your toyboy. Let me in!' There is a furious drum roll of noise which Madge perceives is the man pounding on her neighbour's front door.

Anna opens her bedroom window and hisses, 'Ron, are you out of your mind? It's two in the morning, everyone is asleep.'

'Christ, I wish I had my bloody key. MADGE YOU OPEN THIS DOOR!'

Anna makes an instant decision. She knows Madge is in bed with Juan Carlos, and though the woman has every right to be there with him, Ron is not in the mood to listen to reason. He has obviously been drinking heavily, and he is as erratic as he is obnoxious when he drinks. Juan Carlos, on the other hand, is young, presumably dead sober at the moment, and volatile. Neither Madge nor the sleeping inhabitants of Richmond Road would benefit from a confrontation between the two.

She pulls on a white towelling dressing gown and flings open the door. 'You'll never wake Madge; you know how soundly she sleeps. Come in here and I'll give you coffee.'

After some obligatory grumbling and threats against his wife, Ron complies and starts to follow Anna. Before he does, however, he pounds one more time on Madge's faded dark green door and shouts, 'I'll get you, you fucking toy-boy, you bloody coward, you foreign git! I'll get you.'

A window flies open from the building opposite and a deep voice shouts, 'Shut the hell up or I'll phone the police!' Ron turns wildly to confront the voice but before he can begin hurling abuse at complete strangers, Anna grabs him by his leather jacket and pulls him into her house.

'Now just sit there and shut up before you wake up Sophie,' she orders him imperiously, quickly making coffee to sober him up a bit. 'Who the hell do you think you are, making a scene at this hour?'

'Someone just told me, at the pub. Madge's fucking lodger is a South American bastard, and like I suspected all along, he's not just a lodger, he's screwing her. In *my* house, and in *my* bed.'

'Ron, if you don't shut up I'm throwing you out of here.'

'Not only that, he's the same age as my kids! God, when I see that little shit, I'll – '

The front door, which Anna forgot to lock, crashes open and Juan Carlos, dressed only in jeans, his chest naked and vulnerable in the cold, late autumn night, rushes up to Ron, grabs him by the neck of his jumper, and snarls, '*Hijo de puta.* Son of a whore. Scum. *Que te jodas,* you impotent shit. *¡Sin cojones!* A coward, eh? Foreign git, uh? Toyboy? I'll show you who is a boy, who is a toy.' With this he lunges at the older man, grabs him by shoulders, and shakes him as if he were indeed a soft rag toy.

At this, all the fight drains out of Ron like water from a leaky tap and when Juan Carlos scornfully lets him go he collapses like a boneless thing on to the nearest kitchen chair. 'You go near my woman again and I will kill you.'

This rouses Ron and he mutters a curse as he starts to get up, but Juan Carlos sneeringly gives him a tap on the chest and he slumps down again. The older man is quite drunk and rather unsteady. At that moment the door bangs open a second time and Madge is there. 'Ron, have you gone bananas? Don't you dare hurt that boy, d'ya hear me? He's only a kid.'

She's shouting this as she runs into the house, but stops dead when she reaches the kitchen. 'It's your ex-husband I should worry about, not the kid,' Anna says mildly.

'Kid, kid, kid – boy, boy, boy!' There is another torrent of Spanish expletives. 'I've had enough.' He stalks out of the house into the night.

'Oh dear,' Madge exclaims. 'Poor boy, he'll catch his death. It's freezing out there.'

Ron groans. 'Madge, baby. How can you do this to me?'

'Oh, honey, you did it to me first.'

'Nah, Madge. Not my little Madge.' He gropes for her hand, strokes it like the paw of a puppy.

'You treated me real bad, sugar,' Madge says, stroking his other hand with her other hand so that they look like children about to play that game where they all pile their hands on top of each other and the one underneath has to pull his out quickly.

'Barf,' Anna says under her breath, waiting for the coffee to filter.

Ron, hearing this, glares meanly at Anna before turning back to Madge and his hand stroking. 'Madge, I wanna come home.'

Madge pulls away as if she has touched a viper. 'What?'

'I'm lonely, sweetheart.'

'With all your under-age bimbos?'

Ron sniffs. His eyes are red and his jaw slack and trembling like jelly. 'All that's over,' he mumbles. 'Wanna go home to my Madgie.' He closes his eyes. Anna wonders if this is for dramatic effect or whether he has gone to sleep.

Madge is standing up and looking as if she's had a nasty shock. She grabs one of the mugs of coffee that Anna has poured, adds an inordinate amount of milk to cool it off, and holds it to Ron's lips. 'Drink this, sunshine. You'd better sober up quick and go home.'

'He can't drive in this condition.'

'He can walk.'

But as she says this there is a bump and a crash as Ron falls off the chair and passes out on the floor. The two women look at each other with dismay. 'I'll shove a blanket over him,' Anna says. 'As long as he's out of here first thing in the morning.'

'Don't worry, I'll come over and make sure of it.' Madge takes the other two mugs to the kitchen table, stepping over Ron's inert body as she does so. He has started to snore. She sighs. 'Am I an idiot or what? Do I really want this character back in my life and in my bed?'

'Wait until morning. Don't make any decisions like that until morning.'

But in the morning, by the time Anna and Madge are up, Ron has disappeared, leaving on the floor a crumpled blue blanket, the only sign that anything untoward happened the night before.

Around the same time that Ron, shame-faced and hung over, gropes his way through the dark pre-dawn streets trying to remember where he left his car all those hours ago when he first went to the pub, Steve is awakened by the telephone. 'Hello?' he says sleepily, thinking it is Anna.

'Steve. It's Tess.'

He is instantly awake, alert. 'Christ, Tess. It's bloody early.'

'Not working?' The voice is cool with irony.

'This is a bit early even for me.' Then: 'Sam? Is he all right?' The fingers of panic begin tapping on his back, for why else would Tess phone at this time?

'Yes.' Impatient now. 'He's fine. Steve, I want to see you. Now, today.'

'What are you talking about? Are you sure Sam is okay?'

'Forget Sam for a minute. He's still asleep but soon he'll be up and getting ready for school. I'll take him there, then come straight down to you. The child-minder will pick him up as usual.'

'I don't understand – '

'I have two days' off, holiday time I never took. See you later then?'

'I'm . . . I don't know.'

She takes his hesitancy for consent. 'See you later,' she says, hanging up before he can speak again.

She arrives in a few hours, looking stunning all in black: leggings, boots, long cashmere jumper. Her dark hair is pulled straight up to the top of her head and fastened with a black velvet bow. Steve, who has been unable to work since the phone call, is jumpy, on edge, and annoyed with himself for being this way. Belligerently, he offers her coffee and some lunch.

'Coffee, thanks, no lunch.' She settles into a kitchen chair, looks around approvingly. 'I like this house. I always have.'

Steve grunts, makes coffee.

'Sam loves it,' Tess goes on. 'He goes on and on about it after he's been here.'

'Uh huh.'

'Steve, will you stop it, please? Being so surly?'

He hands her a bright red ceramic mug full of dark coffee. 'I want to know why you're here, Tess.'

She clicks her varnished fingernails nervously on the mug for a moment. 'I can't just spill it out baldly. Not when you're acting like this.'

'For Christ's sake. You left me for another man. Took my son. Acted like shit whenever I tried to talk to you sensibly about seeing Sam. How the fuck do you think I should act?'

To his amazement Tess bursts into tears. 'Oh, Steve,' she finally gasps while he stares at her, unable to go to her, unable to comprehend what is happening. 'I've been so bloody mixed up. I know I was shitty to you, and I'm sorry.'

This completely unbalances Steve. He has never known Tess to say she was sorry to anyone, least of all him. 'Forget it,' he says gruffly, for she is looking at him and waiting for a reply. 'All water under the bridge anyway,' he mumbles banally.

Tess seems content with this and stops crying, taking some sips of her coffee. 'Look,' she says at last, 'it took a lot of nerve for me to come here today and I'm still pretty shaky. Could we postpone the talk until later, just kind of get to know each other again for a few hours?'

Steve wants to say, *but what's the point?*, but the combination of her tears and apology have unnerved him. 'Okay. If that's what you want.'

They sit in silence for a few minutes, drinking their coffee. It is an uncomfortable silence and finally Steve says, 'Look, should we go out somewhere?' He is beginning to feel awkward and gauche in his own home and needs to get out, needs a drink. 'I'd like some lunch. There's a pub in the village that does decent food; we can just about get there before they stop serving.'

Tess agrees, and they go to the pub, drink Guinness and eat mushrooms and melted Stilton on toast. They talk mostly about Sam, but after a while Tess tells him about Carl. Steve finds he doesn't want to hear, but doesn't know how to stop her. He feels out of his depth in these murky deep waters.

'I was a fool to marry him,' Tess says now, staring gloomily at the open log fire. 'He's bad-tempered, arrogant.' She is too proud to tell Steve of the other women.

Steve says nothing. He wonders what he is doing here, what *she* is doing here. The moments slip by like eels, too slippery to hold on to. He feels she is telling him something, but he cannot grasp quite what it is.

She asks to stay the night, and they go to the nearest town to buy seafood, vegetables, rice, for Tess insists she will cook them a meal. As they wheel a basket around the supermarket Steve has a longing for Sam to be with them that is so intense he feels giddy with the emotion and has to grip the wheel of the shopping trolley hard to regain his composure.

While Tess cooks the dinner, Steve works on his guitars for an hour or so. He has made up a bed in the spare bedroom, the narrow single one that Sophie uses when she is here. He tried once or twice to talk about Sophie, and Anna, but the words became lodged in his chest like phlegm, unwilling to be expelled. Tess never mentions either of them, which Steve finds odd because of course she knows of his relationship with Anna. He will tell her of this visit, of course, but he fervently hopes she will not telephone tonight.

She does. Luckily Tess is sitting in the living-room listening to the news, and Steve is able to talk in the hallway in relative privacy. He tells her quickly what has happened.

Anna is shocked, bewildered. 'She's spending the night?' she says dumbly.

'In the spare bedroom,' he says hastily and unnecessarily.

The fact that he needed to state this upsets Anna even more. 'What does she want?'

'I'm not sure. To talk about Sam, I guess. She's in some kind of state of crisis about her marriage breaking up.'

'So she goes to you? You told me you weren't on very amicable terms.'

'I know. We weren't.'

'But she's gone to you.'

'Uh, yeah. She's apologized.'

There is a long silence at the other end of the phone. Finally: 'Oh great. That's great news for you. I'd better go now, since obviously you will have a lot to talk about.' She hangs up before Steve can reply.

He would like to phone her back and indeed begins dialling the Bristol number but Tess suddenly is there. 'Should I make coffee?' she says, and he puts down the phone and follows her into the kitchen, determined to tell her that was Anna on the phone, hoping it will precipitate some comments and discussion about his own relationship.

But Tess has other things she wants to talk about. 'Sam wants us to get back together,' she states without preliminary, as if she has known what Steve was about to say and wants to distract him.

'I know. He told me.'

'Maybe it's not such a bad idea.'

Steve, rinsing out mugs at the kitchen sink, freezes.

Strange noises seem to fill his head, buzzes and clangs and alarms. She is not serious, he says to himself as he slowly turns around.

Tess is looking at him oddly. He finds the look vaguely familiar, then realizes it is lust, mixed maybe with love or perhaps merely nostalgia, and a kind of pleading that he finds hard to handle. Then Tess is in his arms, and he's not sure who is kissing whom, who is clinging to whom. All he knows is that this thing he has longed for for years has finally happened: Tess is his again, and with Tess, he will have Sam.

At that moment Anna is sitting at her kitchen table with Madge raging with anger and despair. 'He couldn't tell her to go,' she says bitterly. 'She snaps her finger and there he is.'

'He explained why he had to see her,' Madge says patiently. 'She will always be the mother of his child, he can't just cut her out of his life.'

'She's staying the night.'

'Anna, stop this. You have to have trust.'

'He never phoned me back.'

'What is this game? Steve loves you, you love him – phone *him*, if you want. You were the one that hung up.'

Anna goes to the phone, clutches it like a lifeline. She dials the number but before it can ring, hangs up. 'No,' she whispers to the dead mouthpiece. 'He has to do it. He has to choose himself.'

Steve breaks away from Tess suddenly. 'Was that the phone?' he says dazedly.

'You're hearing things.' She tries to hold him again but he is looking at her strangely. 'Come up to bed, Steve,' she says coaxingly. 'Remember how it was? We can have that all over again.'

He stares at her, trying to remember how the touch of her

fingertips, the feel of her tongue, used to make him frenzied with want and passion. But all he can see now is an ordinary woman – beautiful, yes; objectively he can see that. But the aura is gone; the magic or chemical or hormone or whatever that made him lust for her, love her, for all those years is no longer present. He can't stop staring at her, surprised at how ordinary she is, how like every other woman with the same number of limbs and eyes and basic accoutrements. Now that whatever made her special is gone, even her beauty seems blurred, opaque.

She is disconcerted by his staring. 'Steve . . . are you all right? What's wrong?'

He begins, as patiently as possible but also as quickly, to tell her. He wants it to be over with, so that when she is at last asleep in the little attic bedroom, he can phone Anna.

'I love you,' he says hours later, waking her up from a weepy, troubled sleep.

'Did it take you this long to figure it out?' Anna says desolately.

'I've known it since Spain. But I got the proof of it tonight.'

Anna closes her eyes, caresses the phone. 'You're not leaving me then?'

He smiles. 'Oh ye of little faith . . . '

It is a feeble attempt but it makes her laugh weakly. 'Have we come through something, Steve? Another crisis?'

'I think we have, love. I think we have.'

'Then let's hope we haven't any more for a long, long time.'

When at last they hang up Steve goes to his bedroom but he knows he will not sleep. He has one more crisis to get through. By letting Tess go he is losing Sam, and the knowledge of this drives into his soul like nails, crucifying him. He knows, rationally, that even if he still loved Tess a remarriage would be precarious; he knows her now, knows that the same complaints she had about him before would re-surface, drag them both down again. He doubts if she loves him; if she does, it is not really him but the successful, ambitious businessman she thinks Steve has at last become. She would soon realize he hadn't changed, not basically, and the animosity and bitterness would begin again.

And yet. And yet . . . Steve allows himself a fleeting moment, a memory of the past, a vision of what might have been. He and Sam, living in the same house, seeing each other every day. Waking up every morning to his son's chatter, tucking the boy in every night and watching for a moment the dreams fluttering behind his closed eyes, his sleeping face. The three of them, he and Tess and Sam, a family again, eating and shopping and doing all the mundane things that families do when they are together . . .

He makes himself stop. Opening the window he sees that there is a thin layer of snow on the ground, thinks how wildly excited Sam would be if he were here to see this rare, early fall. *Sam.* Clenching his fists Steve seems to see his son running through the snow, running away from him, and he knows that tonight he is going to have to let the boy go a second time, lose him again as he lost Sam when Tess left him all those years ago.

For hours Steve lies on the bed, dressed and on top of the duvet, oblivious to the cold coming in from the still open window. It is only when he finally falls asleep that he begins to cry, disjointed rusty sobs that hover between dream and waking, that eventually, after a long, long time, purge him so that he is able at last to sleep deeply and dreamlessly.

Chapter Eleven

CHRISTMAS arrives with particular rejoicing, for Anna and Sophie have just returned from Birmingham where Sophie had a thorough examination. She was pronounced fit and healthy, and Anna was told there was no need to bring her back again for three months as the liver was functioning smoothly.

The family gather in Lyme Regis, at the insistence of Eleanor and Stuart, but for once Anna doesn't resent the summons. She has made it clear that if she and Sophie are to go, then so must Steve and Sam. Tess is flying alone to Rome to visit an old friend for the holiday and says she cannot take the boy. Since the break-up of her marriage and Steve's rejection of her suggestion to attempt a reconciliation, she seems to have plunged into the single state with all the resolution of a swimmer confronted with icy water, determined to quickly get on with the immersion so that an invigorating swim can be enjoyed. And so she has let Steve, to his delight, have Sam every weekend since her visit to Devon while she has thrown herself into the task of revitalizing her social life.

Steve usually spends these weekends with Sam in Bristol. He has talked to his son, explained patiently over and over again why his two parents cannot live together. Sam has wheedled and become sullen, but gradually is beginning to accept the inevitable. Having more time with his father helps, and despite his outburst to Sophie, he genuinely enjoys being part of Anna and Sophie's household. It is Steve perhaps who feels the pang of loss more deeply: though he knows he has done the right thing, knows that he loves Anna and that he and Tess have nothing on which to base a new relationship, yet every Sunday night as he returns Sam to his mother's house he feels a quickening of the pain that he knows will always be there, a stiff, aching, arthritis of the soul which he will have to learn to live with, as people do who have physical illnesses or disabilities.

And there are remissions, many of them. Christmas is one of these. The family gathers on Christmas Eve to the Lyme Regis house which is splendid with red candles and glossy holly and a discreet, symmetrical Christmas tree in the corner of the drawing-room. Anna and Steve and the two children arrive together, for Steve went up the day before to collect Sam. They have barely taken off their coats and settled in when Mike and Mary arrive, the children hyperactive with excitement. For the first Christmas since she became a member of the family, Mary does not feel the prick of trepidation and resentment that has always scratched her when she was with Anna and Sophie, and she kisses her sister-in-law effusively. Why this sharp little thorn has been taken from her she is not quite sure: perhaps it is the fact that she has at last let Anna and Sophie into her life, and rather to her surprise, finds she likes them both. That there are other, darker reasons for her long overdue acceptance of Mike's family – for instance the arrival of Steve in Anna's life, usurping Mike from his surrogate father role; or the fact that Sophie's obvious good health and prognosis makes Mary feel less threatened for her own children – she refuses to acknowledge.

And so Christmas Day goes well and predictably, with too much food and drink which is tempered by a lazy walk on the Cob under a rather dim sun intrepidly trying to burn away a cold, hazy sea mist. Boxing Day is even colder, with heavy grey clouds threatening snow accumulating during the morning. After a late, leisurely breakfast Eleanor says, 'Mary, should you and I give the children an airing in the garden before it either rains or sleets? Ollie can do with some exercise too; we'll take a ball and toss it around.'

Turning to Sophie and Sam she says, warmly, 'Would you older children like to help us with the little ones? You know what a handful they are.'

Sophie and Sam are delighted at being referred to in this manner, and importantly begin helping the younger children put on jackets and gloves. 'Don't forget your hat,' Anna reminds her daughter.

It is refreshingly quiet after they all have gone. Steve and Anna wash up the breakfast dishes and then join Mike and Stuart in the sitting-room, bringing in a fresh pot of coffee. Anna is in a benevolent mood, Christmas being over with no disasters. When she had announced that she intended to spend the day with Steve and Sam, thus forcing her father to invite them also to Lyme Regis, she was aware that she was breaking every family rule. Christmas was, always, for Family, capitalized. Jake had never been invited even though he was living with Anna for those few months, but Anna had never been committed enough to make it an issue. None of the women that Mike had relationships with before Mary ever came, but then he hadn't particularly wanted to bring them, either, preferring to distance them from the scrutinizing attentions of his parents. Besides, it gave him a chance to see Anna and Sophie on their own, see at close quarters how they were coping.

Stuart accepts a cup of coffee from Anna and stirs a tea-spoon of sugar in it. He has already lit the log fire which is decorative rather than functional, the central heating warming the house quite adequately. Sitting back in his favourite seat, an old brown leather armchair, he sips his coffee and gazes into the fire before saying casually, 'I meant to ask you, Anna: how is Rosamund? Have you heard from her lately?'

'Yes, she phoned just before we left for here. She's in France for Christmas, staying with a friend. She'll be back after the New Year.' Anna settles into the soft expansive sofa in front of the large bay windows. In the front garden she

189

can see Sophie awkwardly throwing the ball to Ollie, the dog, who leaps after it with frenetic delight while the other children run after him.

'Do you have plans to go to Malvern?' Mike asks conversationally. 'Rosamund hasn't seen Sophie for a while, has she?'

'No, I must take her up for a few days. The trouble is finding the time. I've got some new adult students and they're very keen, wanting to begin three lessons a week until they go to Spain at half-term, at the end of February.'

Looking up from the fire, which is blazing comfortably now, Stuart says, 'Ah yes half-term. Your mother and I have been making plans for that week.'

'Oh?' Anna looks at her father rather defensively. 'Since neither you nor mother are teachers or students, I gather these plans include me and Sophie?'

'Well, actually they concern Sophie.'

'I see.'

'Though of course you are welcome to come too. But I really don't think what we are planning is quite your sort of holiday.'

'Ah.' Deliberately taking a long sip of coffee, Anna waits a few moments before saying, ominously, 'And what exactly have you planned for my child?'

Steve, sitting next to her, crosses his arms and pinches her ribcage surreptitiously. She looks at him crossly as he winks at her.

'Your mother and I were thinking of taking Sophie to that rather grand hotel in Bournemouth, you know the one – we had a winter break there a couple of years ago. Since you dislike large hotels we thought it would be a perfect time for Eleanor to have her grandchild to herself for a week, and of course I as well would welcome the opportunity to see more of your daughter. Sophie would love it: the hotel has a great deal to offer during these winter breaks – a heated swimming pool, sauna, entertainment. The food is excellent as well.'

190

'You sound as if you have their brochure memorized. But you've left out one thing. Me.'

Stuart puts down his coffee cup and looks up at his daughter, surprised. He has not recognized the sarcasm in her voice and says, mildly, 'Do you want to come? I didn't think it was quite your thing.'

Before Anna can blurt out what is on the tip of her tongue, that her father has no right to plan a holiday for Sophie that doesn't include Anna, Steve tickles her lightly but insistently, his fingers still hidden by her jumper. This diffuses the irritation that was beginning to concentrate against her father and so she says, as conciliatory as she can, because after all this is Christmas, 'It's very kind of you, Dad, but I really can't let Sophie be away from me for a week. Besides, school holidays are the only time Sophie and Sam and I can be with Steve in Devon.'

A flash of annoyance flits, in a most controlled manner, across Stuart's face, but he says nothing for a moment. Mike whistles a tuneless Christmas carol and passes the coffee pot around for refills. Stuart is just about to speak when Steve suddenly says, 'Anna, Sam is not going to be around during half-term, remember? He's off on a school trip. Sophie would be a bit bored without him, don't you think?'

Anna glares at him, but before she can answer Steve continues: 'If Sophie goes to Bournemouth with your parents, you and I could have a holiday on our own together, go away perhaps.'

Stuart looks up at this unexpected ally with surprise, and Anna can see him mentally reassessing Steve's position and influence in his daughter's life. 'A good idea,' he says, nodding sagely. 'I'm sure the two of you could do with a break on your own.'

The two men avoid each other's eyes but Anna senses the unspoken complicity. Get her away, let us have Sophie. You take Sophie and in return let me have your daughter to myself. In a volatile outburst, which has been slowly

191

building during her father's outline of his plans for her child, Anna says stridently: 'So it's all arranged, is it? Is this some kind of feudal throwback I'm witnessing, the men smoothly determining their women's lives without bothering to give her a say? And I'm supposed to meekly accept it, am I? Just like that!'

Knowing she is over-reacting Anna gets up, goes to the French windows, sees Sophie importantly pushing the pram around the garden paths, while Eleanor and Mary play some kind of a game with the others which seems to entail a great deal of clapping and shouting. Mike, trying to tease her out of her anger, goes up to her and puts his arm around her shoulder. 'You've never accepted anything meekly, love,' he says gently. 'The feudal system hasn't a chance with you.'

Anna looks at him gratefully, then with barely-concealed animosity at her father who is watching her smugly, sure that with Steve on his side the holiday is bound to take place. 'Sophie is my child,' Anna says stiffly. 'She may not have a father but she has me, and I know better than anyone what she is ready for and what she is not. I don't need to get away from her, nor she from me. For God's sake she's not even twelve yet!'

'You're splitting hairs,' Stuart mutters. 'She very nearly is.'

'It's not a question of needing to get away from anyone, Anna,' Steve says gently. 'It's just a chance for both you and Sophie to do something different, have a change.'

Anna turns to Mike, her eyes pleading for help. 'She's certainly well enough to go off with the parents, if that's what you're afraid of,' her brother says, and feels like a traitor as she looks at him with hurt, stricken eyes.

'No. No no no no no.' The vehemence of Anna's cry shocks them all, even herself. 'It's too soon yet, okay? Now for God's sake just leave me alone, all of you!' She rushes from the room, grabs her jacket, and joins the women and children in the garden. The overcast day has got colder and Mary takes the pram from Sophie to bring the baby into the house. Turning to her mother Sophie gives her a big bear hug. She is so blatantly happy and healthy that for a moment Anna's eyes sting with unshed tears as she clings tightly to her daughter.

Only a sudden jubilant shout from Sam forces Anna to break away. It is starting to snow, great thick furry flakes, and the children are going demented, rushing about shrieking and trying to catch them. Even before Anna has loosened her hold on Sophie her daughter is stretching out her hands away from her, trying to catch the first longed-for snowflakes.

Standing back, watching the frenzied exhilaration in the garden, Anna is oblivious to the thickly-falling snow settling on her bare head, on her shoulders. From the French windows Steve is watching her, but she doesn't see him. She has eyes for no one but Sophie.

The snow doesn't amount to much in Lyme Regis, but there is more in Bristol. It keeps coming down intermittently during the week after Christmas, both enrapturing the children with each sudden flurry, and frustrating them because it doesn't last as long as they would like.

It is the last day of the year and Steve and Anna have taken Sophie and Sam to Daphne's Café down the road for steamy hot chocolates after a walk through Ashton Park, the woodland and deer park not too far away. It has begun to snow again, nice dry flakes which stick to the ground and refuse to melt. The café is crowded, with only two spare tables, each with room just for two people, so Sam and Sophie rush with alacrity to the table in the back where they happily play at being adult and independent.

'They get on so well,' Anna comments as the frothy chocolate in glossy dark green mugs arrives at their table.

'Amazingly so,' Steve agrees. 'Sam had a wonderful time over Christmas. He loved not being the youngest, with all those children of Mike and Mary's around.'

'Look at them.' They both gaze fondly at the children who are blowing effusively on their hot chocolates to cool them down before drinking. They are intense and serious, concentrating on the job in hand. 'They'd much rather be on their own than with us,' Anna says without thinking.

'So they should, it's natural. Just as it's natural for you and I to want to be alone sometimes, without them.'

Anna does not reply but spoons some frothy cream melting on top of the mug into her mouth. 'Hmm, good.'

'I'd like to get away with you. Just the two of us, alone.'

'Yeah, well, maybe one day,' Anna replies vaguely. 'Piping hot, this. I feel like blowing on mine like the kids are doing.'

Looking carefully at her Steve says gently, 'Think about it again, Anna. Letting your parents have Sophie during half-term.'

Anna reaches into her jacket pocket and gets out her glasses, puts them on, takes them off and polishes them with a paper napkin, then finally puts them on again and looks at Steve. 'Don't,' she says at last. 'Please don't.' She takes away her hand and places it with her other demurely on her lap, looking like a terrified, recalcitrant schoolgirl waiting to be reprimanded.

Steve momentarily retreats. 'Do you know that often when a conversation gets too difficult for you, you put on your glasses?'

'Do I?'

'I've never quite figured out whether it's because you hide behind them, use them as a barrier – or whether you want to plunge right into the situation, seeing everything clearer so to speak. I rather think it's the first one.'

'When you've finished analyzing me,' Anna says acidly, 'maybe you should drink your chocolate. You haven't touched it.'

'I think you are going to have to listen to me, Anna, glasses or no glasses. I have a friend, a musician, who has a house in the Wye Valley. An old, isolated farmhouse, the

194

river in front and woodlands behind. He's only there Christmas and summer, and lets his friends use it the rest of the time. Let's go there in February, just the two of us. We can take long walks, and when we come back exhausted, make love for hours in front of the fire without having to worry if the kids are going to suddenly wake up.'

Anna shakes her head regretfully. 'Sophie – ' she begins.

'Sophie would love it in Bournemouth, your father was right about that. It would be something different, a treat – all that luxury: warmth and plush carpets and lots of good food, you know how Sophie loves food. It would make her feel terribly grown-up, being there without her Mum.'

'Not yet, Steve.' Anna looks trapped, uncomfortable. 'Not yet, maybe someday – someday for sure, okay? But not yet.'

'For God's sake! Not yet? What the hell are you waiting for, Anna? Sophie is as healthy as she has ever been since she was born, even the doctors don't want to see her until March, and then it's only to be another routine check-up. Why the bloody delay? What are you doing to her, and to yourself – and to me, for God's sake? What the hell are you doing to all of us?'

He keeps his voice down so his anger seems almost detached, measured, cold, frightening Anna who has never seen him like this before. She glances over at Sophie, as if she would grab her daughter and run, but Sophie is engrossed in something Sam is saying and doesn't even look their way. Steve is speaking again, his voice clipped and strange with restrained acrimony. 'I'll tell you what you are waiting for. For Sophie to become ill again, for her to need you as desperately as she did before the transplant.'

'That's not true! Of course I still worry about her but – '

'You don't know how to handle the fact that she doesn't need you so much, that she's growing up, becoming a healthy normal child. That she's starting to grow away from you, like normal healthy twelve-year-olds do.'

'Eleven. Christ, why does everyone keep rushing things?'

'Oh, God, Anna – '

'I'm *not* waiting for her to get ill, but yes, of course the thought is always there. Will her new liver continue to function normally? What about all the drugs she is still on, are they affecting her in some way we don't realize, will they suddenly make her ill again? Anything could happen, anything – '

'Christ, Anna, don't you see that's the whole point? Of course anything can happen, but not just to Sophie, to any child, to anyone, any time. Sam can get run over on his way to school. He could fall off his skateboard – he's already had one accident with it. There have been a few cases of meningitis in the city hospital – how do I know Sam won't get it, hasn't been exposed already? When he was younger he was plagued with earaches and on constant antibiotics – how do I know they haven't weakened his immune system, played havoc with his body so that he'll succumb to the first dangerous virus that comes his way?'

Anna shakes her head distractedly. 'I know, I know, but it's not the same, it's – '

Interrupting again Steve says grimly, 'It *is* the same, Anna. Of course it's worse for you because of Sophie's history, but the fear is the same fear, every parent has it. We just try not to think about it; we walk on the edge of the abyss and only occasionally, very occasionally, do we look down, and recoil with horror at what we see. So then we try to forget, try to ignore it. We have to, or we'd go mad.'

He sighs and leans back in his chair, closing his eyes for a brief moment. His drink has become cold and congealed in the green mug but he absentmindedly picks it up, drains it all at once. Anna is silent, unable to speak. The babble of the other customers seems suddenly unbearably loud and she wants to get outside into the silence of the snow still falling gently on the city. Steve says, calmly now, 'You have to stop anticipating, you know. Imagining. You've said yourself how you've never known Sophie to be so well. You have to see her as a whole, healthy child, and not look into the abyss any more than you have to, like the rest of us. Sophie is growing up – you'll have to start letting her go.'

They look at each other sadly, contemplatively, for a few seconds then Steve says, 'I'll see if the kids are ready, settle up for the drinks.' Abruptly he stands and leaves the table, but Anna doesn't move, staring unseeingly out of the window at the snow still falling, people walking by on their way to the bakery or the Italian deli. She thinks about going away without Sophie, of Sophie going off with someone other than herself, and she knows she cannot do it: she *would* be staring at the abyss the whole time, wondering if Sophie was all right, terrified that something was happening and she would not be near to protect, to console – to *will* her daughter well again if everything else failed.

The children have run out of the door and are making faces at her in the window. When Steve touches her shoulder she stands up slowly, facing him. 'I can't do it, Steve, I'm sorry. I can't go with you yet, not without Sophie. She's all I have; she's all that I've ever had. Can't you see that?'

'Oh, God.' Steve is looking at her strangely; she can't quite interpret his expression. 'God,' he repeats, shaking his head.

'I'm sorry,' she says dully.

'You don't even realize, do you . . . you don't even know what you said just now. Sophie's not all you have, Anna. For what it's worth, you have me. Obviously it's not that important or you'd have mentioned it.

'Steve, I didn't mean – '

He doesn't let her finish. 'You've had other people too, but you've chosen not to let any of us count. There was Richard, but you wasted years resenting him for dying. You had Rosamund, who wisely never interfered but would have clearly loved to have more to do with bringing up Sophie. And your parents, misguided though they are at times, love you dearly, as well as Mike who would probably abandon his own wife and children if either you or Sophie needed help.'

'But they have their own lives, don't you see? In the end my life is Sophie's: it always has been.'

They are still standing, facing each other, and at the window the children are beginning to tap impatiently. Other customers in the café have begun to surreptitiously glance at Steve and Anna; though their conversation cannot be over-heard in the general noise of the café, their intensity and distress is obvious. Neither of them notices; they remain standing face to face, not touching, not moving. Finally Steve says, 'I was hoping it would be *my* life, too, but you're not going to let me in, are you? Not even now, when Sophie is well and happy and the operation has been a success. You still won't let her go, or let anyone else in.'

Anna tries to speak, and indeed he is waiting for her to do so, but in the end she can only shake her head sadly. She watches him leave the café and grab each child by the hand, watches Sophie and Sam try to catch snowflakes with the other. Following them out she joins them, and together they walk the short distance back to the house, the children in their high spirits oblivious to the silence of the adults.

It is five o'clock. In seven hours it will be the start of a new year.

Chapter Twelve

JANUARY is dreary and depressing. Bristol is swamped with slushy snow, grey porridge-like mush that melts into the black streets and sooty footpaths making everything seem sordid and a bit disreputable. Sophie succumbs to a nasty virus that makes her nauseous and dizzy, and though Mike visits every day and insists it is the same bug that half his patients are complaining of, Anna still has to fight the fear which is insidiously telling her it is something much more serious. Will it always be like this, she wonders? Will Sophie's every sneeze, every headache, be for her a signal of this agonizing, barely-controlled panic? When will I have faith in her new health? she asks herself over and over.

Steve is in Devon, working frantically on his guitars. On New Year's Eve, when they got back from Daphne's Café, Steve asked Anna if she would mind feeding Sam and Sophie on her own as he needed to get out for a few hours. Sadly, Anna understood that he was deeply troubled by their relationship and needed space from her.

He returned, as promised, in a few hours, in time to tuck Sam and Sophie into bed. Anna had not eaten and the two sat down to a curry she had prepared with the leftovers from the children's roast chicken. On his way back, Steve had bought wine, the Rioja they had drunk in Spain, and it inexplicably made Anna feel sad.

'Where did you go?' she asked as they ate their curry, drank the wine. A coal fire was glowing in the small grate and they were eating in the tiny living-room, plates balanced on their knees as they sat together on the sofa.

'Nowhere. Everywhere. Just roamed around the streets. It's starting to snow hard; I hope I can get away tomorrow.'

Though Anna knew he.was leaving the next day, she was hurt by the eagerness in his voice. Sensing it, he said kindly, 'I have to go, you know. I have so much work. And Tess wants Sam back tomorrow.'

Anna took a deep breath and said, 'What . . . about us?'

'Us? What do you mean?'

The fire made patterns on Anna's wine glass as she twirled it around in her hands. 'Do you want to . . . I mean, I can't blame you if you . . . '

Steve suddenly understood. 'Oh, Anna!' He would have taken her in his arms but his plate, still half-full of curry, was on his lap. 'I'm here, all right? I'm not going to leave you or Sophie. I love you, idiot, remember? You drive me crazy a lot of the time, but I love you.'

And then Anna was clinging to him, and his curry spilled, and he swore and she laughed and then her glass of wine tipped over, but she didn't care because Steve was not going to leave her, for the terror she had felt when she thought he would was almost as bad as her daily disquietude over Sophie . . .

Steve had been truthful when he told Anna he had been roaming the streets aimlessly. After wandering around Montpelier he went off towards the docks, barely aware of the party atmosphere as people made ready to welcome in the new year. He walked and he walked, not seeing anything except the turmoil in his own heart. That he loved Anna, he hadn't a doubt; that he could cope with the way she sometimes still shut him out, he wasn't quite sure.

He walked miles. The combination of the falling snow and the proximity of New Year's Eve seemed to decorate the city like tinsel: there were great shouts of laughter coming from pubs, and groups of young people festooned with multi-coloured scarves and woolly hats wandered about in a seemingly random but jovial manner.

And then more time passed, and still he didn't stop

walking, until suddenly he realized he was in Clifton, on the street where Tess and Sam lived, only of course Sam was in Richmond Road and Tess would be home alone, no doubt getting ready to go somewhere splendid for the night's revelries. And yes, there was her house, the lights in the bedroom on but the thick curtains drawn tightly so that not even a silhouette appeared in the windows.

Steve stopped, looked up. If he knocked on the door he could have everything again – his son, his marriage, beautiful Tess, a proper family rather than this frustrating relationship with a woman so obsessed by her child that he could be doomed to wait on the fringes of her life for ever.

He stood there for a long time. The light in the bedroom went off and the outside light went on. She was obviously expecting someone; this didn't surprise Steve; Tess would never be alone on a night like tonight. *There is still time*, he thought. He moved slightly then more determinedly towards the door. A woman in glasses passed him as he hesitated on the steps of the house, looking at him suspiciously, peering over the grey rims of her huge spectacles in a myopic mistrust that reminded him of Anna. Grinning impetuously at the woman he lurched around quickly and began walking away, away from the elegant homes of Clifton, through the suburban area of Redlands with its gardens and laurel bushes, on to the less salubrious Stokes Croft with the winos already stumbling down the streets and the prostitutes making ready for a lucrative night, and straight on towards the raucous sounds of Montpelier ready to welcome in the new year, where Richmond Road was palpitating with the beat of life and where Sam and Sophie and Anna, his family now, were waiting for him to come home.

Anna has not seen Steve since New Year's Day. He was going to come up for Sophie's twelfth birthday, but she was so ill and miserable Anna said they would celebrate the occasion later, when she was feeling better. Steve had Sam for a couple of weekends but Tess put him on a train to Plymouth where his father was waiting to pick him up. Anna, understanding that Steve and Sam needed time alone together, was nonetheless irrationally hurt, even though Steve tried to explain. 'If Sam comes to Devon I can at least work while he is asleep. I'm absolutely snowed under with orders,' he said on the phone. He was vague and preoccupied and knew it, and retreated even more into his workshop, to his guitars, something he hadn't done since he had met Anna. He knew it was because he was trying to seal himself off from hurt, from pain, from the rejection he felt emotionally from Anna even though rationally he understood her far better than she thought he did.

But at last January is over. February starts as sodden as a damp tissue, but it is much milder, and Sophie is finally recovered from her viral infection and has begun school: only mornings to start with as she is still not quite strong enough for a whole day. She is glad to be back though is worried that her memory has not improved very much since the operation, worried that she is not able to learn new things as easily as she did in the past.

'Are you sure the doctors said it would get better?' she asks Anna time and time again. 'I can't even remember my tables and I knew them backwards!'

Anna isn't sure, but doesn't say. She fears there has been some permanent damage to her daughter's mental ability, for she has noticed great gaps in Sophie's memory and thought processes. But she keeps telling herself there is plenty of time, and now that Sophie's January illness has totally gone, her physical health is blooming, for which Anna is relieved and grateful.

One morning after Sophie has left for school Madge appears with an animal the size of a pony and with paws as wide as plates. Anna, crouching in terror behind her living-room door, watches wide-eyed as the animal, which looks to her like a monster wolf, rushes into the house, bowls Madge

202

on to the floor and leaps exultantly around her prostrate body.

'Quick, get up, come here behind the door!' Anna calls to Madge, too cowardly to go to her rescue.

'I'm all right,' Madge gasps. 'He's only a bit frisky.'

'Good God. What is it? Help, it's eating my sofa!' There is an awful moment while Anna watches the animal frantically slobbering and scrabbling in the bowels of the old sofa, making an ominous noise like an ancient volcano about to erupt.

'It's okay, he's only after Samantha.'

'Good God!' Anna shoots out of her hiding place.

'Don't worry, he loves cats. See, he just wants to lick her! Aw, isn't that cute?'

'I'm not so sure.'

They watch as a damp, bedraggled Samantha extricates herself with an indignant yowl from under the sofa cushions and races to the top of the book shelves. Joyfully leaping after her, the monster's tail knocks over one or two things in its way – an empty mug, a table lamp – and nearly puts out Madge's eye.

'Look, I'm just about to walk him on the Downs,' she shouts over the animal's foghorn yelps which she assures Anna is just high spirits. 'Want to come? Whoa, easy boy, down, boy. Down, you dumb dopey beast!' She grabs his collar and calls to Anna as she is dragged out the front door, 'Meet you in my car, it's right outside the house.'

Anna cautiously follows Madge outside, grabbing her old cord jacket and locking the front door. 'Is this safe?' she asks as she opens the Mini door. 'What is that monster?'

'He's a Deerhound,' Madge says cheerfully. 'His name is Merlin.'

Merlin, overcome at the mention of his name, howls, and the drivers and passengers in the cars next to them at the traffic lights shudder, remembering old nightmares, old childhood fears. 'He really does make a dreadful sound,' Anna says with a shiver.

Madge drives the three or four miles to the Downs slowly, oblivious to the stares and comments of other drivers and pedestrians. Merlin fills the Mini like an overgrown boy in hand-me-down clothes. Because Madge doesn't like to talk when she is driving around the city, Anna waits until they get there and have begun their walk before asking, 'Where on earth did you get that creature?'

Madge lets Merlin off the lead and he immediately terrifies a mother and toddler merely by wagging his tail and drooling happily at them.

'Juan Carlos gave him to me,' Madge shouts above the noise of the toddler screaming his head off in fright. 'Unfriendly woman, isn't she?' She glares back at the toddler's mother. 'Yes, he found it being neglected somewhere and brought it over, poor thing; it was homeless apparently – '

'Oh no, Madge, you can't! You take in all your sons' friends on the same premise: you can't start accommodating animal strays as well.'

'I've always wanted a dog.'

'A dog? More like a yeti!' Anna eyes Merlin cautiously, and the eye-contact makes him giddy with delight. He leaps happily off the ground once or twice, and Anna, succumbing to this unbridled display of pure joy, says, 'Well, maybe he's not so bad. I guess I'd better make friends with him. Hi, Merlin. Nice doggie – oh hell! Down, you! Help, Madge. Help! Get him off me!'

'Here, Merlin, stop that. He's only being affectionate, Anna. MERLIN GET OFF HER. Sorry about that, honey.'

Anna picks herself up and wipes the mud off her jeans, rubs the dog's saliva from her face where he tried to lick her in a frenzy of comradeship. Flushed with his social success, Merlin is now bounding across the Downs trying to befriend a Jack Russell frolicking in some gorse bushes while its owner, an old man in a shabby raincoat, shrieks with fright. 'IT'S ALL RIGHT,' Madge shouts. 'HE'S HARMLESS.'

'Pigs might fly,' the man mutters, scurrying away in the opposite direction, whistling to his dog to follow. The Jack Russell, his hackles raised in defiance, can hardly walk for the trembling in his little stubby legs. 'Bloody lunatic dog,' the man gibbers to himself and to a couple of teenagers groping each other with great single-mindedness on a damp patch of grass between the gorse. 'Shouldn't be allowed, I've a good mind to call the police.'

'Sod off, granddad,' says the male groper, not moving his hands from their interesting place on the female's body, 'this here's a public place and we ain't doing nothing wrong.'

The old man shrugs. 'Don't say I didn't warn you,' he mumbles as he calls his dog away. The teenagers go back to what they were doing but before they can get very far there is a noise like the wind howling through lonely pine forests, like a typhoon on a vast dark sea in the middle of the night. 'Jesus, it's the hound of the fucking Baskervilles,' the female teenager yelps as a great face tries to nuzzle her neck and, she fears, sink bloody fangs into it.

There is a great deal of swearing and scrabbling as in the distance Madge shouts and yells for Merlin, who finally hears her and is so overcome with pleasure he abandons the teenagers and races back at top speed, frightening Anna out of her wits as she is sure she is about to be flattened. But Merlin stops meekly in front of them, and after being scolded sternly by Madge and told to stay, the dog surprisingly does just that and they walk amicably along for a few moments. When they have calmed down a bit Anna says, 'I haven't seen much of you lately, Madge.'

'I know, this goddamn bug going around, everyone in the library was sick and I had to work six days a week, and some evenings as well. I'm taking some time off now to make up.'

'How's Juan Carlos?'

'Oh . . . good, real good.' Madge hesitates, rather embarrassed. She hasn't told Anna about her young lover wanting to take her to Chile to meet his family. Far from being discouraged by Madge's lack of enthusiasm for his proposal, he has seemed to derive even more fire and passion from the challenge.

'Come on, out with it,' Anna says. 'What's up?'

'He, uh, he wants to marry me.'

'*What?*'

Madge looks offended. 'Plenty of women my age marry younger men,' she says huffily.

'Oh Madge, I didn't mean that. You're a gorgeous woman, I don't blame him. It's just that he's . . . he's . . . '

'The same age as my kids!' Madge snorts, then begins giggling. 'Oh boy, isn't it a gas? All these years I've been making smart-mouth remarks about Ron's bimbos, and here I've got me a lush toyboy all of my own.'

'So what are you going to do?'

'God knows.'

'And Ron? I haven't seen him since the night he got drunk and passed out on my kitchen floor.'

'Nor me. He went away skiing over Christmas and when he got back he collapsed with this flu thing going around. Or so the kids told me. I stayed clear of him. He rang me once whingeing about how he wished I were there taking care of him. "No way, baby doll, no way," I told him.'

Anna stops walking and looks at Madge, astonished. 'Isn't this what you've been waiting for?' she asks quietly. 'To have him back? He obviously wants you – I remember him asking you to take him back that night in my kitchen.'

'He was drunk. I didn't believe him. The second time he was ill and feeling sorry for himself.'

The dog, who has been walking more or less sedately at Madge's side, suddenly spots a jogger in the distance and with a joyful yelp leaps in the air and begins running towards him. 'Goddamn it, I wish this dog wasn't so friendly – he'll scare the hell out of that guy,' Madge says, running after Merlin at full speed and hollering for the dog at the top of her lungs.

Anna follows more slowly, so that Madge and the jogger are already deep in conversation when she reaches them. To her surprise she sees that it is Ron, who does not seem overly pleased to see her. 'Speak of the devil,' Anna says blithely.

'Yeah, I know, Madge has already said that,' he states grumpily. 'Christ, will you call this hound off?'

'He's only licking you, dumbbell,' Madge says fondly. 'He likes you, obviously. But then he likes everyone.'

Ron wipes the mud off his rugby club sweatshirt. 'Why aren't you at work?' he says to Madge.

'Why aren't you?'

'Morning off.'

'Same here.'

There is an awkward pause while Anna is made to feel redundant, so she says, 'I think I'll head back now, I've some work to do.'

'Fine, see ya,' Ron calls, while at the same time Madge says, 'I'm coming with you, Anna.'

'Me too,' Ron says. 'I've had enough jogging for the day.'

The three walk along awkwardly for a few moments, only Merlin euphorically rushing about in obvious high spirits. Anna finds an old tennis ball hidden under some bracken and throws it to Merlin, who is so pathetically grateful he whines and salivates in joyful appreciation as he retrieves it.

Ron and Madge walk along ahead as Anna becomes involved in her game with Merlin. 'Where did you get that revolting dog?' Ron snarls. 'Look at my new jumper: great paw marks all over the front. I'll never get the mud stains out.'

'You need a wife,' Madge says sardonically.

Taking her arm Ron suddenly goes all gooey. 'I have a wife, Madge. The best wife in the whole world, and I want her back. I've been thinking about it for weeks and I know I made a big mistake, leaving you. I'm ready to have a go again.' He smiles at her beautifully, as if he has just given her the most precious gift in the world.

It is what Madge has been waiting five years to hear. Ron is sober, serious, and rational; it is mid-morning and broad daylight – what could be more conducive to earnestness and sincerity? She believes him, believes he truly has had enough of his single life, his searching for eternal youth, and is ready to face growing old with the mother of his children.

He is looking at her glowingly, his red face flushed with love and confidence and a bit of high blood pressure brought on by attempting to jog after a boozy evening the night before. 'No,' she says sadly. 'I'm sorry, but no.'

Later, when Ron has stopped arguing and pleading and swearing and threatening and gone home at last, and the women have driven back to Montpelier, Madge tells Anna, 'Love stops, you know. I never thought it did, but it can sometimes.'

'Not by itself. Something usually wears it away, or smashes it.'

'You're right. Ron's indifference did finally, his callousness all those years when I was alone, trying to cope with all those adolescent sons . . . you know, when I looked at him, really looked at him carefully there on the Downs, looked at who he is *now* and not who he was when I married him, or when the kids were small, I realized he was someone else, someone I didn't love at all, never could love because he wasn't the sort of man I'd like to share the rest of my life with.'

She pauses, and stares at the coffee in front of her. They are in Daphne's Café, Merlin tied to a post outside, staring in mournfully through the window and disconcerting the elderly woman only a pane of glass away who is drinking peppermint tea and reading the *Guardian*.

'And Juan Carlos?' Anna asks. 'Is he?'

Madge beams her wide half-moon smile and says; 'Hey kid, one day at a time, okay? One day at a time.' The two women look at each other and laugh, and Merlin, hearing, howls in misery at being left out. The woman sitting by the window jumps up with a start, leaves some money on the table, and hurries out, crossing the street nervously to avoid the animal she can't quite believe is a dog. Anna and Madge, possessed by the giggles, sprawl over the table while Merlin bays and howls louder until finally the café owner asks them mildly to please remove the animal as he is frightening all her customers away.

As they slowly walk up Richmond Road Madge asks Anna about her plans for half-term, which is only in another couple of weeks. Madge knows about Stuart's offer to take Sophie to Bournemouth, and Steve's suggestion that they spend a week together in Wales on their own. Anna told her flatly about both the offer and her refusal, not seeking any advice – her mind was already made up – and Madge kept to herself what she thought about it. Anna says now, 'Sophie and I are going to Devon, as Steve has some work he wants to finish by the end of the month. I suggested that the three of us go to this farm in the Wye Valley but he wasn't keen. I must say I was a bit hurt – he was perfectly happy to go if it had been just him and me.'

'Oh Anna, be reasonable,' Madge says with some exasperation. 'An idyllic little love nest isn't quite the same with three people, unless it's a *ménage à trois*, I suppose, which is not exactly in Steve's line I shouldn't imagine. Of course he wants you on his own! I don't blame him in the slightest for taking your father's side over that Bournemouth suggestion – it would have been ideal for everyone.'

'Oh Madge, not you too? I feel like I'm being pulled apart sometimes. My parents are still trying to run my life and now Steve is getting this possessive streak, wanting me alone all the time – '

'Possessive? Don't kid me that you believe that, please. He's been great with Sophie and more patient than a lot of men and you know it. All he wants now is some time alone with you. It's perfectly normal!'

'But that's the point,' Anna says irritably. 'We're not normal.'

Madge stops walking and turns to Anna in frustration. 'Christ, Anna, what a mass of contradictions you are. Ever since I've known you, you've been trying to make Sophie feel like a normal kid, giving her a so-called 'normal' life, in spite of her illness. Then along comes someone who is trying to treat both of you that way and you freak out. Don't you think you're a bit screwed up?'

They are at Anna's house now and she puts the key in the door, unlocks it. 'I don't know,' she says miserably. 'I don't know anything any more.'

Following her inside the house Madge says, 'Look, you've had a hard time with Sophie, raising her all these years on your own. And you've done a wonderful job, everyone knows that. God knows I couldn't have done it. But like all mothers, like me, you have to face that your job is changing, has changed already. Sophie is growing up, and healthy for the first time ever.'

'So what does that mean? That she doesn't need me any more? Everyone is trying to tell me that lately.'

'Of course she'll still need you. But differently. Like the normal adolescent you've always wanted her to be.'

Shaking her head Anna says, 'I'm such a mess, so full of doubts! I used to follow my instincts, but they seem to be all tangled up these days.' She paces the floor of the living-room restlessly for a few moments then says, 'I can't brood about it now. I've got to get Sophie from school.'

The misery and confusion in Anna's heart is so apparent on her face that Madge goes to her, hugs her warmly. The two women cling for a moment: old friends – there is no longer any need for words. Then Madge says, 'Should I come with you to collect Sophie? Show her Merlin?' The dog, who has been lying at her feet, wags his tail in gratitude at hearing his name, and clouds of ashes rise from the dead fire of the night before. 'Oh damn. Merlin, cut it out.

C'mon, Anna, let's get out of here before he destroys the place.' They go out of the house again and walk the short distance to Sophie's school, Merlin bounding at their side. Anna is quiet, preoccupied, and Madge is silent too, letting her think. She worries about her friend constantly. This is what love is, Madge thinks as they approach the school. Sod men, sod sex, sod Ron and Juan Carlos and all the other lovers she's had since her husband left her – a good woman friend is all she needs. She smiles to herself as she thinks this, but she's quite, quite serious.

That evening Steve phones, saying he'll be up the next weekend. The relief and joy Anna feels when she puts down the phone is overwhelming: it has been a long time, and though she has talked to him almost every day, she has nonetheless felt a fragility in their relationship that was not there before.

Sophie too is pleased, she's missed Steve, and says so. 'Well, we'll have a whole week with him soon, at half-term,' Anna says reassuringly.

To her surprise Sophie does not light up at this but says, almost sullenly, 'It won't be the same without Sam there.'

Anna goes to her, strokes her unruly hair which had been pulled back neatly in a pony-tail for school but is now falling out of the band and around her face, and says, 'It'll be fun, you'll see. You and I can do things while Steve works on the guitars. We'll take walks, go out for lunch and Steve said he'd give you guitar lessons, remember? You said you wanted to learn.'

Sophie turns back to the homework she had been struggling with when Steve rang. The sprawling oak table under the long windows in the living-room is chaotic with school-books and pens and pencils, drawings and paper. Sophie is taking her return to school seriously, in spite of her struggles with her memory loss. 'I wish I could go on a trip like Sam is taking,' she says finally.

211

Anna smiles. 'Sam is going to stay with a French family; it's all been arranged by his school. But Rosamund has friends in France and maybe one day we all can do something like that. You and I and Steve and – '

'I'd rather go on a school trip,' Sophie interrupts. 'Like Sam.'

Anna looks stricken and Sophie, noticing, smiles reassuringly at her. 'Oh, it would be fun to go with you,' she says consolingly, 'but I'd also like to go with all my schoolfriends.'

'Well . . . maybe some day.'

Mother and daughter go back to their work but neither seems able to concentrate. Anna cannot summon up energy or enthusiasm for her latest translation, a book of short stories by an Andalucian journalist, and Sophie sits morosely and doodles. Finally they both give up and spend the rest of the evening watching television, forgetting their preoccupations in a particularly banal television comedy.

Even Sophie is glad of the respite when the telephone rings, and rushes to answer it. It is Rosamund, and Anna can hear the animation in Sophie's voice as she talks to her grandmother. When they have finished Sophie hands the phone to Anna and says she is going upstairs to get ready for bed. She looks excited, pleased. 'Something you said has delighted Sophie, it seems,' Anna says into the receiver.

Rosamund laughs. 'I'm afraid it is the cat, Grey, that Sophie found for me. She has had kittens, three of them. Sophie is eager to come see them. I don't expect you could – ?'

She breaks off apologetically. Rosamund, unlike Sophie's other grandparents, is aware of boundaries. She has never crowded Anna, nor made demands, and Anna has been aware of this, and grateful. But now, as the silence between them goes on slightly too long, Anna has a fleeting moment

212

of dismay, as if there is a price she, and Sophie too, must pay for this tact, this reservation that she herself has imposed. She has the sudden, rather unpleasant feeling that Rosamund is, with discretion of course, trying to make an appointment with her own granddaughter. 'I was thinking,' the older woman is continuing, 'that perhaps you could come here for half-term? Sophie said it's only a fortnight away, and the kittens will be at a delightful age then.'

Anna, dismayed, begins babbling. 'Sophie must have forgotten we're going to Devon, to stay with Steve. We haven't been there for ages, and Steve hasn't been here because he's had so much work on. It seems impossible for us all to get together these days! Maybe we can come up the weekend after half-term, how would that be?'

'Whenever,' Rosamund says kindly. 'Whenever it is convenient.'

She is glad that Peter is there for she feels oddly bereft when she gets off the phone. She hadn't realized how much she was hoping to see her granddaughter over the half-term. 'She's not coming?' Peter says, looking up from the newspaper he was reading. He can tell it by her face, for he has not been listening to her conversation.

'No, they're going to Devon. Anna wants to be with Steve. I can't blame her, but it's a shame for Sophie. She says Sam wouldn't be there and she'd rather come here and see the kittens. Oh dear, I hope I haven't caused dissension.'

'Why don't you have Sophie on her own? Then Anna and Steve could have some time together.' He looks so pleased with himself at this solution that Rosamund smiles.

'Of course that would be the thing to do,' she says thoughtfully. 'But one could never tell Anna. There are some things she must discover for herself.'

'For what it's worth, I'm here,' Peter says comfortably. 'I'm not going back to France for almost three weeks.'

'It's worth more than you'll ever know,' Rosamund answers. 'More than I usually admit to myself.' She goes

213

over to him and kisses him spontaneously, delighting him more than *she'll* ever know.

Sophie is hovering at the top of the stairs, having listened to her mother's conversation. When Anna hangs up she calls down, 'Why can't we go to Malvern for half-term? I'd love to see the kittens. And the twins – they'll be off school as well and we could have such fun! I want to see Grandma, too. We haven't seen her since way before Christmas.'

'We're supposed to be going to Devon, Sophie. You know that.'

'Do we have to, Mum?' She comes slowly down the stairs. 'If Sam won't be there, I'd rather go and see Grandma.'

'What about Steve? You know he'd like to see us; you know he gets lonely in Devon on his own. We've not seen much of him lately either, and he's counting on half-term.'

Sophie is torn at this, and Anna feels suddenly guilty, for she knows she is using emotional blackmail here. There is a short silence while Sophie turns things over in her head before finally saying, 'I've got it, Mum! You go to Devon. I know you want to see Steve and he wants to see you. I'll go and stay with Grandma!'

She looks so pleased with herself, so proud of this solution, and starts chattering verbosely: 'Mum, isn't that a good idea? Everyone will be happy, you and Steve and me and Grandma . . . and you and Steve can go on long walks – I know you take me but I still can't walk as far as you – and I can see the kittens!' She looks so radiant that Anna feels both dismay and pride, that the child feels strong and confident and grown-up enough to want to venture somewhere without her.

Sophie is looking at her mother expectantly. She has brushed her thick dark hair and for once it falls obediently on to her shoulders instead of flying fractiously all around her head. Anna wants to gather her into her arms like warm eggs from a clean sweet-smelling henhouse, wants to run her

214

fingers through her daughter's shining hair. She does neither, instead she says, gently, 'Look, love, it's all very awkward. Your other grandparents have already asked to take you away for the half-term.'

'Where?' Sophie asks, surprised.

Anna tells her about Bournemouth. 'You'd hate it, Mum,' Sophie laughs. 'Stuck in a posh hotel like that in the middle of lots of hotels, with Grandma and Granddad.'

'That's why they didn't invite me.' Anna hesitates then says, 'Would you have liked to go, Sophie?'

After thinking about it for a moment Sophie says, 'It would be a giggle, I suppose. I've never stayed in a fancy hotel, and eating out every day would be fun, and so would the swimming. I'd love that, being right near a swimming pool. But I think I'd rather go when it's warmer, you know? So that I can paddle about in the sea as well. Easter time would be nicer.' She looks at Anna carefully. 'When did they ask, Mum? What did you tell them?'

Suddenly Anna feels uncomfortable. She refused her parents' invitation without even consulting Sophie, treating her as if she were still a very young child unable to make any decisions for herself.

Deciding to be honest she says now, 'I told them we were going to Devon, Sophie. I didn't feel it was quite time yet to have separate holidays.'

Sophie looks at her mother with frustration and is about to protest when something in Anna's face, the look of defeat, perhaps, etched into the curves and contours on her face like scratches on a pane of glass, moves the child to say, 'I guess we'd better go to Devon. Steve will be lonely without Sam and he'll need me to cheer him up.'

Now Anna lets herself be embraced by her daughter. Arm and arm together they go upstairs and Sophie gets into bed. Her mother sits on the edge and they talk languidly about nothing much of importance until the child falls asleep. Nothing more is said about half-term, and

Sophie seems resigned and contented enough about going to Devon.

And yet. And yet . . . Anna goes downstairs and thoughtfully puts on the kettle, feeling suddenly chilly and needing a hot drink of some sort. As she rummages through the cupboard looking for a herbal tea she thinks about her daughter, how animated Sophie became when she suggested going on her own to see Rosamund, how grown-up, how confident. There was more there, too: an anticipation, an excitement, the thrill of adventure, of striding out on her own on to that frightening but beguiling path of independence.

And yet she withdrew, retreated, because of me, Anna thinks sadly. She was willing to hold herself back, submerge her own wants and needs, because she knew I wasn't ready to confront them yet . . . Suddenly, Anna understands what a burden it must often be for Sophie, to be responsible for her mother. She must know how Anna's life has revolved solely around her daughter, how for years she was the core of Anna's life, and it must be beginning to oppress her now that she is growing stronger, growing older. *Oh, Sophie*, Anna thinks. We love each other so and we don't know how to cope with it now that things are changing.

Abandoning her search for tea Anna goes back upstairs to look at her daughter. She is peacefully asleep, her mouth slightly open, and Alice her doll, which she has still not outgrown, is by her side. Anna sits lightly on the edge of the bed, holds Sophie's hand gently, taking care not to awaken her. She would like to stay there for ever, just Anna and her daughter, cocooned by love: a magic circle, a moment of time stopping, never ending.

It's late when she finally stands up, kisses her daughter one last time, and walks slowly downstairs again. It's late but Anna has to make some phone calls: now, before she changes her mind. Hoping that the people she is going to ring at this hour love her enough to forgive her, she takes the phone and begins dialling.

Stuart is still awake, his hip having been troubling him, but he is gruff with fear at the lateness of the call. Anna soothes him and says what she has rung to tell him: that she would like Sophie to go on holiday with them, but during the Easter break instead.

'Actually, it would be much better,' Stuart says, convinced by this time that it was his idea anyway. 'It would be rather cold in Bournemouth in February and we'd have to stay indoors most of the time. We could use the beach more in spring.'

Rosamund is asleep when Anna phones. Peter, beside her, is asleep also. He is staying the night again, much to both of their surprise. Rosamund is finding it more and more difficult to let him go after a day or an evening together, even just to his own flat in Malvern.

'Anna?' she says, picking up the phone by her bed. 'What's wrong?'

Anna begins softly crying, terrifying Rosamund out of her wits. 'My dear, what's wrong? Is it Sophie?'

'I had to phone now or I'd change my mind. I'm sorry I've been difficult sometimes.'

Rosamund doesn't understand, doesn't know what to say. Anna goes on, 'Sophie would like to stay with you over half-term. On her own. I'd like it too.' She wishes she could stop crying.

'My dear, are you sure? I've never wanted to pressure you – '

'You never have! That's why I want Sophie to go to you. Sorry about the tears. It's bloody hard, this letting go.'

Now Rosamund understands. 'Oh, my poor Anna.' The tears prick her eyes also, for she knows what her daughter-in-law is going through, knows that the pain of separation, even a temporary one, can be unbearable if one has gone through other, more final severings.

And so they talk: Rosamund reassuring, Anna slowly calming down. After they have hung up Peter, also wide

awake by now, says, 'I hope you were paying attention to
what you said, all that quoting of Blake about destroying joy
if you cling too hard to it, that you should kiss it and let it
fly away and you'll be blessed eternally.'

'Well, it's true,' Rosamund says, snuggling under the bed-
clothes with him.

'Will you remember that? I've always let you go, you
know. I've never clung.'

'I know.' She kisses him fondly.

'Will I be eternally blessed, then?'

'Hush. It's late, let's sleep.' They lay side by side holding
hands until Peter drifts off, but Rosamund stays awake for
some time longer. She wonders whether it is always wise to
let go: are there not some things that should be held on to
and cherished? Turning over she holds on to Peter, and is
still clutching him tightly as she finally falls asleep.

Steve also forgives Anna for waking him out of a sound sleep
and telling him she wants to go with him to Wales for the
half-term. But he says, 'You don't have to do this just for
me, love. It's for yourself too.'

'I know. I want to be with you. I've missed you. And
Sophie . . . Steve, tonight when I held her hand and wanted
to hold on to her for ever, when I knew I could never let her
go . . . I realized then that I *had* to. Stop clinging to her, you
know?'

Steve knows. 'Listen,' he says. 'You sound a bit weepy.
And I'll never go back to sleep. Why don't I drive up to
Bristol right now? It's only a couple of hours.'

'What about your guitars?'

'Sod the guitars. I love you.'

'Drive carefully. I love you too.'

They hang up and Anna joyfully dances into the kitchen,
puts the kettle on a second time. Before it boils she goes up
once more to see Sophie. She is still asleep, her tangled hair
covering her face, her mouth slightly open to reveal white,

gleaming teeth. Anna takes her hand again, then kisses it lightly and puts it down. I love her more than my life, she thinks, but then she's never asked for it. Slowly she leaves the bedroom and goes downstairs where the kettle at last has begun to boil. Making herself tea she sits down with it at the kitchen table, waiting for Steve. She feels balanced now, refreshed and positive, ready to take the next step in her future whatever that may be. *At last*, she says to herself. *For the first time ever, I am getting on with my own life*. The thought brings her a calm, confident satisfaction.

Chapter Thirteen

'STOP fussing so,' Peter says kindly. Rosamund is checking the refrigerator for the third time, wondering if she has forgotten any of Sophie's favourite foods. 'Here, taste this.' He hands her a spoonful of leek and potato soup and then ladles a tiny amount into a cup for himself. 'Hmm, I must say my leek and potato soup is like no other! Do you know that my neighbour in France, Madame LeLeannic, accepts a bowlful for her supper every time I make it? She calls it *un potage formidable!*'

'It's delicious, Peter, as it usually is,' Rosamund says distractedly. 'I'm so glad the bakery saved us a seedy loaf, Sophie loves them.'

Putting his hand on her shoulder Peter says, 'You are terribly tense, you know. Is it because Sophie is coming to stay on her own? Or is it perhaps me, that at last the two separate parts of your life are going to meet?'

'A combination of both, I suspect.'

Keeping his hand on her shoulder he scrutinizes her carefully. Her face looks drawn, her remarkable blue eyes worried. 'I don't have to be here for lunch, you know. I needn't meet Anna this time. If you'd still like me to get to know Sophie, we have all week.'

'On the contrary,' Rosamund says thoughtfully, 'I find I need very much for you to be here.'

'Perhaps that is worrying you too?'

Smiling up at him Rosamund says, 'Yes, perhaps it is.'

The sound of Anna's 2CV raspingly choking to a stop outside the cottage sends Rosamund rushing out of the house. Sophie and Anna get out of the car and after many embraces and exclamations the three finally go inside. Peter, tactfully remaining in the kitchen to stir the soup, has his first glimpse of Sophie as she comes running in looking for the kittens which are with Grey in an unobtrusive box in the corner. 'Oh, how sweet! Oh Grey, you are such a clever cat! Look, their eyes are already opened, I thought they'd still be shut. Hello, Grey, do you remember me? I found you!'

After a few minutes she becomes aware of Peter. 'Oh, I didn't see you there. Grandma said there was a friend of hers in the kitchen.'

'The kittens are much more important. You are Sophie, is that right? I'm very pleased to meet you. My name is Peter.'

Still with the kittens in her lap, she smiles at him and Peter's heart lifts. It is Rosamund's smile, the same reckless turning up of the mouth, the same spontaneous outburst of warmth and delight spreading over the whole face. Peter is so moved he has difficulty in turning away from the child as Rosamund comes into the kitchen to introduce Anna.

Lunch is pleasant, easy. After the soup there is salad and cheese, and then Sophie's favourite rich chocolate ice-cream. When Anna discovers that Peter lives for most of the year in France, she begins making the connection between this man and the frequent visits her mother-in-law makes to that country, 'to stay with a friend'. Rosamund has over the years never volunteered any other information about the 'friend' but to be fair, Anna thinks now, I never asked, never showed much interest. I was too wrapped up in Sophie to pay much attention to what was happening around me.

She makes up for it during the next hour or two, watching Rosamund with Peter, asking in the most tactful manner how they met, how long they have known each other – innocent questions, which Peter answers easily and Rosamund, more hesitantly. When it is time for Anna to leave she realizes that the surprise of finding a strange man so intimately stirring leek and potato soup in her mother-in-law's kitchen has pre-occupied her to such an extent that her fears of leaving Sophie have not had a chance to surface. Now, however, as she stands outside ready to get into her car, reminding Rosamund for the third or fourth time about Sophie's drugs – the dosage, the timing – all her old dreads and forebodings claw at her like familiar birds of prey and she clings to Sophie for longer than necessary. As she kisses her she sees in her daughter's face a mirror image of her own terrors, and knows that the child, despite her bravado, is as apprehensive of the parting as she is. Sophie, though wanting to take a step on her own, is suddenly desperately afraid of falling. Through all her life of illness and hospitals and operations, it has been her mother who has always been with her, holding her, encouraging her, willing her own strength into the frail body of her child. Clinging to her mother, Sophie tries not to cry. It is not easy, this first little step. It is much harder than she had thought.

The moment expands. *I cannot go*, Anna thinks. *I cannot leave her.* And then there is a whoop and a holler as the door bangs at the house next door and the Anderson twins are running across the front lawn crying, 'Sophie, Sophie! Mum said we had to wait till after lunch to come over. Have you seen Grey's kittens? We have a whole week off school, do you? Mum said she'd take us all to the swimming pool at Worcester one day, the really warm one!'

Sophie breaks away and turns to greet them. *Now. Go*, Anna says to herself. And somehow she does it. Somehow she gets into her car, waves frantically and drives off. Sophie, waving away with the twins and Rosamund and Peter, is smiling, and Anna feels almost sick with relief.

After a while, to prevent herself thinking, she turns on the car stereo and the tape Sophie had put in is still playing. Roy Orbison, of course, and here it comes again: 'You're not alone, you're nooot alone, you're noooot a-lone, any moooore . . . ' It makes Anna smile. I'm *not*, she thinks, I'm really not. The odd thing is, I never really was, only I couldn't see it. She thinks of the generous amount of love and support she has had since Richard died: Mike, and

Rosamund, and dear kind Madge . . . and even her parents; though she found Stuart's authoritative manner and abrasiveness overbearing at times, she can understand now that he was acting in what he thought was the best way for both his daughter and granddaughter.

And Steve. Thank God for Steve, she thinks sombrely. Suddenly she cannot wait to see him, cannot wait for him to hold her and so lessen the gap she is beginning to feel widening between herself and her child as she drives away from Malvern and towards Bristol.

'Happy?' Steve says that night as they cuddle on the big sofa in front of the fire, warming each other with their skin and hands and breath. There is a frost outside, and they have just come in from the garden where they were watching a new moon appear over the valley.

'Hmm. Yes, I suppose I am.'

'You've done very well. You've only rung Sophie once and we've been here four whole hours.'

'She sounded so at home, Steve, so contented,' Anna repeats for the third time. 'Rosamund has made the spare bedroom into a perfect little room for her, with a desk for her books and drawing materials, and a duvet cover with kittens on it. Peter stayed for dinner, apparently, and played Monopoly with her afterwards for almost two hours. He claims to love Monopoly!'

'I love *you*,' Steve murmurs, his breath sweet and warm in her ear. Anna forgets Sophie for the first time that day as she says softly, 'And I love you, Steve.' She realizes as she says it that she doesn't find the words threatening; on the contrary, they feel comforting, reassuring. Another first, she thinks with satisfaction.

Another first.

The week goes quickly, and Anna is amazed that she is able to relax, enjoy being with Steve on his own. The weather remains dry and frosty, perfect for walking in the woodlands behind the farmhouse or in the valley along the river. Some days they never take the car out, on others they explore a bit: a walk in the Forest of Dean, a day in Hay-on-Wye where they buy a dozen second-hand books between them.

There is a connected phone in the farmhouse, which relieves Anna for she has given the number to Rosamund and knows if Sophie needs her she is only a few hours' drive away. But Sophie has been fine, and seems to be enjoying her visit. Anna had forebodings only on one day, when she knew they were all going to the swimming pool in Worcester. 'I hope it's not too crowded,' she fretted to Steve as they threw some bread to the two swans which had followed them as they walked along the river. 'Sophie's still not that strong. I hope no one pushes her.'

'Rosamund will be there, as well as the twins' mother.'

'She can't really swim well. I hope Rosamund remembers that. Sophie loves pools, but never goes into the deep end. I hope the twins don't try to entice her out of her depth.'

It wasn't until that evening, when Anna phoned and spoke to Sophie, did her uneasiness disappear. 'She loved it, Steve. Mrs Anderson chose a time when the pool was practically empty, and it was warmer than a bath, Sophie said. Afterwards Peter took everyone to some jolly Italian restaurant where there were posters all over the walls and the waiter actually tried to teach them Italian. Apparently they had the most enormous pizzas "in the whole wide world".' Anna smiles. 'Oh, I'm so glad, Steve. I'm so very glad it is working out all right.'

When the holiday ends they both drive straight from the farmhouse to Malvern to collect Sophie. 'Happy to be getting back?' he says to her as they drive along the winding road through the Wye Valley towards the Severn Bridge.

Anna looks guility at him. 'Well, I . . . it's been such a wonderful week, Steve.'

'That's not what I asked,' he says gently.

'I'll be happy to see Sophie.' She starts to say something else, then stops.

Reaching for Anna's hand with his left one, Steve says, 'It's okay, love, you can say it. You've missed Sophie and can't wait now to get back to her. It doesn't cancel out the good time we had together. If it's any comfort, I missed Sam too. It's the first time I haven't had him during half-term, the first time he's been out of the country without me. I didn't like the fact that Tess let him go on that trip, you know. I realize it's his last year at primary school and all that, and it's the big outing for the school leavers – but it did worry me somehow. Sam is so shy with new people, and to stay with a strange French family – '

He breaks off, and Anna looks at him with interest. 'I never knew you felt like that. I'm glad you told me – it makes me feel less possessive.'

'It'll get easier as they grow up, I hope.'

'Then we'll be worrying about their driving cars and smoking cigarettes – '

'And dope and drugs, and alcohol – '

'And sex, of course. Parents always get frantic about sex. Too young or not emotionally ready. Relationships. The Pill, pregnancy – '

'AIDS, condoms.'

'Stop! I'll never cope, Steve, never.'

'Of course you will. We'll do it together.'

They drive along in silence for a while, thinking of the future. Anna realizes that she is looking at it calmly, with measured optimism; that it does not, as it used to, loom like a black hole threatening to annihilate her.

Once again it is lunchtime when they arrive in Malvern, and once again Peter is in the kitchen, this time stirring a thick ham and pea soup. 'Sorry, I didn't hear you come in,' he says as Anna introduces him to Steve. 'I seem to be relegated to the kitchen. I hope you don't mind soup again, it's the only thing I do well in the cookery line. The other two are next door; Sophie is saying goodbye to the twins, I believe.'

And then the door bangs open and there she is, looking both grown-up and endearingly child-like, her hair neatly pulled back in a plait, her smile excited and joyful at seeing her mother again but also somehow serene, contented.

It is a happy luncheon party. Sophie talks almost non-stop; she is full of things she must tell Anna and Steve at once. Rosamund too seems relaxed, tranquil. There is an easy rapport between her and Sophie – the week has been good for both of them, Anna thinks. Peter does not say much but just watches everyone calmly, ladling out more soup when necessary, or cutting more bread. He and Sophie share the odd joke, the occasional giggle; they seem quite at ease with each other, as if they have known each other much longer than a week.

'When are you going back to France?' Steve asks Peter.

'In a couple of days.' He looks at Rosamund as he says this but she appears engrossed in buttering a slice of bread. Though he tactfully tried to stay away from the house during Sophie's stay, not wanting to infringe on the privacy of grandmother and child, he was pleased to find that both were eager to see him when he did arrive. And in the evenings, after Sophie had gone to sleep, Rosamund seemed to want him there, to talk to him about Sophie, about what they had done when he wasn't with them.

'It's odd,' Rosamund had said when once again she found she wanted Peter to spend the night instead of returning to his own flat. 'It's odd how addictive companionship can be. I have Sophie, yet I find I very much want you here as well. And yet I have been quite happy at other times, being alone.'

This hurt Peter, and he said, 'I always miss you when I am in France, or in my house here alone.'

'You shouldn't say it like that – so lovingly. You will make me admit that I miss you too – that I am content without you only by deliberately casting you out of my mind, making myself concentrate on my pots or a riveting book or whatever.' She didn't add that she felt a rather self-satisfied complacency during those times when she was on her own, knowing she could survive without intimate contact with other human beings. There is less risk, she thought, when one is self-contained, when one can be reposeful even though one is totally alone.

Peter was looking at her oddly. 'I'm going back to France soon. Will you come with me, stay with me?'

He had asked her before, of course, but not lately. Reiterating the answers he knew well she said lightly, 'My workshop is here. What about my pots? I already spend far too much time with you in France; each year I am further behind with orders.'

'I'm not asking you to give up your work. I would make you a pottery in France and we could bring the things over when I have to return to England for a few weeks. We'd work it out.'

Rosamund, saddened that this conversation had come up again, patted his cheek gently before saying, 'I prefer it this way, Peter. We love each other, we are lovers – yet we have our own homes, our own work, our own space. This way we shall never irritate each other.'

Or rely on each other too much, she said to herself. Rely on the other always being there, like I did with both Richard and Tony, so that when they weren't there, I came close to madness.

Now as Peter tells Steve and Anna he will soon be returning to France she knows he is looking at her, knows he is willing her to change her mind, go with him. Deliberately she avoids his eyes, intently buttering her bread, and so the moment passes.

Steve, Anna and Sophie leave after lunch, after Rosamund promises to drive to Bristol for the weekend in a few weeks' time when Grey's kittens are old enough to leave

228

their mother, for Sophie is, of course, going to have one. 'Samantha will hate the kitten,' Anna warns. 'She's old and set in her ways.' But Sophie, with her usual optimism, is sure that both cats will love each other once they get to know each other, and Anna relents.

As they drive away Peter says, 'You'll miss the child, now you've had her to yourself. Now you've lived with her, been together twenty-four hours a day.'

The 2CV turns a corner, vanishes out of sight. 'You see?' Rosamund demands, brusquely wiping away a recalcitrant tear. 'You see now why I won't live with you? One so quickly, so pathetically, begins to rely on other people.' Furiously she walks away from him, into the house. When he follows her and tries to take her in his arms she says, 'Please don't say anything, all right? Let's get our coats and walking shoes and go to the hills for a nice brisk walk and not speak at all except for the occasional comment on the weather or landscape.'

Peter, understanding, says, 'Your favourite tea shop will be open, and blissfully empty at this time of year. I will buy you an immense tea, with scones and a slice of carrot cake.'

Rosamund squeezes his hand gratefully. 'I do love you,' she says. 'That's the trouble. Far too much.' Before he can answer she puts her finger to her lips and rushes out to collect a scarf and a woolly hat, for it is after all only February, and though the daffodils are already out there is still a distinct wintry chill in the afternoon air.

March continues cold, but dry and frosty. Sophie steadily grows stronger, and at the end of the month returns with Anna to Birmingham for a few days for her appointed check-up and routine tests. 'Sophie, how well you're look-ing!' Belinda cries as she hugs and kisses her former patient. Later, when Sophie is in the day-room talking to some of the other patients, Belinda says to Anna, 'She's marvellous. So full of energy and fun.'

'She was actually looking forward to coming up here, to show off her new liver, she told me.'

'It's obviously been accepted by her body. You can tell just by looking at her.'

'I know.' The two women smile at each other.

'I don't know how you coped, Anna. I couldn't have.'

'You would have, you know. None of us think we can, but something happens when it's your child. You cope because of her.'

Belinda says nothing but thinks of Max. They are still meeting once a fortnight or so for the odd lunch or dinner, but they are very careful with each other now, after the earlier squirmishes and subsequent stalemates: polite and solicitous. Max sometimes tells her about the women he occasionally takes out but admits there is no one with whom he would like to have a deeper relationship.

'They won't have babies, you mean?' Belinda teased him one day recently when they were in the hospital cafeteria having a late afternoon tea. Max had been visiting a post-operative friend in another ward and had called in unexpectedly to find Belinda, who was just going off-duty.

'On the contrary, they're almost too eager to settle down and have kids. We just don't click, that's all.'

'We did.'

'I know.' They looked at each other sadly, each thinking how much they still loved the other, until Belinda said, 'Don't you think it's a bit bizarre, this? A bit calculated? Deliberately giving up someone you say you love because she refuses to breed as you want her to?'

'Belinda . . .' Max looked at her warningly. 'We promised not to talk about it any more.'

Something in the way she swallowed her sudden anger, attempted to smile, touched him, and for a moment he was assailed with doubts. *What if she is right?* he thought suddenly. *What am I giving up for some wistful dream of children, a family?* He reached over and took Belinda's hand, and as

230

she looked at him with love and expectancy he nearly said: forget the babies, it's you I want, only you.

But the words wouldn't come, remained unsaid in the depths inside him, and though he knew he really did love Belinda, he loved his dream more: the house in the country, banal though it might be; the toddler waiting for Daddy at the front door when he came home from work, the son to take to the county cricket matches, the daughter who would wrap him around his little finger with her loveliness and charm. He would have liked their mother to be Belinda, but because she refused, he hardened himself against her.

In the long stretch of silence Belinda slowly removed her hand, watching his set, determined face, feeling him draw away from her. 'Must be off,' she said lightly. She walked away, still loving him, but suddenly realizing she didn't very much like him right now. It was a new feeling, and she was thoughtful and contemplative as she left the hospital and slowly made her way home alone.

Now, looking into the day-room, Belinda sees Steve, who drove Sophie and Anna to Birmingham and is staying with them until Sophie's tests are over. Steve is reading a newspaper and Belinda watches as he looks up, catches Anna's eye, and they smile at one another. 'He's nice, your Steve,' Belinda says. 'Sophie adores him, and he's so good with her. Has he children of his own?'

'A son, eleven now. Sam. He lives with his mother.'

'You can tell he likes kids.'

'I know,' Anna says. 'He'd like more.' She looks troubled at this and Belinda is moved to say, 'That must be hard on you. I can understand not wanting any more, after Sophie.'

Looking again across the ward at Steve, Anna says softly, 'I'm not sure now. I felt like that before, but now I'm not so sure.'

Later, over a meal in the cafeteria, Belinda says to Jim, 'I

231

can't believe it. I just can't believe that after all she's gone through with Sophie, Anna can even consider having another child.'

'The next one would be all right – a different father. Steve can be tested beforehand to make sure he hasn't the same gene and, if not, their baby could not have the same genetic fault as Sophie. Anyway, there are tests – '

'Don't be so clinical, I know all that. I wasn't thinking of the physiological problems – it's the emotional traumas that kids put you through.'

'They say it's worth it.'

Belinda thinks of Sophie's healthy pink cheeks, her happy abandoned laughter, her enthusiasm for school and her new kitten and the huge Deerhound next door, and wonders whether in the end it *is* all worth it. Who knows, she thinks: perhaps sometimes it is? She becomes so absorbed in this thought that Jim has to prod her to finish her lasagne.

Later, watching Sophie attempt a drawing of her mottled rag doll, noting the transparent expressions on her face – irritability when something is going wrong, sheer rapture when things come out right – Belinda feels such an over-whelming surge of unfamiliar emotions that she is moved to go to Sophie, hug her impetuously. 'Is that because you like my drawing?' Sophie says with a grin, holding it up for Belinda to see.

'Yes,' Belinda says. 'And because I like you.' This time it is Sophie who embraces Belinda, then pulls away to add another few lines to her drawing. 'Here, you can have it,' she says. 'I have Alice so I don't need her picture.' She elabo-rately signs her name at the bottom and hands the drawing to Belinda.

As she takes the drawing from Sophie, the strange feeling stirs in Belinda again. *I'd love a daughter like you*, she wants to say but the thought is so overwhelming she cannot artic-ulate it, so she just kisses Sophie briefly, thanks her for

232

the drawing, and rushes away to the nurse's station to compose herself.

'The doctors don't want to see me for six months!' Sophie shouts as soon as Madge and Juan Carlos and Merlin walk through the door. They have just returned to Bristol and Steve has gone to collect Sam.

As everyone enthuses over this news, Merlin begins howling happily, thinking he is being praised. Sophie, giggling, rushes to him and hushes him up. They adore each other, this slight, slim girl and the gargantuan dog. Sophie makes a tremendous fuss over him, rubbing his stomach for hours while he grunts and whines and snorts in ecstasy and gratitude. In return he never leaves her side when he sees her. One night while Madge was drinking coffee in the kitchen with Anna, Merlin tried to get into bed with Sophie, but she laughed so hard he made do with lying on the carpet beside her.

Samantha and the new kitten hid away upstairs when Merlin bounded in, and Sophie now runs up to look for them. 'Do you two want to stay for dinner?' Anna asks Madge and Juan Carlos. 'Steve has done a pasta dish; it's already in the oven. We're all starving.'

'Ah, Steve is the cook in the family, yes?' Juan Carlos asks.
'We share.'

'I shall have him teach me. I am not like my father and grandfather and brothers back in Chile who think it demeaning to go near the kitchen. For Madge, I shall learn to cook.' He beams at her tenderly. He is wearing black jeans, a headband of the same colour, and a red shirt, and gleams with vitality and energy. In contrast Madge seems pale, tired. 'Are you all right?' Anna asks her friend.

'Fine. I think I just need a good night's sleep. The kids seem to be up half the night playing their music, talking . . . ' She breaks off as she catches Juan Carlos's eye and smiles briefly. It's not just the children tiring her out, Anna thinks.

233

There is a party atmosphere at Richmond Road that night. Madge brings over the casserole she had prepared and two of her sons come over with their girlfriends, bringing wine and cheese and several French sticks from the bakery down the road. Mike and Mary, with all the children, call in to see how Sophie had got on in Birmingham and are promptly invited to stay. 'It's up to Mary,' Mike hedges, looking at his wife. Mary, marvelling at Sophie's health and euphoria, says they'd love to stay, and sends Mike down to the Italian delicatessen for cold meats and fresh cheeses and any other goodies he can find.

After dinner Juan Carlos insists on the men washing up. 'This is good for me, to become anglicized. To work in the kitchen, so. I do not wish Madge to be a slave to me.'

'Fat chance, sweetheart,' Madge shouts from the living-room.

'You equate domesticity with Englishmen?' Mike asks, reaching for a tea towel.

'Us, domestic?' Steve grins, up to his elbows in soapy water.

Juan Carlos carefully dries a plate. 'You joke, but my mother, an intelligent woman, does nothing but cook and wash and care for my younger brothers and sisters all day. My father, he comes home from work early and talks politics half the night with his friends. He would never think to help my mother to make coffee, wash up a plate.' He pushes a tea towel down into a long glass, trying to dry it properly. 'I should never wish this same fate on Madge.' He pulls out the cloth and the glass falls to the floor, shatters into tiny shards. Juan Carlos looks at it mournfully. 'You see? I have so much to learn!'

That night he makes love to Madge for hours, and though she loves every minute of it, she is rather nonplussed when, instead of turning over and going to sleep like any self-respecting Englishman, he sits up, turns on the light, and begins to talk.

234

'*Encanto mio*, I have written to my father in Chile, for a loan of money to buy you an air ticket to Santiago in the summer,' he states. 'I have told my father I love you and wish to marry you.'

Madge wakes from her half-sleep and sits up also. 'What? You had no right. I can't go to Chile and I can't marry you. I'm married already.'

'You can divorce him now. You have said you no longer love or want your husband.'

'For Chrissake, Juan Carlos! What will your father say, if you roll up with a divorced woman of almost forty-six with four grown sons of her own?'

'He will be furious,' Juan Carlos says smugly. Madge looks at him and groans. 'Oh, I get it. This is your little act of rebellion, is it? There's no revolution in your country this year so you'll have your own mini one in the bosom of your family. No thanks, leave me out of it.'

'We needn't stay in Chile, though I have been offered a job with my old university doing research. I love England, I would be happy to live here. Until I can find a job I should be happy to be the house-husband, you know? I shall learn to cook, look after the children – '

Madge sits up in horror. 'Are you nuts or what? I've had my children.'

'You are not too old to have mine. My aunt had twins when she was fifty-two.' He starts caressing her breast with great deliberation, as if laying the ground for immediate conception.

This so terrifies Madge that she jumps out of bed, wraps a dressing-gown around her, and goes off to the kitchen to make a cup of tea. It is so late that the whole house is at last still and quiet, all the occupants asleep, even Merlin who is uncharacteristically subdued tonight after a long walk on the Downs and merely wags his tail at her from his bed in the corner. Following her downstairs Juan Carlos shouts, 'Where are you going? Come back to bed, Madge! There is so much to talk about.'

'For God's sake put on some clothes. There is *nothing* to talk about. I don't want to get married again, ever. I most certainly never want more children. And I am not going to Chile just so you can show your family how modern and liberated you are and how you have rejected their feudal patriarchy.'

Juan Carlos is so indignant at the unjustness of this that he swears vociferously in Spanish for a moment or two, then says, 'You don't love me, Madge. If you loved me, you wouldn't say such things.' Suddenly all his anger is spent and he stands there, naked and detumescent and somehow so pathetic-looking that Madge wants to cradle him in her arms like one of her children. 'Go to bed, sweetie, okay?' she wheedles gently. 'You're getting goose-bumps. I'll just wait until the kettle boils and bring us both a cup of tea upstairs.'

But when she goes up with the tea Juan Carlos is sound asleep, curled under the covers and breathing deeply. Once again she feels a maternal urge to take his hand, stroke it tenderly. He looks rather like her son Tom when he is asleep, she thinks; and then: Oh God – does that mean I am committing emotional incest?

Getting into bed quietly so as not to waken him, Madge sits up, trying to be very still, drinking first her tea, then his. She suddenly very much wants her bed to herself, her heart to herself. Even, her thoughts continue, her house to herself. She has never lived alone, going straight from her mother's home to marriage with Ron, and when Ron left there were the children, filling every room, every available space – crowding Madge both physically and emotionally.

But it wasn't just the boys and their friends, she admits ruefully to herself. There were also the men she filled her life with, hoping one day someone would scrub out the love she still felt for Ron. There is no more love now for Ron, but it wasn't Juan Carlos who eradicated it. It was time, and resignation, and the changes within herself that turned her into a woman no longer satisfied with living in the past, with loving a man she now saw as shallow, incapable of deep commitment.

Turning out the light Madge silently slides down under the blankets. Juan Carlos turns over in his sleep and puts his hand on her stomach. Tenderly she removes it and rolls over. She is sorry for him, and knows she will have to handle him tactfully, but he is young and passionately wants to be in love – she has no doubt that soon he will find someone else.

How quiet the house is, she thinks as she closes her eyes. How peaceful. She thinks she would quite like to live alone now, for a time, anyway. After she has dealt with Juan Carlos perhaps she should begin to make negotiations with her children – perhaps it is time to give them a gentle shove off the perch, encourage them to flap about on their own wings for a bit.

She has never had such truant thoughts before, and they strangely excite her as she tentatively dreams about an independent future, a future in which her life belongs to her and not an army of men plaguing her for food or comfort or shelter or sex. As she finally falls into a deep, untroubled sleep the dream stays with her, leaving her curiously sated and refreshed the next morning, in spite of only three or four hours' sleep. As she dresses quietly to go to work, careful not to wake Juan Carlos, she feels light and exuberant and full of anticipation, as if she were a child again and today were her birthday. Catching her mood Merlin tries to leap into her lap in affectionate excitement and is blissfully delirious when she doesn't chide him for nearly knocking her off her chair at the kitchen table. Miles away in thought, Madge absentmindedly scratches his chest, absorbed in herself, absorbed in this new day which holds such infinite promise.

Chapter Fourteen

'I don't want to move to Devon!' Sophie cries, spilling her drink of pineapple juice as she vehemently sits down in the deckchair out in the tiny garden. Reggae music is once again flowing over the high brick wall that separates the house from the pub behind it, and the shouts and murmurs of the clientele can be heard clearly through the open windows. It is early April, and unseasonably hot. Anna is hanging clothes out on the line to dry and Sophie has been talking to her. It is Sunday afternoon and there is the smell of beer permeating their patch, and something suspiciously like cat pee.

Since their holiday together, Anna and Steve have found it difficult to be apart. During the week they spend long hours on the telephone and race madly back and forth between Bristol and Devon to be with each other at weekends. 'This is daft, Steve said one Monday morning as he sleepily pulled on his clothes and thought of the boring motorway drive ahead of him. 'Why aren't we living together?'

Anna, cleaning her teeth, said from the bathroom, 'I wish we were. I hate it when you leave. Why don't you stay with us permanently?'

'How can I live a hundred miles from my work place? Why don't you and Sophie move in with me?'

Anna stared at him. Why not indeed, she suddenly thought, and felt a rush of exhilaration and anticipation flow through her. But there was no time to talk – Sophie was waking up and looking for her school things; Anna herself was in a rush for she was supply teaching again. But that night when Steve rang she said joyously, 'I've thought of nothing else all day.'

239

'Me too. Come to Devon, please do. I want to be with you. Both of you.'

'Yes. And me.'

They talked for an hour, made plans. Sophie could go to school at the comprehensive nearby, where Anna could perhaps find work. 'The question now is when,' Steve said at last. 'How about tonight?'

Anna laughed. 'I'd love to.' She knew as she said it that this was true: all day long she had been thinking of it, of leaving Bristol and moving to Devon. She was ready to go; she knew it from the sudden flicker of excitement she had felt when Steve first mentioned it. Bristol had been her home for a long time; she had met Richard at the university here. But they had never intended it to be a permanent home – they had stayed on because there was work for them both and it was convenient to stay in one spot for a year or two, until they could save enough money to travel. Yet here she still was, all these years later. It was time for a change, time to move out of the city and into the country, where Sophie could grow up surrounded by green fields and trees, where the only noise at night was the occasional sound of an owl or a sleepless lamb. In the past couple of years the commotion next door from the pub on Friday and Saturday nights had worsened, keeping her awake sometimes for hours, and there was an uneasiness, a feeling of barely-lidded violence, in the city now that made her suddenly eager to leave. Madge too was saying the same thing a few days ago, saying that she was thinking of selling her house, finally divorcing Ron, and buying someplace 'big enough for one', preferably out of Bristol. It was time for all of them to begin looking towards an alternative future.

'A garden, Steve,' she said to him happily, still on the telephone. 'I'd love a garden, a proper one and not a postage stamp with one scrubby clematis, two yards of grass, and a brick patio large enough for two deckchairs only if they're pressed close together.'

'We could grow things. Garlic and green peppers.'
'Masses of sunflowers, like in France.'
'Leeks. Oh Anna, come soon, come soon!'

But now it looks as if they will not come at all, for Sophie is bellicose and obstinate, insisting she will not move, and Anna is fighting both irritation and frustration. Trying to stay reasonable she says, 'I've told you, Sophie, that Steve and I decided we wouldn't move until the summer. So you still have several months yet to get used to the idea.'

'I love this house.'

'I know, so do I. We've been happy here. But we're outgrowing it. You need a bigger bedroom, and with Steve and Sam here nearly every weekend it's cramped, crowded.'

'I don't want to change schools.'

'I know, it's hard, but even if we stay here, you will have to anyway.' This is Sophie's last year in primary school – because of her illness, she did not move up with the rest of her group but opted to stay where she was another year, to try and make up the work she missed. The operations had sapped her confidence, made her less able to cope with new situations. She would have liked to stay a second extra year at her old school but was aware of how much taller, older, more physically mature she would be to the other students.

'I'll miss Madge, and Mike and the kids, and my friends – '

Trying to be as patient as she can, Anna says, 'I really do understand how you feel, love. I'll feel strange leaving here too. But Madge is probably moving away anyway, and you know Mike and Mary would love to stay with us in Devon for holidays. I want to move, Sophie. I want to live with Steve all the time now, and he does with us. We might . . . we might even get married one day, would you like that?'

This cheers up Sophie enormously, and Anna feels with relief that the battle has been won. 'Oh Mum, really? You'll marry Steve? Can he be my father? Oh, I'd love a father!'

This nearly breaks Anna's heart but she manages to say, albeit shakily, 'And he'd love you for a daughter.'

Sophie thoughtfully goes into the kitchen, pours herself some more juice, and returns to the garden to drink it. Thinking the crisis is over, Anna begins pegging out more clothes on the line. Then Sophie states, 'He'll have to move here, of course.'

Anna groans, 'Sophie – '

'Oh, Mum, we can make do, I don't need a bigger room, and Sam is happy enough in the tiny bedroom when he comes to stay.'

'Steve can't move here; he's got his workshop – '

'He worked here before when he was married to Sam's mother.'

'Sophie, you can't go moving a workshop back and forth as if it were a game of Monopoly,' Anna snaps impatiently.

Sullenly wiggling her fingers at the kitten who is playfully trying to grab them, Sophie says, 'As you said to me, there's plenty of time to think about it.' She gets up and goes to the kitchen door, the cat following along behind trying to grab her ankles.

Anna, thinking Sophie is beginning to capitulate, agrees. 'Yes, there is, lots of time.'

'I'm sure you and Steve can work something out. If he really wants to marry you he'll move to Bristol.' Having had the last word she flits into the house, turns the telly on far too loudly.

She's growing up, Anna thinks with amazement: something I feared would never happen. She's actually becoming adolescent. Staring into the house at her wayward daughter she doesn't know whether to laugh or to cry.

That weekend Madge spends an evening with Sophie while Steve and Anna go to the cinema, watch a French film. 'Enjoy it?' Steve asks when they come out.

'Mmm, brilliant.'

'Let's not rush home. Fancy a drink?'

They stop at a pub nearby and order cold lager, for it is still unseasonably warm. Finding a table away from the crowds they take their drinks and settle down. 'Okay, what's up?' Steve asks.

Anna smiles. 'You always know when I'm preoccupied.'

'You're totally transparent. Come on, tell me.'

And so she does: all about Sophie, her reluctance to move, her surprising obstinacy. Then tentatively she says, 'Steve, we've never really discussed the possibility of you moving back to Bristol.'

'Oh Anna! You know that's not on. You *want* to move, you've said so.'

'I know, I know. But I can't do it unless Sophie wants to. She's had such a traumatic life so far, in and out of hospitals – I can't subject her to another upheaval yet, I'm sorry. She doesn't need to get stressed and upset; she needs calm and an uneventful life now for a year or two.'

Steve is dismayed, but tries to be precise and logical as he explains to Anna why he cannot move back to the city. 'I'm expanding the business, you know that – I've already begun enlarging the workshop – and I'd never be able to find anything remotely as suitable here. I'd have to sell the house if we were to buy something big enough for all of us, as well as workshop premises. It would be impossible now, with house prices so low. Besides, I'm fond of the place, and so are you and Sophie. It would be madness to sell it.'

Morosely, Anna says, 'You're right, of course you're right. You can't sell. Oh God, what a dilemma.'

'Look, don't worry, it's early days yet. Sophie'll come round to the idea, you wait. I'll have a chat with her this weekend, see if I can persuade her.'

But he can't: not Steve nor Anna nor Madge nor even Mike, who comes around on Sunday morning on his way from seeing a patient. Sophie is adamant she does not want to move, and her distress at even the thought of it is upsetting to all of them. 'You come and live with us, Steve,' she wheedles at one point on Sunday evening, when he mentions how he dreads those early morning drives back to Devon.

'You know I can't, Sophie. We've explained why. I'm stuck where I am.' He looks at her grimly. 'But there's no reason why you and your mother – '

'Oh stop it, stop it! That's all everyone has been talking about all weekend, moving to Devon.'

'It's important, that's why we're trying to talk it all over reasonably,' Anna says. 'If we move we want to go in the summer, give you plenty of time to settle before school begins. You can't do things like that in a hurry; I'll need to decide whether to sell or rent the house here – '

'Sell it then! *You* go move to Devon and I'll stay here and live with Madge and Merlin.'

'That's not very sensible,' Anna says crossly. 'You know Madge is moving to somewhere smaller.'

Steve sighs and says, 'Let's forget it for now, shall we? Just think about it for a bit, Sophie, that's all.'

'I'm not going to think about it! I don't want to think about it or talk about it again – I'm not going and that's that!'

A sudden spasm of anger against her daughter takes Anna unawares, and before she can stop herself she says harshly, 'Aren't you being a bit selfish? What about me, what about what I want?'

'Oh, go then! But I'm staying here. If Madge won't have me, Uncle Mike will!' She stomps across the living-room and out of the front door, slamming it hard behind her.

'Leave her,' Steve says as Anna starts to rush after her. 'Look out the window, see? She's gone into Madge's. Let her cool down over there.'

'I've never had a fight with Sophie before,' Anna says weakly, collapsing into a chair. 'Look, I'm shaking. I've never, ever lost my temper with her.'

'You only did slightly. And so what – you were both feeling strongly about things. It didn't hurt to show it.'

'I've never seen her like that, except when the drugs made her so volatile that time in hospital. But this was totally different.'

'It was a totally normal outburst from a normal healthy adolescent. She's growing up, Anna. She's going to row with you occasionally.'

Anna groans and puts her head in her hands. 'She'll never move, never.'

'She will if you do. She has to. She won't be the first child who didn't want to move house, but had to when the parents went.'

Looking at him despairingly, Anna shakes her head. 'It's no use, Steve. She's been through too much – I won't ask her again. I can't force her to make a move she is so dead set against. You'll have to try and understand.'

Steve does and he doesn't. He tries, but all he can see is the fact that Sophie has put a stop to any chance of a life together for himself and Anna.

'You'll have to just wait for me, okay Steve?' Anna says, trying to be light. 'Like you said, Sophie is growing up.' She frowns, suddenly becomes sombre. 'You *will* wait, won't you?'

'I haven't any choice,' he says bitterly. 'I haven't any bloody choice at all.'

Easter is late this year, and the warm weather holds for Sophie's week at the seaside with Stuart and Eleanor. Sophie, getting ready to go, kisses Madge goodbye, reminds her again what to feed the cats, and clings to Merlin tenaciously before she gets into the car. 'Oh, Madge, you're not really going to get rid of Merlin, are you?' she asks.

'I'll try not to, honey, but I don't know. He's not really happy in the city. He was brought up on a farm, you know, and isn't really settling. What he'll do in a smaller house,

245

I don't know. I won't be able to afford anything with any kind of a garden or space, even if I do manage to get out of town.'

'Maybe we could have him, Mum?' Sophie asks not very hopefully as they drive out of Bristol.

'You know it's not possible, love. If he's outgrowing Madge's house, think what he'd be like in ours!'

When they are on the motorway Sophie laughs. 'I was just thinking about this holiday, at this luxury hotel. Do you think I should take a tent, in case I don't like it?' She giggles again. 'Our poor dear useless tent, that leaks all over the place. Remember in Spain? What a fun holiday that was! No posh hotel could beat that.'

Anna is moved. 'You think that, Sophie? But you were so ill.'

'Not every day. It was still fun. The three of us were so happy.'

She's right, Anna thinks. In spite of illness, fear, uncertainty, we managed to be happy. I'm so glad she remembers that, and not the other.

The afternoon with her parents is spent pleasantly, walking Ollie the dog, taking Sophie around the town visiting her favourite spots – the Cob, thronged with people at this promising start to the Easter holidays, the dim, musty second-hand book shop near the beach, where Sophie likes to rummage through old children's books, and the treasure-crammed fossil shop where Sophie buys her mother a necklace of polished stones the colour of amber. 'Because I'll miss you in Bournemouth,' she says, putting it around her mother's neck.

That night when Sophie is in bed Anna settles in the sitting-room with her parents as Eleanor brings out the ritualistic whisky on a tray. After they have sipped their drinks Stuart says, 'About Sophie's education.'

Her spirits quickly dropping, Anna replies warily, 'What is there to say?'

'She is finishing primary school, dear,' Eleanor says cautiously. 'Your father would like to discuss what is to happen next.'

Stuart nods solemnly. 'It has been remiss of us not to discuss her education before.'

Anna's determination to remain unruffled by whatever her parents have to say disintegrates. 'For God's sake! Sophie has been wavering between life and death for years. Her education has not been exactly first in our priorities.'

Ignoring this outburst Stuart says, 'I phoned Harold Wright in Birmingham. He feels the operation was a success and doesn't want to see Sophie for six months.'

'I told *you* that,' Anna says petulantly. 'Don't you listen to me?'

Appearing not to notice her truculence, Stuart continues: 'Your mother and I feel that now is the time to concentrate on the best possible education for Sophie, and we are willing to pay all her school fees. Naturally you would not want her far away.'

'I don't want her to board at all. Full stop.'

Stuart and Eleanor exchange glances. 'I have been investigating private schools as near to you as possible. There is one excellent one only a forty-five minute drive away.'

'I said she's not going to board. Neither she nor I want it, even if she were entirely well and did not need any special attention.'

'Very well.' Stuart looks resigned and long-suffering. 'There is no reason, then, why you could not drive Sophie to school every day. Provided you get a decent car, of course. That ridiculous 2CV is an anachronism on the road.'

Anna takes a long sip of her whisky before saying, 'You know very well that's not on. It will still be a long time before Sophie has the strength and stamina of other children her age. I'm not subjecting her to a long drive every day.'

When her parents are silent Anna, hoping the topic will

be closed, adds, 'Sophie will be quite happy with her friends at the local comprehensive.'

Eleanor, who has been, so far, only listening, leans forward in her chair and says quietly, 'It's a terribly large school, dear. Not right for Sophie at all. Your father has already investigated it.'

'It's an over-crowded urban institution with few facilities, harrassed and overworked teachers, and a student population mostly just killing time until they are sixteen. Hardly the environment for Sophie.'

The anger is rising in Anna like a fish floating to the surface, slowly but steadily. 'It's where Sophie wants to go,' she says in a precise, unnatural voice. 'Her friends are there, she's planning on it. She has a right to go where she wants after all she has been through. Even if I wanted her to go to a private school – which I don't – Sophie herself would refuse to go. She hates change, hates meeting new people now, since her operations.' Anna stops, glances at her parents. Her mother looks resigned; her father determined. Anna takes a breath and says, 'Both Steve and I tried to get Sophie to move to Devon. I wasn't going to tell you because there was no need, it hasn't worked out. Sophie does not want to move, and one of the reasons is that she wants to move up to the same school as her friends. So you see, there is no point in continuing this argument.'

She looks dully at her empty glass. Arguing with her parents wearies her, saddens her, and infuriates her all at the same time, and she wonders sadly if it will ever be anything different. She is so lost in her own thoughts that she has not even tried to anticipate her parents' reaction to the news that she was contemplating moving to Devon. Finally she looks up warily, flustered by their silence. Stuart and Eleanor are staring at her, completely stunned, Stuart for once speechless. It is her mother who finally says, 'You are thinking of – moving in with Steve?'

'I wanted to. We even talked about marrying.' Anna looks

at her, suddenly shy. She cannot look at her father. 'I didn't tell you because it all fell through. Sophie refuses to move. It's a shame, because there is a small but excellent comprehensive school right near Steve's village. It would have been ideal for Sophie.'

Eleanor is both moved and torn. She feels a sharp bracing joy for her daughter, who is willing to risk marriage again, who has at last found someone to love as she once loved Richard. Yet she also feels a dull sadness, almost a nostalgia perhaps, that she has not been able to share all this with Anna. She would like to embrace her daughter, but feels restricted by her husband's presence, by her own inability to express the emotions so well hidden, so sealed and locked, inside her. So she does not move; but she hears herself saying, in a surprisingly strong and clear voice, 'I am so very pleased for you, Anna. I like Steve very much, and I would be happy to have him as a son-in-law one day.'

Anna nods briefly, grateful for this support, and for a moment their eyes meet in some kind of acknowledgement, some kind of awkward understanding. It is not an embrace, Eleanor thinks, but it is something. It is the best I can do, but at least it is something.

Stuart still has not said a word. His first reaction, one of outrage that Anna was planning such an enormous change in her life without consulting him, has been supplanted by the germ of an idea incubating in his mind. Anna, relieved not to be subjected to a barrage of questions, accusations, or advice, says hastily, 'Anyway, there's no point in discussing it, it's not to be, not for a long time anyway. Sophie and I will be staying put, and so will Steve. We'll keep on as we were, for a while at any rate.'

Anna and her mother begin to talk of other things, but Stuart remains aloof, preoccupied. Anna thinks he is probably sulking because he has not got his way over his granddaughter's education, but on the contrary, his mind is wholly engaged, contemplating contingency plans. Eleanor, glancing at him, realizes this and is uneasy. She wonders what in God's name he is up to now, and wishes he would just let Anna and Sophie alone. Some day, she is sure, she will tell him so.

Chapter Fifteen

THE phone wakes Anna from a deep sleep. *Sophie,* she thinks frantically – something is wrong with Sophie. She is miles away from her mother, in Bournemouth with Eleanor and Stuart. *I never should have let her go.* Her heart is racing like the drumbeat of a demented musician; she is sweating and dizzy as she answers the phone. 'Yes, hello?' Her voice is cracked and trembly. *I never should have let her go.*

'Anna, were you asleep? I'm sorry I didn't realize it was so late.' There is a pause. 'Anna, are you there? This is Rosamund.'

Anna feels her whole body grow limp, flaccid with relief, and wonders if the sudden passing of terror is going to make her faint.

'I'm sorry I phoned so late,' Rosamund says again. 'It's after midnight, I didn't realize – '

'It's okay. Sorry I'm a bit dopey. I thought it might be about Sophie, that something was wrong.'

There is a slight pause. Anna, pulling herself together, realizes that something *is* wrong, only not with Sophie. 'What is it?' she asks her mother-in-law. 'What's happened?'

'I'm phoning from hospital. It's Peter. He just got back from France, came straight to my place, not very long ago. He was unloading his case from the car and suddenly collapsed, with terrible pains in his chest.'

'Oh God. Heart?'

'Yes, it must be. I drove him here – oh Anna, it was dreadful, he was clammy white and his lips were blue – and he was having trouble breathing. The doctors are with him now.'

251

'I'm coming up. I'll be there within an hour, there won't be traffic now.'

'Oh no, I didn't mean – '

'Sophie is in Bournemouth, and Steve and Sam are having a few days on their own, camping. So I'm totally free. Where are you?'

Rosamund tells her. When she hangs up she realizes how very much she wants her daughter-in-law there; how she knows she would not be able to bear it alone if anything happened to Peter. Oh God, she thinks distractedly, *it is not easier.* She thought that by living apart from Peter she could protect herself against possible loss, yet now as she prowls around the hospital, unable to sit still, she is full of bitterness and regret that they have wasted so much precious time when they could have been together. *I am a fool*, she says to herself over and over. I have withdrawn and isolated myself, thinking it would spare me pain, but now the pain is greater because of the things I could have shared with Peter and didn't, the moments of growing intimacy which were severed at every separation, every parting. And now if he dies, instead of having those moments to wrap around me like a warm patchwork quilt made up of memories and love and closeness, all I'll have is bitterness and anger and regrets at my own stupidity.

Just over an hour later Anna arrives at the hospital and is surprised to see Peter dressed and sitting in the main reception area, Rosamund holding his hand and looking incandescent, euphoric. They do not see her at first, and as she watches them Peter takes his free hand, strokes Rosamund's hair carefully. They are oblivious to the night sounds of the hospital around them, oblivious to the world outside whatever plane it is they are at this moment inhabiting. For a brief moment Anna feels fiercely envious.

'Anna!' Rosamund cries, seeing her at last. She goes to her daughter-in-law, embraces her. 'I feel such an idiot, getting you all the way up here! I was in such a panic.'

'It was good of you to come,' Peter says, kissing her also. 'Rosamund seemed to think I was on the way out.'

'You looked as if you were.'

'I must say I felt it. Such excruciating pain. Still rather sore, but it's amazing how the pain lessens once you know it is not terminal.'

'I tried to phone you, Anna, as soon as the doctors told me what had happened, but you were already gone. How sweet you are to come up all this way!'

'It's not far and there wasn't any traffic. I was happy to come. But what was it? Obviously they are not keeping you in, thank God!' She smiles warmly at Peter, who certainly does not look like a man suffering a heart attack. He looks amazingly young and benign, and heartily pleased with himself despite the obvious pain he is in when he moves too quickly, or takes a deep breath.

'I feel a fraud.' He smiles back at her. 'It's not my heart at all. Apparently I sprained a chest muscle when I lifted the suitcase out of my car.'

'It was terribly heavy, I tried to move it when we rushed off to hospital. Peter says it's filled with chunky earthenware pottery he found somewhere, thought I'd be interested in.' She smiles at him joyously, and touches his face lightly, as if she still can't believe he is there.

'The pain was rather sudden and quite nasty. It totally took my breath away. I was sure it must be a heart attack. Sorry to have been so disruptive.'

The three walk slowly out of the hospital, into their cars. Rosamund insists Anna is to spend the night with her and not travel back to Bristol, and Anna agrees. When they get there Peter decides to have a long soak in a hot bath to try and ease his chest, and Rosamund and Anna settle down with a cup of tea because they are still too wound up to be ready for bed.

'I thought I had lost him,' Rosamund says, staring into her teacup as if Peter were drowning there. 'I thought I had lost him irrevocably.'

253

'But you didn't,' Anna says gently.

'No. But I could have. All I could think of, besides the impending loss, was how foolish I had been, to waste all those weeks, months, when we could have been together.'

'I know. I think that about Steve and myself.'

'They are not infinite, our weeks and months. I realized tonight that we are only allotted a certain amount, and if we don't use them wisely – ' She breaks off, shaking her head. 'There are times when it is necessary to hold on to things,' she says finally. 'But it is so difficult to know when.'

They are silent, hidden in their own thoughts; their own reflections. Then Rosamund looks sombrely at Anna and says, quietly, 'Don't leave it until it is too late, my dear. As I almost did. Hold on to Steve, if you want him. I am lucky – I have been given another chance. It does not always happen like that.'

As Anna drives back to Bristol late in the afternoon of the next day she wishes with all her heart she could ring Steve, see him. She is going to tell him that she will join him in Devon, live with him, marry him, whatever. Sophie will be distraught, but she will get over it. The child's life in Bristol will be changing anyway, with Madge moving away, with the changeover to another, less cosy, school. The quality of life for her child will be better out of the city, at least for the next few years. Sophie does not see this now, but she too will have to learn to let go of the past, to accommodate the future.

Steve arrives a few days later, having dropped Sam off with his mother after a successful camping and fishing expedition in Cornwall. He and Anna are now going to the farmhouse in Wales for the next couple of days, until Sophie returns from Bournemouth.

Anna waits until they have arrived, had a bite to eat, explored the house again and the woodlands around it before she tells him. It is evening and they are by the river, sitting on a log waiting for the swans, who have produced four downy signets. The larger one spots them and glides across to them as Anna says, 'Do you remember once, in the hospital at Birmingham, you asked me to marry you? I believe it was so that you could hang around me and Sophie. But never mind your motives: it was a real proposal, I remember quite distinctly.'

Steve laughs, throws some bread to the male swan. The mother has not left her nest on the other side of the river; not even the temptation of free tidbits can entice her away from her young. 'I remember too,' he says. 'You told me not to be daft.'

Fumbling about in the pocket of her thick plaid shirt Anna finds her glasses, puts them on, and becomes intensely interested in some wild violets growing in the grass at their feet. 'Well, I've thought about it,' she says studying the flowers and nervously plucking the fat blades of grass surrounding them. 'The answer is yes,' she finishes at last.

Steve looks at her, at her frizzled hair pulled back in a tie-dyed scarf but oozing out of the edges like foam out of a beer mug; at her great huge glasses with the fat lenses, and feels quite weak with love and lust and desire for her. 'Anna,' he says gently, blowing the grass out of her hand and kissing the palm. 'Anna, I want to marry you too, but I can't come to Bristol. We've been through all this. It would be wrong for all of us.'

She looks at him with such an eager naïve smile that he feels flushed with tenderness. Her large eyes are luminous, deep, magnified a hundred times by the glasses. 'I know,' she tells him. 'We can't possibly live in Bristol. Sophie and I are moving in with you.'

He is hugging and kissing her so frantically that he knocks off her glasses which fall into the shallow edge of the river and nearly get eaten by the male swan before Steve leaps in and rescues them. The swan, indignant at this intrusion into his waters, agressively draws up his wings and hisses at them challengingly. 'When did Sophie change her mind?' Steve is asking. 'What made her do it?'

'She hasn't. She doesn't know. I'm not going to tell her on the phone; I'll wait until she returns home.'

Steve groans, disappointment hitting him like a fist. 'So nothing's changed!' The swan hisses, wings erect in battle position, daring them to go near the water again.

'Everything's changed,' Anna murmurs, holding him closely to her. She explains everything: about Rosamund and Peter, about holding on sometimes, about priorities. 'Sophie will come around,' she says at last. 'She'll love it in Devon, once she has settled into the new school.'

As they have been talking the sun has set and a great round globe of a moon is glowing at them. The air is warm and heavy with the scent, the feel, of spring. 'Is the grass dry?' Steve says softly, his hand on the warm skin in the small of her back. 'Or should we head for the house?'

'I don't think we'll make it.' She has lost her glasses again but doesn't notice. The grass is damp but warm, and laying there with Steve she feels the same strange oblivion she sensed in Rosamund and Peter at the hospital: as if there were no one else in the world, as if no one existed but two people, entwined and touching.

The swan, watching, regains his equilibrium and lowers his wings. Calmly, gracefully, he swims back to his own mate, who is still waiting silently in the soft green shadows.

'Mum, Mum, look! I've got a suntan. It was so warm, I even paddled in the sea!'

Sophie is back from Bournemouth and Steve and Anna have gone to Lyme Regis to collect her. She has had a marvellous holiday, and so apparently have Eleanor and Stuart. 'Oh my dear, it was so good of you to let us have Sophie,' her mother enthuses uncharacteristically as Anna helps her prepare lunch. 'We had such fun with her; she's such a delightful child. She made your father laugh and feel years younger.'

256

'You're looking years younger yourself,' Anna says truthfully. Her mother seems more defined, her soft face firmer and more positive. Looking at each other the two women smile, then tentatively move towards each other and touch. It is both slight and spontaneous, a movement of hands to shoulders, nothing more, but it gives them both enormous, if shy, satisfaction.

After lunch Steve and Anna and Sophie take Ollie out for a walk while the older couple rest, having only just arrived from Bournemouth that morning. Sophie wants to look for fossils, so they go on the beach carrying a couple of small hammers and a bucket to carry their prizes. Though it is still warm, the sun of the past few days seems hazy, opaque, and there is a mist coming off the sea.

As they walk towards the soft rocks and cliff face where the fossils are, Anna begins to broach the subject of moving to Devon. She has not been able to relax since she has been reunited with Sophie, knowing they will have to talk about the move. She feels it saliently prodding her, urging her to get it over with, so she begins: 'Steve and I have been doing a lot of talking about next September, and we've been making plans.'

'Oh, that reminds me!' Sophie picks up a small stick, throws it into the sea for Ollie. 'Granddad and I did a lot of talking too, about my schooling and everything.'

'Oh?'

'He's done some investigating into comprehensive schools for me, 'cause he knows you don't want me to go away to school – I don't want to either, yuk! I told him no way; I was going to the same school as all my friends. Then he started telling me how awful it was, how I'd hate it.'

Anna opens her mouth to indignantly interrupt but Steve warningly squeezes her shoulder. 'I told him I didn't care what the school was like as long as my friends were with me, but then he started really worrying me, telling me how large it was, how rough and over-crowded, how I'd be lost after my small primary school.'

She pauses to throw another stick for the dripping, yapping Ollie as Anna, extremely angry, says, 'He shouldn't have said all that, Sophie.'

'I thought that at first, and told him if it's that bad I just wouldn't go to school at all, I could stay home and Mum would teach me! But then he said I'd miss other kids my age, and started going on about compromise, what it meant and how we had to do it sometimes to get the best out of life. I didn't understand half of it, but then he came up with a good idea.'

Anna and Steve exchange glances. 'I'll bet he did,' Anna says grimly.

'What was it?' Steve asks.

'Granddad said he has investigated all the comprehensive schools in the Southwest, especially the smaller ones because he knows I hate large schools. He has a friend in Devon, another retired surgeon like himself, who has lots of grandchildren at school and this man said the best comprehensive around is the one in Steve's town! It's small, and Granddad even phoned the headmistress who is ever so nice, he says, and will make sure I'm happy there.'

She looks at them complacently and innocently. 'So you and Steve can get married now. Can I be a bridesmaid? Oh, I'd love that!'

She runs down the beach after Ollie, who is holding a rotten tree branch draped with seaweed and ambling up the sand with it. 'Look,' Anna says, her eyes filling with tears. 'She's running, Steve.' He puts his arms around her wordlessly. 'That's all she wanted, you know? To run, like other children.' They watch as Sophie catches up with the dog, grabs the stick from him and throws it into the sea, laughing as Ollie happily paddles after it.

Later, after they have found some fossils and are heading home, for the mist has come up rather heavily from the sea, Anna asks her daughter: 'You're quite willing to leave Bristol, then? Try this new school that your grandfather seems to know all about? What made you change your mind?'

'I don't know, I think maybe it was being away from home, being in a strange place, without you, and meeting all the new people staying at the hotel. It wasn't that terrifying, it was even fun.' She grins at her mother. 'And Granddad can be very – you know.'

Anna grins back. 'Persuasive?'

'Yep, that's the word. Besides – ' She suddenly breaks off and looks down at the sand sheepishly, and just the tiniest bit guiltily.

'Uh oh,' Anna says. 'Besides *what*, Sophie? Come clean.'

'It's, uh, Merlin.'

'What?'

'Madge's dog, Merlin. I told Grandma all about him one day, how Merlin and me are such mates, how he loves me more than anyone and I love him almost more than the cats. Grandma said that if I agreed to move to Devon, she was sure you and Steve would let Merlin come too, since there would be plenty of room. She said if I asked you both nicely, you were sure to say yes.'

In the silence that follows Sophie does not dare look up, until finally a kind of strangulated sound comes from Anna, and a whoop of delight from Steve, and then the two adults are laughing and laughing, clutching their sides, sitting down weakly in the sand and flopping about giggling so hard Sophie is rather glad there is no one about to see them. She doesn't think it's that funny, but she knows it means she can have Merlin. Joyfully, she begins to run again, slow awkward ungainly steps but running it is. One day, she thinks, one day soon, I shall be running with Merlin on the fields around Steve's house – *our* house, or up on the moor where there is plenty of room for us both to run about. The thought fills her with happiness, and suddenly she can't wait to get out of Bristol, begin her new life. She feels very grown up, very mature and very contented as she slows down and waits for her mother and her new soon-to-be father to catch up to her. When they reach her she takes each of their hands and together the three walk slowly across the sand, through the thickening mist towards home.

Chapter Sixteen

SINCE the property market has dropped, Anna decides not to sell the house on Richmond Road but rather arranges to have it let. She feels this would also be less of a wrench for Sophie, who, though in general is looking forward to the move, still has moments of regret and nostalgia for the house she has known all her life. Madge's place next door has been miraculously sold to the wealthy parents of a university student wanting a 'little place' for their daughter and her friends for the next three years. Madge has found a tiny one-bedroom house on the outskirts of the city while her bemused sons are forced to make accommodation arrangements for themselves. Excited as a teenager leaving home for the first time, Madge finds the idea of living alone exhilarating. She has already made up a list of library books she is going to borrow, classics she has been meaning to read for a long time; and she has bought a compact disc player with all her favourite jazz albums on discs. 'I never had a chance to listen to what I liked,' she explained to Anna: 'First there was Ron with his old Carpenters or Neil Diamond records, then came the kids with their reggae or rock, and lately Juan Carlos with his South American tapes blaring day and night over the pop and reggae.'

There are other changes this spring and early summer. As Anna winds up her life in Bristol, beginning already to move things bit by bit to Devon, in Malvern Rosamund prepares to set up house with Peter. They are selling his flat, but keeping her cottage and the workshop, for they plan to divide their time between the two countries. Rosamund looks at Peter often as he moves his personal belongings from his flat to her home, looks at him as if he were a luminous gift of light and sunshine suddenly presented to her after years of shadow. Having accepted him in her life totally, she now simply cannot get enough of him, which delights Peter no end. They too are like adolescents in the throes of a first love-affair – they cannot keep their hands off each other, and are forever touching, clutching, holding hands, wrapping their arms around each other when they are alone and unobserved.

Anna and Sophie are to move when Sophie finishes school, only a couple of more weeks now. Most of their books, clothes and favourite possessions have already been moved into Steve's place, so that when the term ends, they can fill the 2CV with what remains and close the house. Mike is seeing to the rental; he has a young colleague doing locum who will move in for at least six months from July.

Stuart and Eleanor are, contrary to Anna's expectations, rejoiced that their daughter and Steve are establishing themselves as a couple. When Anna and Sophie thwarted Stuart's plans for private education, this unexpected alternative seemed an ideal solution, for he was genuinely worried how a child with Sophie's history of illness, with her still severe memory lapses, would survive in a huge sprawling inner-city comprehensive. Eleanor is relieved and grateful they are moving out of the increasing dangers of city life; Stuart, with his Victorian leanings, is pleased his daughter and grand-daughter have a man to lean on, to protect them from life's blows and cudgels. Though a part of him is loath to relinquish this role for himself, he is feeling older these days, his hip more painful. Eleanor on the other hand has a buoyancy far younger than her years as she contemplates another wedding, secretly hoping that Anna and Steve, when they get around to it, will do it properly, with Anna at least festive in a pretty dress and Sophie all flowery as a bridesmaid at her side, and of course a nice reception somewhere with good food and wine and conviviality.

'Two weeks, Steve,' Anna says on the phone. 'I can't wait.

This house seems so dead now, we've cleared out just about everything but the furniture we're leaving behind.'

'And here it looks full of you already: Sophie's room already cluttered with her books and old dolls and pictures, and in my bedroom – our bedroom – the bedside table is filled with books in Spanish: Lorca, Lope de Vegas, Calderon . . .'

'Oh, Steve! That reminds me. I had a letter back from the comprehensive near you – remember, I wrote to the head-mistress? – she said she has been thinking of starting the Spanish GCSE course and wants to see me to discuss it as soon as we move. Perhaps I'll find work there!'

'Don't you want to sit at my feet while I make guitars – "can you cook and sew, make flowers grow . . . ?"'

'Don't sing Dylan to me – this is not the sixties; I want to earn my keep! But I'll share the cooking with you, how's that?'

Their phone bills are exorbitant, they talk so long and so often. But like Rosamund and Peter, they are discovering each other anew in their plans and dreams and sanguine blueprints for the future.

And then one day Sophie's teacher phones. Luckily Anna is home; it's midday and she is not supply teaching but in her kitchen working on a translation. 'Sophie's not well; she feels feverish, wants to go home. Perhaps it is the flu. Can you collect her?'

Anna grabs a cardigan, for the weather has turned cool and windy, and races in the 2CV the couple of blocks to the school. Sophie is in the nurse's little cubbyhole lying on the bed, talking laconically to her teacher. When she sees Anna she smiles weakly, and Anna's heart contracts, shrivels. Under the feverish flush on her daughter's face is an umis-takeable tinge of yellow. *No*, Anna thinks. *No, no, no, no.* Gently she leads Sophie to the car and races as fast as she dares for home.

Mike is on his lunch hour; he is actually at home and Mary, her own heart palpitating with fear and empathy at the panic, the urgency in her sister-in-law's voice, calls him shrilly to the telephone. He goes to Richmond Road at once and examines a grumpy Sophie, who was dozing, exhausted, in her bed with the cats. 'I don't know,' he says when he has come downstairs. 'This is out of my scope. Sophie has still had these temperatures occasionally, since the operation – '

'Not like this. Not so debilitating.'

'And I suppose it could be the flu.' He sounds doubtful. Alarm and trepidation eat at Anna's gut like a parasite; she can feel them there, gnawing and clawing and churning her insides until she feels she is going to be sick. 'Her skin is yellow, Mike,' she says flatly. 'That hasn't happened since the last transplant.'

Mike phones Birmingham, is told to take Sophie to the children's hospital in Bristol for blood tests. 'We were told everything was fine, not to come back for six months,' Anna jabbers compulsively to her brother after he has arranged for the tests.

'We don't know yet if anything's wrong,' he says soothingly. 'Try not to jump to conclusions until we have the results of the tests.' Anna looks at him with such despair that he feels as if the coldness, the hopelessness of that look will freeze him for ever in this moment.

Hope has weakened Anna over the past few months; when the results of the tests come through she curls up in a foetal ball and weeps and weeps for hours, while Mike and Mary have Sophie, who is feeling slightly better, to stay for the afternoon at their house. 'What exactly is happening?' Mary asks her husband when Sophie is out in the garden with her young cousins.

'Her blood chemistry is showing rejection. The liver is somehow malfunctioning. God knows what will happen now.' He looks haggard and draws a stark contrast to the rosy and vibrant face of his youngest child sitting in the high chair between them. He wants to go to Anna, alone in the house on Richmond Road, but she has insisted on being alone, needing a few hours' time and space to assimilate this new blow before she can face Sophie again. Yet it is Mike who also needs to be alone; he has failed Anna, failed to protect her. He feels a lightning flash of anger that his profession has failed her also, the profession he so touchingly believed in for so many years. Lately he has been becoming more disillusioned with orthodox medicine, with its reliance on potent and dangerous drugs, on extensive surgery, on the treatment of the body as if all the parts were separate, bearing no relation to the whole. He always had simple, unquestioning faith in his profession, which withstood the death of favourite patients, the lack of response at times to impeccable treatment, the frustration sometimes of not being able to diagnose a pain, an illness, of the human body. His faith was able to carry him through all these things, but now it was wavering. And yet it was not this fresh setback to Sophie causing him to doubt but the desolation in Anna's eyes, the desperation in her face. Above all else in his life he wanted to help her, but in this he was impotent.

'Mike?' Mary says tentatively, afraid for him, afraid for the havoc she sees reflected in his face. He moans and she goes to him, holding him while the baby laughs and merrily throws bits of banana all over them and on the floor.

Steve and Anna and Sophie go to Birmingham. 'Oh hell,' Belinda says to Jim when they arrive. 'It's not going to start again, is it? Not Sophie, please God, not Sophie.' Jim looks at her and shakes his head. He too is more distressed than he should be.

Hope courses once again through Anna as new and more powerful drugs are given to Sophie in a last desperate attempt to save her liver and her life. The doctors are optimistic, for at first Sophie responds and seems less tired, less yellow-skinned. Her blood chemistry cautiously improves and after a week they are discharged, as Sophie is restless and unhappy at the hospital. At home she seems stronger, healthier, and Steve returns to Devon to make guitars while Anna tries to wind up her work in Bristol. There is no question of Sophie returning to school, so there is no reason why they cannot move now.

But before they have a chance, Sophie begins to relapse. Though Anna curses and prays, makes bargains with every deity she can think of, wills every ounce of her own strength into her daughter to make her whole again, the yellow flush on Sophie's cheeks is deeper, more pronounced; she is excruciatingly tired and weak, and her fevers have returned.

Sophie seems resigned, and almost cheerful in her inimitable, courageous way, for she is surrounded by people she loves, by laughter and affection. The house is crowded nearly every day with all her young cousins, or friends from school, or Madge and her sons. Merlin and the cats fill up her bedroom, and Sam is in there often now that school has stopped for the summer. She has been more ill than this in the past, more times than once in her young life, and has got over it.

But when it looks inevitable that they must return to Birmingham, her optimism fades. 'Do I have to go?' she asks Anna, her dark eyes round and troubled.

'I'm afraid so, love. We want your liver right again, and that's the only place it can be done.'

Sophie accepts this, as she has had to accept many unpleasant things. She nods her head but a tear falls unbidden from her eyes. 'No more operations, Mum, okay? I couldn't bear any more operations.'

'No operations,' Anna promises. 'We'll get this liver right.'

Sophie is quiet on the way to Birmingham, but when they arrive she clings to her mother and Steve, frightened and lost. 'I hate hospitals, I really do,' she says vehemently as the three of them once again walk into the liver unit. 'I've had enough.'

She is put on a drip for a week, with massive dosages of the anti-rejection drugs. Once again hope, watered and fertilized by activity, by busy medical staff doing numerous critical things to her daughter, flowers in Anna's desolate, frightened heart and she becomes almost euphoric, sure that this time it is going to work.

'God, I can't bear it!' Belinda cries to Jim. 'Anna is so pathetically hopeful, so reliant on us here, so sure we are going to save Sophie.'

'She has to be. This is Sophie's last chance.'

Belinda closes her eyes. 'I think I'm in the wrong profession,' she says slowly as she opens them. 'I can't handle all this. I get so angry, then so depressed. Every death is like a bit of me dying.'

He looks at her ashen face, her haunted eyes, and for the first time is inclined to agree.

On the third day of the drip Sophie turns sleepily to her mother and whispers, 'Can I go home after this? I miss Merlin. And the cats.'

'Soon,' Anna promises. 'Soon.'

On the fifth day while Anna keeps watch as Sophie dozes, the child wakes and says sleepily, nonchalantly as if she were talking about the weather, 'It's not so hard to die, I don't think. It's the people left behind who have the hard time.'

She is asleep before her mother can answer. Sure that the words are an omen, Anna sits up all night at Sophie's bedside, Steve beside her, holding her when she falters. But in the morning Sophie wakes refreshed and cheerful. It's her last day on the drip, and the prospect of going home has made her stronger and healthier, at least momentarily, than all the drugs medical science can offer.

But they cannot go just yet, for more blood tests have to be taken. The results are slightly more promising because of the drip, but it is early days yet and Sophie must be observed, monitored. She talks incessantly about going home. Having been in and out of hospitals all her life, and tolerating them, even at times enjoying them, she has now had enough.

'She's panicking about another operation,' Jim says to Belinda who is at the nurses' station making some notes. 'She's absolutely terrified of having another one.'

'I know, poor thing. Well, can you blame her? They are long horrific operations and she's had two already.'

'Her mother looks dreadful. So pale and ill herself.'

'I'll go talk to her while Steve is playing cards with Sophie.' Belinda goes to Anna, sits down beside her. 'Sophie seems brighter,' the nurse ventures.

'Her colour is worse,' Anna says tremulously. She has been crying.

Sharp unexpected tears prick Belinda's eyes and she thinks: God, how unprofessional. But all she can say is, also unprofessionally, 'Do you not despair of the day you ever had a child, the day Sophie was born?'

Anna looks at her with bewilderment. 'How could I? How could anyone, knowing Sophie, ever wish she had never been born?'

She really means it, Belinda realizes. After all that has happened, would still happen, Anna would not have forfeited the experience of having Sophie. The thought awes her, and makes her feel slightly bereft, slightly lost, as if there were signposts she has missed, maps she has misread.

That night she sees Max again, for neither has as yet put a stop to their regular meetings despite the unsatisfactory manner in which they often end. Max had phoned to arrange supper at the little Italian restaurant which used to be a favourite of theirs before they split up. After ordering, Max, feeling nostalgic and relaxed after a couple of glasses of Chianti, says, 'Odd, how in the past few months these meetings with you have been the highlight of my week.'

'Oh?' Belinda murmurs, surprised. She is feeling limp and listless, and too downbeat to be anyone's highlight. She has no idea how her vulnerability, her temporary fragility, stirs him, gives him hope. Perhaps time and their separation has softened her, he thinks, made her pliable.

'I think we should give it another try, Belinda,' he says softly. 'I'd like to move in with you again.' As he says it he realizes it is true. They have been apart for over a year; he has seen other women but none have really interested him. What he has been doing, he understands now, is to subtly try to convert Belinda, wear her down with love and persistence, with the withdrawal of himself so that in her loss and loneliness she would come around to his – quite reasonable – demand to start a family.

'What about your two point four babies, or has the national average changed since we discussed this before?' she says curiously. She is surprised she feels nothing else, just curiosity.

'Don't take the piss,' he says tetchily.

'Sorry. But babies were the issue, remember?'

'Well, they still are. I still want them. But I'm getting the feeling that you might be changing.'

Belinda says nothing, surprised at his perception. She has not mentioned Sophie to him for months, only once when she was feeling low, but Max had discouraged her, changed the subject. 'There you go again,' he had said, 'talking about illness, about ill children. Save that for work, okay? That's where it belongs, not here with us.'

You were wrong, she thinks now. *It was all part of it, somehow. My fears. Facing them through Sophie, through Anna.*

Max is looking at her with eager hope, confidence. 'We were so good together, Belinda. We'll carry on being good-together. We'll marry, have that baby. You know I'll help – change nappies, look after it with you, give you time for

269

yourself. And if you want you can even carry on with your job – '

She shakes her head abruptly. 'I'm quitting it,' she interrupts, not knowing until she says it that this is so. 'I'm not right for it. I get too involved.'

He is delighted, thinking this means she will settle down with him, be enticed into motherhood. And indeed she knows now that maybe one day she *will* have a child, but not now, and not with Max. She realizes she wants a man who will love her first, for herself and not for her potential as a mother of his children. A man who, if the babies didn't come or God forbid were ill like Sophie, wouldn't desert her for someone more fertile, more fecundly promising.

'Let's try again,' Max is saying coaxingly. 'All this time and we haven't been able to let each other go . . . it must mean something.'

Belinda, in spite of the wine, the atmosphere, the nostalgia, feels more lucid and clear-headed than she has for a long time. 'It means only that we've been too afraid to make a permanent break, one we both know is inevitable. We've moved on, Max. Away from each other. It's time we acknowledged it, came to terms with it.'

She pours herself some more Chianti and hurriedly begins discussing her future, which will not include him. She feels light and vital with having made the decision to leave her job, even though she is not sure what she will do. Go back to college, she feels: train for something else, perhaps some kind of mental health nursing, or counselling – there were all sorts of possibilities.

Her lethargy evaporates and she begins to glow with the wine, with the future. Max sadly drinks and wonders what went wrong, how he so misjudged her, how he never realized that the change he perceived in her was a change *away* from him and his dream, not towards them.

★

The doctors at last give up; they say Sophie's liver is irrevocably damaged and there is nothing more they can do to save it. By the time they gently break the news to Anna, she knows, she knows. She has seen the yellow creep from Sophie's skin to the whites of her eyes, has noticed the swollen abdomen.

Marvin Templeton summons Anna to his office, and Steve goes with her. The small stuffy room seems crowded, for there is another man taking up space whom Marvin introduces as Ian Ronson. 'Ian is one of the surgeons on our team,' Marvin explains with easy familiarity. 'He was in the States while Sophie had her last two transplants, working with one of the largest liver units in America.'

While Marvin pours them all coffee from the percolator steaming on a corner table, Anna studies Ian Ronson closely. He is not very old, but his slim, elegant body oozes with rich clothes and a glossy self-assurance. He lights up a Marlboro and Marvin disapprovingly opens the tiny window above his desk, letting in a strong, warm breeze. The young surgeon inhales deeply, then spoons two heaped spoonfuls of sugar into his coffee. 'I've had a look at Sophie's medical records,' he says when he is finally ready to give Anna his attention. 'And also the results of her latest tests. Your daughter's liver is, as you know, failing. We've done all we could to save it, but nothing has worked, and there is nothing more that can be done.'

Anna nods wearily. 'We know all that. We've known for days.'

Ian drags on his cigarette like a man gasping for air, and Marvin moves to stand by the window. 'However, there is no need to despair,' he continues as he exhales. 'There is no reason to believe a third transplant won't be successful.'

Anna stares at him, then at Steve, who is looking as shocked and stunned as she is. Neither of them had even considered a third transplant. For a moment hope flies wildly inside Anna like a young bird caught inside a room: then she opens a window and lets it out. 'It's impossible,'

271

she says dully. 'Sophie would never stand another operation, neither physically nor psychologically.'

'That's for me to decide.'

'She doesn't want one.'

'Then she'll die.'

The tears run down Anna's face but she says, with dignity, 'She'll die anyway. I want her to die in peace, not punctured and bleeding and torn to shreds by your operations.' She gropes for Steve's hand, holds it tightly.

Ian Ronson lights another Marlboro and puffs on it for a few moments. Then he says kindly, 'You're too distraught to make the decision now. Think about it for a while.'

'I can't do it to her,' Anna whispers, still clutching Steve. 'I promised. No more operations.'

Ian's face darkens, the easy charm gone. He is not used to being said no to. His next words are cool, measured: 'You're denying your daughter a chance to live, is that what you're saying?'

At this Marvin protests. 'I hardly think Anna – '

Ignoring him, Ian interrupts. Talking directly to Anna he states brusquely, 'You must know that there isn't much time. If there is going to be another operation, it must be done soon before your daughter is too weak to survive it. Don't leave it too long before giving me your decision.'

He leaves the room. Steve holds on to Anna while she shakes and shakes and shakes. He feels she will never stop trembling.

The next twenty-four hours have a surreal, nightmarish quality for Anna. Her parents insist on driving to Birmingham at once when Anna phones and Stuart, as soon as he arrives, insists on talking to anyone available: Marvin, Harold Wright, and the new surgeon who is so keen to perform a third transplant on Sophie. 'I don't know how to advise you,' he says finally, as he and Eleanor sit with Anna and Steve in the cafeteria, an untouched meal in front of them. 'I just don't know what to say, Anna. Everyone gives such conflicting advice. I don't know what to tell you to do.' He has tears in his eyes, and his daughter is unbearably moved. Reaching over to him she takes his hand, which seems gnarled and old compared to hers. 'Whatever you decide will be the right decision,' he says at last, awkwardly and sadly. He knows he can no longer handle Anna's life and his defeat is palpable.

They leave, and Mike arrives. 'No one seems to hold much hope for a third transplant,' Anna tells him. 'The general consensus is that it will never work. The only one who seems to believe another operation should be attempted is Ian Ronson, who is positively flushed with his successes in America. But I wonder if he really thinks Sophie will survive another one, or if he just wants the chance to perform something as tricky and spectacular as a third transplant.'

'I've talked to him. He's quite fired up about it.'

'He's young. He wants to make his mark.'

'I've also talked to Harold Wright. He disagrees with Ronson, doesn't think it should be attempted.'

'I know. He told me Sophie's chance of surviving a third operation is questionable. And he doesn't have much hope that another liver will take after two have been rejected.'

'All the surgeons say that, except Ian.' Mike begins pulling at his thick curly beard in absentminded agitation. 'What does he know of Sophie anyway? Look what just two operations have done to her – she went through hell, she is permanently damaged mentally, physically she is no better off than before the transplant – '

'That's what I keep saying.'

Mike and Anna talk and talk, endlessly circling the same questions over and over again. Yet whatever is said, the words of Ian Ronson go round and round in Anna's head: 'You're not going to deny your daughter a chance to live, are you?'

A chance to live. A chance to live – but at what price? A damaged body, a damaged mind?

A chance to live: but for how long? A year, a month, and that full of pain, of fear?

In the end Anna does the only thing she can do, she goes to Sophie. The child is in bed now, ready to drift into sleep. Steve is sitting with her, talking to her quietly about Merlin, about Devon. Sophie's face is scrubbed clean, her shaggy hair brushed back and falling on the white pillow. 'Oh Mum,' she says, smiling her wide, warm smile, 'there you are!' She takes Anna's hand as her mother sits next to her on the bed.

'Sophie,' Anna begins softly, 'they want you to have another operation.'

Sophie looks at her serenely. 'You promised me, Mum. No more operations.' There is such trust in her voice: no fear, no questions: only a deep, unshakeable trust.

'I know I promised. It's just that the doctors don't think your new liver is doing that well.'

Sophie registers this. There is no panic, no fear, not even any surprise, just a sad ancient resignation which Anna recognizes. It has been part of Sophie since she was old enough to understand she was not like other children, would never be like other children. 'Well,' she says at last, and even smiles as she speaks, 'the doctors have always said that, since I was born. Let's just go home and see what happens, like we've always done.'

Anna squeezes her hand and they sit there, the three of them, and after a time Sophie drifts off into sleep as if she hadn't a care in the world. Anna stands up, kisses her gently, and leaves Steve with her as she goes to look for Ian Ronson.

He is not pleased with Anna's decision, but no longer tries to dissuade her. He is young and bright and will go places, Anna thinks, but Sophie is her daughter, not a statistic on liver transplants. Because he is young and has stopped pushing her, she tries to explain. About things like the quality of life, and wanting Sophie's to be the best possible in whatever time she has left, not scarred and slashed by useless operations, by fears and pain and terror. About letting go, about how important it is to know when you can no longer hold on to something you love dearly, how you must let it go when it is time. He listens, this surgeon, but Anna can see he doesn't understand. Perhaps he will one day, but he doesn't now.

A few days later they leave the hospital. They were urged to stay, but Sophie couldn't bear it; and anyway, there is nothing else they can do for her here. Sophie says her goodbyes radiantly, transformed with joy at being allowed out, and hugs Belinda effusively. 'Visit me!' she cries, snuggling in Belinda's arms, 'Come to Devon when we finally get there and meet Merlin.'

'I just might do that,' Belinda replies. She wishes they would hurry up and go, before she bursts into tears in front of her colleagues.

As they drive out of the city Sophie suddenly asks, 'What home are we going to?'

'What do you mean?'

'Are we going to our old home or our new home?'

'I thought we were going to Bristol,' Steve says, looking at Sophie in the rear view mirror. 'You still have stuff there, and Madge has Merlin and the cats.'

Anna turns to look at her daughter, who already looks less tired and frightened since they left the hospital. 'Where do you want to go, Sophie? Would you rather go straight to our new home?'

'I think I would, I really would. It would be much better to leave Bristol like this, don't you think? With no goodbyes? We can start our new life right this minute!'

'Great!' Steve exclaims. 'I can collect the dog and cats this

275

weekend, when I bring Sam down. He's spending some of his holiday time with us.'

They by-pass Bristol and head for Devon, laughing and making plans on the way down. 'What a brilliant idea, Sophie,' Steve exclaims as they get their first glimpse of Dartmoor, clear and powerful in the summer sunlight, the sheep sprawled over it like basking tourists. 'This is after all our future down here, whatever it may be.'

Whatever it may be, Anna repeats to herself. At the hospital she asked Harold Wright how long he thought Sophie had, and though at first he tried to hedge, he finally admitted it would probably not be more than a few months. No matter: as Sophie would say, we've heard it all before. We'll just get on with it, this business of living, in the best possible way we can, as long as we can, as happy as we can.

When the car stops in Steve's drive – their drive now – Sophie gets out and heads for the duck pond, carrying a paper napkin full of bread crumbs she salvaged from the snack they had at a motorway rest stop.

'Sophie,' Anna calls. 'Come back for your cardigan. The wind's come up quite chilly.'

She hasn't heard. 'What's that, Mum?' she shouts from half-way down the garden.

Anna begins to call her back, but then stops. Letting go, she says to herself: that's what life is all about. Knowing when not to hold on, when to open your arms and let go.

'It's all right, Sophie,' Anna says letting her go, her dear darling daughter with her skimpy T-shirt, her unruly hair, her indomitable spirit. 'You go on, love. You go.'

She does, and the evening seems colder. Steve takes Anna's hand and together they watch Sophie run away from them.